BUILDINGS
OF PITTSBURGH

Top: Bridges on the Allegheny River, with Pittsburgh's North Side on the left.
Bottom: Hillside houses, South Side in the Beltzhoover neighborhood.

BUILDINGS
OF PITTSBURGH

Franklin Toker

A volume in the
Buildings of the United States series

SOCIETY OF ARCHITECTURAL HISTORIANS, CHICAGO,
and
THE CENTER FOR AMERICAN PLACES,
SANTA FE AND STAUNTON,
in association with
THE UNIVERSITY OF VIRGINIA PRESS,
CHARLOTTESVILLE AND LONDON

PUBLISHERS NOTES: *Buildings of Pittsburgh* is the eleventh volume in the Buildings of the United States (BUS) series, founded and sponsored by the Society of Architectural Historians (SAH). The book was brought to publication with the generous support of those organizations that are listed on page xi, for which the SAH is most grateful. Portions of this book are excerpted from *Buildings of Pennsylvania: Pittsburgh and Western Pennsylvania* by Lu Donnelly, Franklin Toker, and H. David Brumble IV, a forthcoming volume in the BUS series. For more information about SAH and the BUS series, go online at www.sah.org. For more information about the publication of *Buildings of Pittsburgh* and the Center for American Places, please see page 200.

Society of Architectural Historians
1365 North Astor Street
Chicago, Illinois 60610–2144, USA
www.sah.org

The Center for American Places, Inc.
P.O. Box 23225
Santa Fe, New Mexico 87502, U.S.A.
www.americanplaces.org

Distributed by the University of Virginia Press
www.upress.virginia.edu

15 14 13 12 11 10 09 08 07   1 2 3 4 5

ISBN-10 0-8319-2658-0 (HARDCOVER)
ISBN-13 978-0-8139-2658-2
ISBN-10 0-8139-2650-5 (PAPERBACK)
ISBN-13 978-0-8139-2650-6

Library of Congress Cataloging-in-Publication Data

Toker, Franklin.
   Buildings of Pittsburgh / by Franklin Toker.
      p. cm. — (The buildings of the United States series)
   Includes bibliographical references and index.
   ISBN 978-0-8139-2658-2 (hardcover) — ISBN 978-0-8139-2650-6 (pbk.)
   1. Architecture—Pennsylvania—Pittsburgh. 2. Pittsburgh (Pa.)--Buildings, structures, etc. I. Society of Architectural Historians. II. Center for American Places. III. Title. IV. Series.

NA735.P53T65 2007
720.9748'86—dc22
                                        2007022859

CONTENTS

FOREWORD   IX

LIST OF FUNDERS   XI

AUTHOR'S ACKNOWLEDGMENTS   XIII

HOW TO USE THIS BOOK   XV

INTRODUCTION TO PITTSBURGH'S ARCHITECTURE   3

CHAPTER 1: THE GOLDEN TRIANGLE   11

CHAPTER 2: OAKLAND   41

CHAPTER 3: SOUTH SIDE AND THE MONONGAHELA VALLEY   63

CHAPTER 4: NORTH SIDE AND THE ALLEGHENY VALLEY   83

CHAPTER 5: MCKEES ROCKS AND THE OHIO VALLEY   115

CHAPTER 6: THE PITTSBURGH NEIGHBORHOOD: A QUESTION OF PHYSIOGNOMY   123

CHAPTER 7: ON THE PARKWAY EAST   157

CHAPTER 8: EARLY SETTLERS AND TROLLEY SUBURBS   165

CHAPTER 9: DAY TRIPS FROM PITTSBURGH   175

GLOSSARY OF TERMS   183

SUGGESTED READINGS AND FILMS   189

ILLUSTRATION CREDITS   193

INDEX   195

ABOUT THE AUTHOR   199

Other Books in the Series

Buildings of Alaska, Alison K. Hoagland (1993)

Buildings of Colorado, Thomas J. Noel (1997)

Buildings of the District of Columbia, Pamela Scott and Antoinette J. Lee (1993)

Buildings of Iowa, David Gebhard and Gerald Mansheim (1993)

Buildings of Louisiana, Karen Kingsley (2003)

Buildings of Michigan, Kathryn Bishop Eckert (1993)

Buildings of Nevada, Julie Nicoletta, with photographs by Bret Morgan (2000)

Buildings of Rhode Island, William H. Jordy; Richard Onorato and William McKenzie Woodward, contributing editors (2004)

Buildings of Virginia: Tidewater and Piedmont, Richard Guy Wilson and contributors (2002)

Buildings of West Virginia, S. Allen Chambers, Jr. (2004)

FOREWORD

The primary objective of the Buildings of the United States (BUS) series is to iden-
tify and celebrate the rich cultural, economic, and geographic diversity of the
United States of America as it is reflected in the architecture of each state. The series
was founded by the Society of Architectural Historians (SAH) of Chicago, a nonprofit
organization dedicated to the study, interpretation, and preservation of the built environment throughout the world.

Buildings of Pittsburgh is the first city guide to be published in the BUS series, which
eventually will comprise more than sixty volumes documenting the built environment
of every state. When completed, the series will provide a detailed survey and history of
the architecture of the entire nation, including both high-style and vernacular structures. The idea for such a series was in the minds of the founders of the SAH in the
early 1940s, but it was not brought to fruition until the SAH was challenged by Niko-
laus Pevsner—the eminent British architectural historian who had conceived and carried out the Buildings of England series, originally published between 1951 and
1974—to do for the United States what he had done for his country.

The authors of each BUS volume are trained architectural historians who are thor-
oughly informed in the local aspects of their subjects. In each volume, special conditions that shaped the state or part of the state, together with the building types necessary
to meet those conditions, are identified and discussed: barns and other agricultural
buildings, factories and mining structures, warehouses and conservatories, bridges and
transportation buildings take their places alongside the familiar building types conventional to the nation as a whole—courthouses, libraries, city halls, religious buildings,
commercial structures, and the infinite variety of domestic architecture, from workers'

houses to mansions. Although the great national and international architects of American buildings receive proper attention, outstanding local architects, as well as the buildings of skilled but often anonymous carpenter-builders, are brought prominently into the picture. Each book in the series deals with the very fabric of American architecture, within the context of a time and place for each specific building and within the entirety of urban, suburban, and rural America. Naturally, the series cannot cover every building of merit; practical considerations dictate difficult choices in the buildings that are represented in this and other volumes. Furthermore, only buildings in existence at the time of publication are included.

The BUS series has received generous and ongoing support from the National Endowment for the Humanities; the Graham Foundation for Advanced Studies in the Fine Arts; the Ford Foundation; the Samuel H. Kress Foundation; and the National Park Service, HABS/HAER/HALS. For this volume, SAH is also enormously indebted to an anonymous donor and to the many individual members of the SAH who have made unrestricted contributions to BUS.

The SAH expresses its appreciation to the author, the Center for American Places, the University of Virginia Press, the SAH Board, the current members of the BUS Editorial Advisory Committee (listed on page VII), and that Committee's former members.

Karen Kingsley
Editor-in-Chief
Buildings of the United States

LIST OF FUNDERS

The Society of Architectural Historians gratefully acknowledges the support of the following, whose generosity helped bring *Buildings of Pittsburgh* to publication:

Anonymous
The Heinz Architectural Center
National Park Service, Heritage Documentation Programs, HABS/HAER/HALS Division
National Endowment for the Humanities, an independent federal agency
Friends of the Center for American Places
Vira I. Heinz Endowment

Initial and ongoing support for the Buildings of the United States series has come from:

National Endowment for the Humanities, an independent federal agency
Graham Foundation for Advanced Studies in the Fine Arts
Pew Charitable Trusts
University of Delaware
Ford Foundation
Samuel I. Newhouse Foundation
Samuel H. Kress Foundation
David Geffen Foundation
Furthermore, a program of the J. M. Kaplan Fund
University of Missouri
Richard H. Driehaus Foundation

Top: North Side houses, with the Heinz plant in the background.
Bottom: The Tenth Street Bridge crossing the Monongahela River, with South Side in the background.

AUTHOR'S ACKNOWLEDGMENTS

I was honored when the Society of Architectural Historians (SAH) invited me to partic-
ipate in its Buildings of the United States series. My initial assignment from the SAH was
to join Lu Donnelly and David Brumble in writing the forthcoming BUS volume, *Buildings of Pennsylvania: Pittsburgh and Western Pennsylvania*. Later, the Society asked me to
write on the architecture of Pittsburgh as an independent volume, and this is the result.

It has been a pleasure working with George F. Thompson, president and publisher
of the Center for American Places, who served as the book's project director and man-
aging editor. In writing this book, I used the indispensable research sources at the Pennsylvania Department of Carnegie Library, Heinz Regional History Center, Architecture
Archives of Carnegie Mellon University, and Pittsburgh History and Landmarks Foundation. I am indebted to the librarians and research staffs at those four societies and,
above all, to Martin Aurand, the late Walter Kidney, and Al Tannler. Thanks, also, to
Barry Bergdoll, for his insight on the Frank House.

It is no cliché to say that I have learned much from my students at the University of
Pittsburgh and, naturally, from my teaching colleagues there as well. But one of my
debts overshadows all: Lu Donnelly left me alone to deal with Pittsburgh while she
(aided by David Brumble) wrestled with the remaining thirty-two counties of western
Pennsylvania. But any number of times Lu generously rescued me from research or
logistical dead-ends in my own territory. Lu also superintended the maps for this volume by Ken Steif and Mark Mattson and the photography by Nicholas Traub, and she
materially aided in assembling older illustrations and in writing *Chapter 9: Day Trips from
Pittsburgh*. I thank her for being such an exemplary colleague.

The title *Buildings of Pittsburgh* was used once before, not for a book but for a detailed article on the city's architecture in *Architectural Record* 30 (September 1911): 204–82. The author was the eminent architectural critic Montgomery Schuyler, and his survey is generally regarded as the best essay written on Pittsburgh. My hope is that readers of this book will profit from it as much as generations of us have gleaned from Schuyler's work.

Franklin Toker

HOW TO USE THIS BOOK

For touring purposes, *Buildings of Pittsburgh* organizes the city into neighborhoods and districts and outer Pittsburgh by river and turnpike. It starts downtown, as do most visitors, with the Golden Triangle, then moves to the adjacent neighborhoods or districts, and concludes with two day trips from Pittsburgh.

An entry's heading information includes the current name of the building or site (often followed in parentheses by the earliest known name); the beginning and completion dates of construction; the architect, if known; and the dates of major additions or alterations and their architects, if known. In an entry's location information and in the text proper, federal highways are labeled either as interstates (e.g., I-376) or as "US" (e.g., US 40); the designation PA with a number (e.g., PA 68) applies to all state or local roads.

Pittsburgh has a very dense and irregular urban street network. For this reason, every building or site included in a chapter's text is keyed by a number to an overview or street-level map; that is, the numbers in the maps correspond to the respective entry numbers in the chapter texts. The maps included in this volume are intended to be supplemented by commercially published highway and street maps.

Almost all the sites discussed in this book are visible from public roads or public property, and readers no doubt will respect the property rights and privacy of others as they view the buildings. Some properties and buildings that are inaccessible to the public are included because of their significance to understanding Pittsburgh's architecture; some of them may be open at limited or irregular times or by arrangement. Local historical societies and visitor information centers offer additional information on historic buildings and sites, including times of operation.

Volumes in the Buildings of the United States series are intended to include only extant buildings. Some of the structures described here, however, will unfortunately have been altered beyond recognition or even demolished by the time this book is released to the public. The Society of Architectural Historians (www.sah.org) welcomes comments and suggested updates and corrections for future printings or editions of this work.

BUILDINGS
OF PITTSBURGH

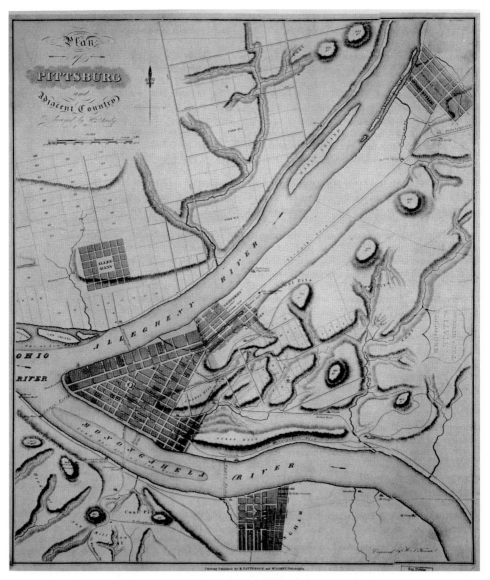

Fig. I.1 Plan of the cities of Pittsburgh (Woods-Vickroy, 1784) and Allegheny (David Redick, 1788). Engraved plan by William Darby, 1815.

INTRODUCTION TO
PITTSBURGH'S ARCHITECTURE

I took four tries to establish Pittsburgh. The Point—that literal point in downtown Pittsburgh at which the Monongahela and Allegheny rivers meet to form the Ohio— was fortified both by a party of Virginians and by the French in 1754, then by the British in 1759–1761. But these military settlements were not in city form, even if a 1760 census counted some 200 squatters living in houses around the British fort.

Pittsburgh was laid out as a city in 1784 by surveyor George Woods for the heirs of William Penn, founder of Pennsylvania, but it was unclear to which county it belonged and even to which state, since it was claimed both by Pennsylvania and Virginia. Logically, when Pennsylvania carved out Allegheny County in 1788, it ought to have designated it Pittsburgh County, as a western counterpart to Philadelphia County in the east. That would have integrated the state's concern for the administration of justice with the city's concern for its own power base. But Allegheny County was created not to exalt Pittsburgh but to curtail it: the rival city of Allegheny was laid out by David Redick on the opposite bank of the Allegheny River in 1788. Pittsburgh stole the dignity of county seat from Allegheny City almost at once, and in 1907 it gobbled up the rival settlement to become its North Side. Merely looking at the layouts of Allegheny City and Pittsburgh shows a striking difference in character (Fig. I.1): Allegheny City was broad, elegant, even utopian in its mix of buildings and green pastures in a perfect square, whereas Pittsburgh was cramped, overbuilt, and somewhat crooked in a jumbled street plan that shoehorned commercial enterprises along the richly profitable Monongahela and Allegheny riverbanks.

As it rose in its industrial wealth, Pittsburgh appeared uncultured and brash to the rest of the nation. What was not obvious then, and remains too little studied now, is that, as a trade and distribution center, Pittsburgh and the whole of western Pennsylvania had roots both old and deep. When Europeans came here, they found only modest Native American settlements of the Delaware in modern-day Lawrenceville and McKees Rocks and smaller transient groupings of the Seneca and Shawnee. Probably gone by then was a Late Prehistoric village that had flourished at McKees Rocks from about 900 BCE (Before Common Era). Still visible today is the natural base for what was once McKees Rocks mound—the largest in Pennsylvania—which had been occupied by Native Americans during the Early and Middle Woodland Periods, possibly as early as 1,000 BCE. What these remains show is an extensive trade network along the riverine systems of the mid-continent; in those remote pre-European days, it was not the Ohio Valley but the East Coast that was hinterland. The rise of industrial Pittsburgh as a global center of exchange thus followed an ancient template.

The role of Pittsburgh in western Pennsylvania would always be one of dominance, but the metropolis had to be interdependent with the small towns surrounding it. They were literal feeders during agricultural days, then allegorically so, when immense amounts of industrial production—often carefully and precisely orchestrated from one mill to the next—came from those same sites that were now turned into industrial satellites. Consequently, Pittsburgh's growth pattern was organic rather than orthogonal, as seven expansion rings spread out from the Point in the next two and a half centuries.

The first of these seven expansions was the creation of the rivalry between Pittsburgh and Allegheny City in the 1780s. Architecture in those two pre-industrial towns overwhelmingly followed the sober Federal and Greek Revival styles from the 1790s to the middle of the nineteenth century. The city had two professional architects early on, both British-born, in the visiting Benjamin H. Latrobe and the permanent resident John Chislett. The most impressive of the city's buildings from this era are mainly lost, as one would expect, but a few reconstructed walls and the Blockhouse remain from Fort Pitt (1.1); the Neill Log House still stands in Squirrel Hill; and south of the city, "Woodville" (8.6) survives as a surprisingly high-style exemplar of domestic architecture on the fringes of the frontier settlement. Otherwise, we have to depend on lithographs to acclaim Latrobe's Allegheny Arsenal, Chislett's second Allegheny County Courthouse, and the massive "Homewood" house that gave its name and social cachet to the city's eastern suburbs. Bedford Square (3.5) on the South Side survives to give the general massing if not the specific structures of that part of the city around 1815, and the nearby Bedford School of 1850 (3.4) and its contemporary, the Mexican War streets district on the North Side (4.18), are good representatives of Greek Revival in Pittsburgh.

Around 1800, there was a second expansion from the core, resulting in the creation of a half-dozen detached settlements along Pittsburgh's riverbanks. Along the Allegheny River, Bayardsville (now the Strip) was platted around 1800 and William Foster's Lawrenceville followed in 1812. On the south bank of the Monongahela, Birmingham was platted by Dr. Nathaniel Bedford on land owned by his father-in-law, John Ormsby, in 1811, while on the Ohio River the settlements of Manchester, Sewickley, and Economy (this last just north of Allegheny County) were founded between the 1820s and mid-nineteenth century.

Like so many overcrowded and poorly built American cities, Pittsburgh suffered a calamitous fire (recorded locally as the "Great Fire" or "Big Fire") on 10 April 1845. It burned through fifty-six acres in twenty-six blocks, about a third of the Golden Triangle, as well as a quarter-of-a-mile along the Monongahela shore. About a thousand buildings were lost (thankfully only two deaths were recorded). As one would expect, new wooden buildings became extremely rare in Pittsburgh after mid-century, though it was generally held that this was more a consequence of the power of the brick trusts than of farsighted city planning.

A third expansion, from mid-century to around 1875, was sparked by the arrival of the Pennsylvania Railroad in Pittsburgh in 1852. This led almost immediately to the formation of a string of railroad suburbs east of downtown, in Shadyside, Homewood, Point Breeze, Wilkinsburg, Edgewood, and Swissvale. Some aesthetes preferred to live at even greater remove from Pittsburgh, at Evergreen Hamlet and Sewickley in the Allegheny and Ohio river valleys, respectively. These near and far suburbs showcased the Gothic Revival, which had earlier manifested itself in Pittsburgh in such works as John Haviland's Western Penitentiary of 1828 (now demolished).

This post-Civil War era saw the predictable importation of new styles in the Romantic tradition: Italianate and Renaissance Revival, Second Empire, and the beginnings of the Romanesque Revival. Topographically, the period marked the integration of the building and landscape architectural traditions, as in Allegheny Cemetery (6.7). Some downtown relics from this era are Dollar Savings Bank (1.8), the cast-iron facades on Wood Street (1.10) and Liberty Avenue (1.39), and the Italianate storefronts around Market Square. Even richer are three long, crowded streets that testify to post-Civil-War prosperity and which have recently sprung vigorously back to life: East Carson Street on the South Side (3.6), East Ohio Street on the North Side, and Butler Street in Lawrenceville. While Philadelphia designers such as John Notman and Isaac Hobbs had much influence on the mid-century city, Joseph Kerr, Charles M. Bartberger, and other local architects led the outsiders in terms of volume.

The stage was now set for a fourth expansion from the core, in the industrial satellite communities in the Allegheny, Ohio, and Monongahela river valleys. From 1875 to 1910, industrial Pittsburgh reached its apogee, both in its factories and the huge institutional buildings created from its new wealth (Fig. I.2). Virtually all the early mills were later cannibalized or razed, but certain archaeological survivals still stand in the Strip and Lawrenceville. Just two mills keep some of their original functions on their original sites today: Andrew Carnegie's Edgar Thomson Works in Braddock (3.16) and H. J.

Figure I.2 Lithograph view by Otto Krebs, 1874.

Heinz's food-processing plant on the North Side (4.25), but the whole Pittsburgh district resonates with hundreds of factories and thousands of worker houses that survive in mill towns such as Natrona, Homestead, Turtle Creek, and Wilmerding, and a little later in McKees Rocks, Duquesne, Clairton, Ambridge, and Aliquippa—these last two over the county line in neighboring Beaver County.

The tremendous wealth from industry flowing into the city from the 1890s until World War I refurbished Pittsburgh's downtown, and made the Triangle truly golden. After the creation of the industrial plants, the spending by the robber barons of their vast wealth is the second most characteristic moment in the architecture of Pittsburgh. The new governmental and commercial architecture featured both medieval-based styles, such as the train station by Frank Furness (demolished), and the Beaux-Arts idiom. The latter was the style of choice for Carnegie's partners—Henry Phipps, Henry Oliver, and Henry Clay Frick—for the skyscrapers they commissioned from New York City's George Post, Chicago's Daniel Burnham, and others. The masterpiece of the era remains H. H. Richardson's Allegheny County Courthouse and Jail (1.15), which combined elements of both stylistic camps. The Courthouse and the sumptuous corporate buildings gave Pittsburgh national and international prominence in architecture.

The same years preceding World War I saw a fifth major expansion from the downtown, setting an elegant ring around the old urban core through the application of City Beautiful ideas to the middle- and upper-management neighborhoods of Oakland, Shadyside, Squirrel Hill, Highland Park, Point Breeze, and the North Side. A score of mansions survive on Fifth, Penn, and Ridge avenues from the years in which those streets held the highest concentration of millionaires in the United States.

What best survives from City Beautiful Pittsburgh are three city parks and their linked thoroughfares, all laid out by city planner Edward Manning Bigelow between 1890 and 1925. The parks are Schenley, Frick, and Highland; the thoroughfares are Bigelow Boulevard, Boulevard of the Allies (conceived around 1910 but delayed until the 1920s), Beechwood Boulevard, and Highland Avenue. These four carriage roads— probably originally planned as five—would have formed a twenty-mile ring around that portion of Pittsburgh lying between the Monongahela and Allegheny rivers. The best of Bigelow's roads today bears his name, though it was initially called Grant Boulevard. This stylish roadway was opened in 1901 to lead motorists from Grant Street in the Golden Triangle, to Schenley Plaza in Oakland and beyond into Schenley Park. The road still branches off at Grant Street at Seventh Avenue (today marked by the USX Tower (1.36) instead of the Beaux-Arts pylon once proposed) and snakes for about six miles along a cyclopean retaining wall cut into an escarpment some 100 feet above the Strip. This is the best part of Bigelow, aestheticizing the industrial districts of the Allegheny River valley and Polish Hill.

After Polish Hill and a picturesque swerve over Bloomfield, Bigelow Boulevard awkwardly picks its way through the then-new development of Oakland—whose growth it had spurred enormously—into Schenley Plaza. The boulevard then snakes its way from west to east through Schenley Park (under the new name of Schenley Drive), then changes name again for a third serpentine run across Squirrel Hill as Beechwood Boulevard. The fourth element is Washington Boulevard, picking up from Beechwood in Point Breeze at the intersection of Fifth and Penn avenues, whence it took pioneer motorists down a wooded ravine to the Allegheny River shoreline. The fifth element would presumably have been a return boulevard along the Allegheny to downtown: Butler Street does this functionally, but without Bigelow's characteristic aesthetic touch.

Egged on by Bigelow, Pittsburgh's industrial elite began to endow the East End with a string of monuments that would end only with World War II. Andrew Carnegie took the lead with the creation of his Library, Institute (2.14), and Technical School (today Carnegie Mellon University) (2.16–2.19). The entrepreneur Franklin Nicola doggedly pursued the concept of the City Beautiful until the Oakland district yielded a baseball park, society hotel, fashionable clubs, model homes of the Schenley Farms district (2.3), and Beaux-Arts Acropolis-style campus for the University of Pittsburgh (Figs. I.3 and I.4). The Mellon family contributed heavily to Oakland's medical complex, then took

Figure I.3 Henry Hornbostel's proposed "Acropolis" plan for the University of Pittsburgh, 1908.

the lead in three monuments of still eye-catching scale: Mellon Institute (2.9), the Cathedral of Learning (2.10), and East Liberty Presbyterian Church (6.11).

From roughly 1910 to 1940, there was a sixth expansion from the downtown core, this one also to accommodate the motorcar. A set of ambitious road and public works projects turned a set of discrete urban sites into a loose web of suburbs. First came the Liberty Tubes, tunneling under Mt. Washington to reach Mt. Lebanon and the nearer South Hills. Two picturesque expressways followed: Allegheny River Boulevard, leading to the wealthy suburb of Oakmont, and Ohio River Boulevard to the even more glamorous Sewickley. These were the years that left Art Deco buildings in almost every corner of the city: the Allegheny County Airport (3.19), Allegheny General Hospital, the Art Deco storefronts on East Carson Street (3.6), New Granada Theater on the Hill (6.44), and a sort of institutional Art Deco in Buhl Planetarium (4.16). Modernism came to the fore in the 1930s with Frank Lloyd Wright's office in Kaufmann's Department Store (1.20) (moved in 1974 to the Victoria and Albert Museum in London), and the world-famous Fallingwater for the same Kaufmann family in nearby Fayette County (9.2).

The seventh expansion from Pittsburgh's core paralleled post–World War II growth across the nation and gave the city a whole new chain of suburbs in the South Hills, North Hills, and suburban corridors branching off the Pennsylvania Turnpike and the Parkways East and West. But the Pittsburgh Renaissance from 1945 through 1969 (known as Renaissance I) had even greater impact on the rebuilding of the Golden Triangle, in what was one of the most massive reconstructions of a city core in the nation.

"Renaissance" is an important term in Pittsburgh history, but its local meaning is a postwar movement that was crucial to the survival of the city. Pittsburgh reached its highest rates of industrial production in World War II, but even by 1944, when the local politicians, academics, and business leaders formed the Allegheny Conference on Community Development (ACCD), it was clear that, without massive redevelopment, Pittsburgh would be bypassed in the postwar economy. The main thrust of Pittsburgh's

Renaissance I involved federally mandated flood control on the three rivers, stringent air pollution controls, and the creation of the nation's first Urban Redevelopment Authority with the power to flatten sizeable portions of the city. The flood and pollution controls reversed the worst environmental effects of Pittsburgh's two centuries of industrial production. For the built environment, the most visible and positive achievements of the Pittsburgh Renaissance were Point State Park (Gateway Center, the Hilton Hotel) (1.1 and 1.2) and Mellon Square, downtown, and their attendant skyscrapers; the worst excesses of urban renewal took place outside the Golden Triangle, on the North Side and in East Liberty and the Hill.

Renaissance II, from the late 1970s to around 1990, operated differently than Renaissance I. The goals and priorities of the first were set by the Allegheny Conference and professional groups and implemented by the public sector; in the second, the public sector did more of the planning and agenda setting, with a diverse power base in the private corporate and neighborhood groups. This Renaissance spawned completion of the light rail system in 1983, rebuilding of Grant Street, an agreement for a new airport (5.8), and several downtown skyscrapers, including PPG (1.5), Dominion Tower (1.26), Fifth Avenue Place (1.3), Oxford Center (1.13), and One Mellon Bank Center (1.19).

Figure I.4 Aerial view of Oakland, ca. 1980s.

Renaissance II also expanded into the neighborhoods, where Main Street and preservation programs worked to encourage contextualism and infill rather than urban expansion—much of which was sprawl by that point. Suddenly Pittsburgh found itself with revitalized neighborhoods, a host of recycled buildings—Heinz Hall (1.29), Benedum Center (1.27), the Pennsylvanian (1.35), the Mattress Factory (4.20), Andy Warhol Museum (4.3)—a new wave of downtown skyscrapers, two sports stadiums—Heinz Field for the Steelers and PNC Park for the Pirates—a convention center, and a mammoth new airport. Pittsburgh's city government states that it remains committed to the integration of its new developments in Squirrel Hill, South Side, and the Hill with their pre-existing old neighborhoods nearby; citizens groups try their best to keep city government to its promise. There have been some notable failures (the Waterfront mall in Homestead being the most prominent), but for the most part the new buildings blend well into old contexts. Prominent examples since the 1980s are Crawford Square (6.45), on the Hill, the South Side Works on East Carson Street, and the Village of Shadyside (6.26). It was only in the 1980s that small communities such as Monroeville, Southpointe, and Cranberry (the latter two in adjoining counties south and north of Pittsburgh) emerged with a character decisively detached—culturally and physically—from the old urban core.

Pittsburgh continues to be an important place for innovative architecture. Since 1993, when several local environmentally conscious non-profit organizations united to open a branch of the Green Building Alliance in Pittsburgh, the city has embraced the ideals and philosophy of environmentally friendly building. As a place degraded by its industrial boom, Pittsburgh learned early and well that cleaning the environment deterred urban decay. With the help of local foundations and the enthusiastic cooperation of local cultural entities, green building techniques are becoming the norm in new building, such as the new David Lawrence Convention Center (1.33), and in additions to older buildings. This city that was famous for embracing its smoky atmosphere, because it indicated that the citizenry was working, is now preaching the gospel of green building and clean air. Pittsburgh, in fact, is consistently among the top three American cities for buildings with the Leadership in Energy and Environmental Design rating.

The 255-acre Golden Triangle is roughly comparable in shape to Lower Manhattan from its tip to Greenwich Village. As with the skyline view of Lower Manhattan, Pittsburgh's creates an equally strong image. Although its skyscrapers are fewer and perhaps their towering scale is less dramatic, Pittsburgh's urban matrix is a good deal tighter, since the Golden Triangle is entirely isolated from the rest of the city by the sharp rise of the Bluff and the Hill and by the intrusive Crosstown Expressway (I-579)—an unsung legacy to Pittsburgh from New York City's famous planner, Robert Moses.

Nature carved out this triangle where the Allegheny and Monongahela rivers join the Ohio, but geopolitics early on shaped it into a miniature city. In 1784, Pennsylvania obliged the descendents of William Penn to sell off their last holdings in the Commonwealth, the so-called Manor of Pittsburgh among them. The rudimentary and illegal settlement around Fort Pitt lacked a coherent street plan and was never platted into saleable lots, so the Penns got George Woods and his teenage assistant Thomas Vickroy to lay out this triangular town in a few weeks in the spring of 1784. The Woods-Vickroy double-grid plan (Fig. I.1)was more expedient than elegant, but it endures today as the sacred cow of Pittsburgh urbanism. Actually, only three projects have dared modify it: Gateway Center (1.2) from 1947 to 1968, PPG Place (1.5) in 1979–1984, and Oliver Plaza at Oliver Avenue and Wood Street in 1968. Pittsburgh's downtown is so small and so walkable that the entire district functions as a well-preserved and cohesive mercantile exchange.

The nickname Golden Triangle was bestowed in the years of feverish industrial expansion following the Civil War. Even as the Triangle's wealth may seem depleted compared to those days, it still serves as headquarters for a significant grouping of Fortune 500

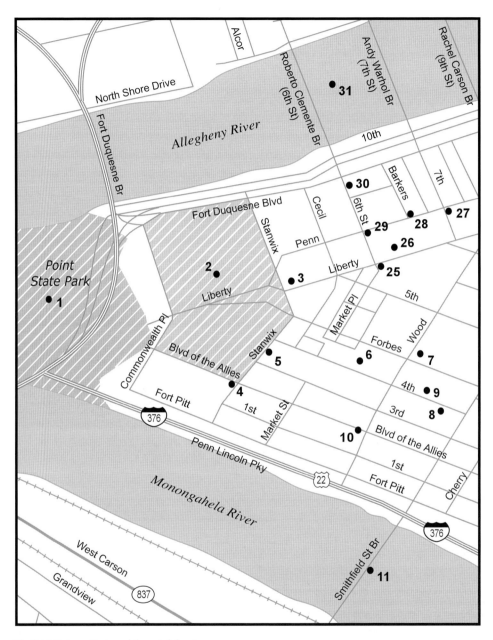

The Point, Gateway Center, and the central downtown.
Approximate walking time: several hours to a half-day.

companies, and there are few American districts that can match its architectural riches. The Burke Building (1.6) is a learned essay in Greek Revival, Dollar Savings Bank (1.8) in Italianate, H. H. Richardson's Courthouse and Jail (1.15) the unparalleled exemplar in Romanesque Revival, a clutch of churches sings the rhapsody of Gothic Revival, and whole blocks of Grant Street and Fourth Avenue shout the excesses of Beaux-Arts. There are varieties of modernism, too: superb Art Deco interiors in the Koppers Building (1.37) and the William Penn Hotel (1.18); the post–World War II classics of Gateway Center (1.2); and worthy contemporary designs in the new ALCOA (4.1), Convention Center (1.33), and CAPA (1.32). The two strongest impulses of the current Golden Triangle are pushing the district back to the future: one is to reemphasize the rivers, which gave the city birth; the other is a push to convert unneeded commercial and industrial space to housing. Downtown Pittsburgh is finally getting what it has most lacked during the last half century: permanent residents.

1.1 FORT PITT AND THE BLOCKHOUSE
1759–1761 (rebuilt 1953), Capt. Harry Gordon, engineer; 1764, Blockhouse. Point State Park.

These remnants are the physical core of Pittsburgh and the metaphorical core of western Pennsylvania. In 1753, a twenty-one-year-old George Washington urged Virginia's Governor Robert Dinwiddie to erect a fort at the Forks of the Ohio. The next year, Virginia constructed Fort Prince George at the Point, but it was replaced almost immediately by the French Fort Duquesne, a four-bastioned fort of which nothing remains today but a few artifacts and a modern stone outline showing the location. When the British dislodged the French in 1758, they put up a hasty replacement but also began construction of an elaborate, five-bastioned, pentagonal fortress with earthen breastworks, thirteen-foot-high brick revetment walls, and stone quoins. The total perimeter of the fort and its escarpments was about half a mile; it was protected on the landward side by extra earthworks and a moat.

The fort barely withstood a siege during Pontiac's Rebellion of 1763, spurring Colonel Henry Bouquet to add two redoubts for sharpshooters; one survives as the pentagonal

Fort Pitt and the Blockhouse

blockhouse. While the blockhouse—probably the oldest building in western Pennsylvania—survives, though almost totally rebuilt, the fort itself was demolished in 1797 and its million bricks went into the town's new homes and warehouses. The fort site was overrun in 1852 by the tracks of the Pennsylvania Railroad, which, for a century, used the Point as a freight depot. When archeologists from the Carnegie Museum of Natural History ascertained in 1941 that the fort's foundations were still intact about ten feet below the industrial detritus, Charles Stotz undertook a meticulous, though partial, reconstruction of its primary walls and two bastions.

Access to Point State Park from Gateway Center is cut off by eight lanes of highway traffic. The park's main entry has such a low clearance that architect Gordon Bunshaft of Skidmore, Owings and Merrill suggested a flattened arch portal to Stotz, who used post-tensioned concrete for its three ribbed arches. The inventor of that concrete technique, the eminent French engineer Eugène Freyssinet, came to Pittsburgh to personally supervise its construction. A wide pedestrian bridge at its center funnels visitors away from the low edges and carries them over a cobble-stoned reflecting pool into the park.

1.2 GATEWAY CENTER

1947–1968. Bounded by Fort Duquesne Blvd., Stanwix St., Blvd. of the Allies, and Commonwealth Pl.

This development saved Pittsburgh as a post-World-War II city. Together with the green acreage of Point State Park, the office buildings of Gateway Center radically transformed the sooty downtown into an approximation of LeCorbusier's towers-in-a-park unbuilt scheme for 1920s Paris. The developer, the Equitable

Gateway Center

Life Assurance Society, had earlier financed Irwin Clavan's cruciform-tower housing estates in Manhattan. Here the modernist designer Clavan worked with the traditionalists Otto Eggers and Daniel Higgins, who had completed John Russell Pope's National Gallery and the Jefferson Memorial in Washington, DC. The towers of One, Two, and Three Gateway (Eggers and Higgins with Irwin Clavan) were drawn up as the beginning of what was intended to be a forest of a dozen or more blocks for leading Pittsburgh corporations such as Jones and Laughlin Steel, PPG Industries, People's Gas, and Westinghouse. Only three of the chrome-alloyed steel uniform designs were realized, but these have proved surprisingly versatile and durable. Their maintenance has been impeccable, and the outdoor plazas function as the lunchtime breathing space they were always intended to be. Interestingly, the more traditional Beaux-Arts style planning of the walkways and fountain of the Gateway Plaza today are more appealing than the informal gazebos and planters of Equitable Plaza on the opposite side of Liberty Avenue.

After this experiment in coordinated design, Gateway Plaza (1950–1953, Clark and Rapuano, landscape architects) was filled out with independent designs for a hotel, an apartment block, and a problematic high-rise of professional offices atop a parking garage. The three-block Equitable Plaza (1955–1968, Simonds and Simonds, landscape architects) attempted no uniformity in design, though there is a loose volumetric linkage among the Post-Gazette Building (a rehabilitation in 1962 of a structure of 1927), the Verizon Building (former Bell Telephone Building, 1958, Press C. Dowler and William C. Dowler), the former IBM Building (1.4), and the Pennsylvania State Office Building (1957, Altenhof and Bown). The distinguished International Style firm of Harrison and Abramovitz took a conventional approach to the design of its Westinghouse Building of 1968, on a podium overlooking the Mononga-

Fifth Avenue Place

hela River, but still striking is the same firm's Four Gateway of 1960, with almost column-free floors served by an extruded—and still glistening—stainless steel service core.

1.3 FIFTH AVE. PLACE
1985–1987, The Stubbins Associates, with Williams, Trebilcock, Whitehead. 120 Fifth Ave.

Fifth Avenue Place is surprisingly unsubtle for a design by the much-respected postwar modernist Hugh Stubbins. Its overscaled windows, arbitrary jumps between glass-and granite-paneled outer skin, and uninspired crowning pinnacle are unavoidable features in the first view any visitor to Pittsburgh gets coming in from the airport.

The adjacent old Joseph Horne department store at the northeast corner of Stanwix Street and Liberty Avenue (1892; 1900, W. S. Fraser; 1922 addition, Peabody and Stearns of Boston) was remodeled as an office block in the mid-1990s and renamed Penn Avenue Place. The configuration left the Beaux-Arts exterior of the old store intact as a dignified visual anchor to the downtown, but much compromised by neighboring Fifth Avenue Place.

1.4 UNITED STEELWORKERS BUILDING (IBM BUILDING)
1961–1963, Curtis & Davis. 60 Blvd. of the Allies.

This was one of the more closely watched construction projects of the 1960s, as it was a landmark in the return of the bearing wall that had done only intermittent structural service since the early steel-skeletoned Chicago skyscrapers of the 1880s. The welded stainless steel web of these thirteen-story truss walls is constructed of three different strengths of steel, which progressively lighten as the building rises and the load lessens. This web is dual-purpose, being both the structure and a sunscreen for the interior. With its floor, wall, and elevator loads all carried on a central core, the open interior, with spans up to fifty-four feet, enjoys the highest possible internal flexibility. Though the fussiness of the

United Steelworkers Building (IBM Building)

honeycomb exterior marks it as a postwar period piece, the structural innovation articulated here has become a standard architectural alternative to the non-bearing curtain wall.

1.5 PPG PLACE
1979–1984, Johnson & Burgee. One PPG Pl.

The ultimate glass house, PPG Place is both billboard and world headquarters for a company founded almost on the same spot a century before as Pittsburgh Plate Glass and today one of the largest glass and chemical manufacturing companies in the world. Occupying five acres carved out of the heart of the eighteenth-century street grid of downtown Pittsburgh, PPG Place is the chief icon among the city's Renaissance II skyscrapers from the 1980s. Profusely pinnacled (231 in all, many glowing at night) and sheathed in a million square feet of PPG's own neutral silver Solarban 550 clear glass, the forty-four-story main tower and its five lower siblings give life—albeit rather stiffly—to Philip Johnson's vision of a glazed

PPG Place

Place des Vosges of Paris. The plaza, laid out around an obelisk, is minimalist and austere, in stark contrast to the architectural hodge-podge of neighboring Market Square, an authentic if over-restored relic of the city plan of 1784.

The central tower is entered through a fifty-foot-high lobby paneled entirely in burgundy-colored glass. The glass motif is carried into the elevator cars, which are sheathed in shattered glass. Behind the tower, toward Stanwix Street, stands a large but underused Wintergarden that continues the pointed-arch motif of the surrounding arcades and reaches a height of forty feet, roughly scaled to match the height of the Gothic Revival St. Mary of Mercy Church (1936, William Hutchins) across Third Avenue.

Gothic veneer aside, PPG Place is a standard International Style product. Nonetheless it has a contextual quality much appreciated by Pittsburghers, since it echoes both Richardson's courthouse tower (1.15) a few blocks away on Grant Street and the Cathedral of Learning at the University of Pittsburgh (2.10), some two miles to the east. Citizens use PPG Place for outdoor concerts and the classic Pittsburgh event: Steeler pre-game rallies. The open space was recently given some year-round excitement with an ice-skating rink that converts to a playful and user-friendly multi-headed fountain during warmer weather.

1.6 BURKE BUILDING
1836, John Chislett. 209 Fourth Ave.

A survivor as hardy as the blockhouse next to Fort Pitt (1.1), the Burke Building has always been one of the most handsome buildings downtown. Built of cream-toned sandstone—luxurious for an office building—the Greek Revival design is taut and well proportioned. This five-bay, three-story pedimented structure with its striking Doric-columned entryway survived the onslaught of the Victorian revivals, escaped the ravages of the Great Fire of 1845 by not more than half a block, and,

Burke Building

finally, has emerged as a surprisingly strong outbuilding to the PPG Place complex that engulfed it in the 1980s. In the 1990s, it was restored using renewable resources, and it is now the headquarters of the Western Pennsylvania Conservancy, which preserves both the natural environment of western Pennsylvania and its single most distinguished building, Frank Lloyd Wright's Fallingwater in Fayette County (9.2).

1.7 POINT PARK UNIVERSITY CENTER (BANK CENTER)
1890s–1920s; 1976, Lorenzi, Dodds, and Gunnill; 1997, Damianos + Anthony. 414 Wood St.

In the 1970s, at the cost of $4.2 million, the Bank Center united five turn-of-the-twentieth-century banks into Pittsburgh's first specialty mall, but the result was a cacophony of styles and materials. The sumptuous marble staircases and columns, the 727-panel stained-glass skylight, and the bronze and steel vaults overshadowed the plain materials and colors used in the rehabilitation. The four-story, three-bay Free-hold Building (1890) is the oldest of the quintet. The B/G Building of 1900 is a small, highly decorated two-story block, while the People's Savings Bank (1901, Alden & Harlow) is a fifteen-story office building crowned in granite. The last two components are the classically

influenced Colonial Trust Company Building (1902, Frederick Osterling), to which Osterling added a T-shaped lobby in 1926 that stretched from Fourth to Forbes avenues and Wood Street, and the People's Bank Annex, which was added by Press Dowler in 1927 as the first attempt at visual unity among these banking prima donnas.

After the Bank Center failed, Carnegie Library and Point Park College rehabilitated the complex again in 1997 as the Golden Triangle's book and electronic information center—a good analogy for Pittsburgh's transition from an industry-based to a knowledge-based urban center.

1.8 DOLLAR SAVINGS BANK
1868–1871, Isaac Hobbs & Sons; 1906 addition. 348 Fourth Ave.

An endearing if hyperkinetic piece of Italianate froth by a major Philadelphia designer and architectural publisher, Dollar Bank is an effective, red sandstone facade superbly conserved. Although downtown Pittsburgh once had similar banks at nearly every corner, today there is nothing like it in town. On what was formerly

Dollar Savings Bank

a restricted site, Hobbs set pairs of over-scaled Corinthian columns to support a high entablature of dramatically projecting stone brackets. The result is a facade that is virtually all detail and almost no wall.

1.9 INDUSTRIAL BANK
1903, Charles M. Bartberger. 333 Fourth Ave.

Although not an especially original design, this is the most handsome of the three bank buildings near the corner of Fourth Avenue and Smithfield Street. Next door at 337 Fourth stands Daniel Burnham's coldly classical Union Trust of 1898, built for Henry Clay Frick; beyond, at 341 Fourth, stands James Steen's overly fussy Fidelity Trust (1888–1889) in Richardsonian Romanesque.

The German-trained Bartberger inherited his architectural practice from his father, Charles F. Bartberger, and passed it on to his son Edward. The three generations practiced architecture in Pittsburgh for well over a century (1845–1956). This bank is one of the most confident handlings of Beaux Arts classicism in the city. Its facade consists of a huge granite arch

Commercial Building (Industrial Bank)

whose voussoirs align with sharply cleft breaks in the horizontal coursing. Above, the windows are set in a dwarf mezzanine.

The two blocks of Fourth Avenue between Market and Smithfield streets constitute the core of Pittsburgh's former financial district, second in capital only to Wall Street circa 1910. Fourth Avenue began life in the Woods-Vickroy plan of 1784, but gained importance only in the 1830s, when the Bank of Pittsburgh and the speculative Burke's Building (1.6) located here. Other banks followed suit after the Great Fire of 1845 and the financial panic of 1873. Imposing structures by George Post and Frank Furness are gone, but Dollar Savings Bank (1.8) remains. By the turn of the twentieth century, Pittsburgh's oil and stock exchanges and the headquarters of twenty bank and trust companies stood here. Eventually bank mergers and the lack of room for growth forced many of the financial institutions off Fourth Avenue. Today, the dominant architectural style on the street is still Beaux-Arts, either in low-rise banking houses or high-rise office towers.

1.10 WATSON-STANDARD BUILDING AND CAST-IRON FRONTED BUILDINGS
1860s-1870s. 101–103 Wood St.

Watson-Standard typifies Pittsburgh's cast-iron fronts of the 1860s and 1870s, with four stories of Italianate lunette windows in imitation of stone. Pittsburgh produced countless cast-iron facades for other cities, but it never developed a great taste for them. Among the few cast-iron fronts still standing downtown are 805–807 Liberty Avenue; 927–929 and 951–953 Liberty Avenue (1.39); 214–218 Fifth Avenue at McMasters Way, probably once gabled over its central bay; and several office buildings or warehouses on Fort Pitt Boulevard east of Market Street. The Triangle Building of 1884 (Seventh Ave. at Smithfield St.) represents a later tendency to limit the cast-iron elements to piers and window jambs.

Smithfield Street Bridge

1.11 SMITHFIELD STREET BRIDGE
1882–1883, Gustav Lindenthal. Smithfield St. and the Monongahela River.

This, the oldest of Pittsburgh's extant bridges, is the third at this site. The first on this site and in Pittsburgh was the covered wooden Mononga-hela Bridge of 1818 built by Lewis Wernwag to replace a ferry crossing, four years after he had completed an unparalleled 340-foot single-span timber bridge in Philadelphia. Destroyed in the Great Fire of 1845, it was replaced by John Roebling's Monongahela Suspension Bridge. When traffic loads reduced its stability a gener-ation later, this second bridge was torn down.

Construction of the present bridge began in 1880 under Charles Davis. Only the sandstone piers of his design were erected when he was re-placed by Lindenthal, who used the piers to carry a combination of an arch and a suspension bridge. This lenticular truss, which resembles a double convex lens seen on edge, is typical of design and engineering of the era, using small pieces that were easily manufactured, assembled, and transported to the site. There are two 360-foot spans, for a total length of 1,185 feet with approach spans. As one of the first primarily steel highway bridges in the United States, Smithfield fittingly marked both the transition of bridge materials from wrought iron to steel and the coming of age of Pittsburgh's steel industry.

In 1889, two trusses were added parallel to the original ones to accommodate horse cars. These were moved to widen the bridge for

One of Pittsburgh's more specialized cottage industries is the counting of bridges. At latest count, there are 446 bridges within Pittsburgh's city limits, while Venice, Italy, has a mere 400 and St. Petersburg, Russia, just 304. But bridges mean far more to a city than just statistics. Since 1818 when the covered wooden Smithfield Street Bridge went up as the first in the city (burned in the Great Fire of 1845), bridges have been not only a prime expression of Pittsburghers pride in their engineering achievements, but also the most visible statement of their wish and need to cement a community broken up by topography and ethnic diversity.

Pittsburgh demonstrated leadership in building bridges with the trio of experimental wire-cable suspension bridges erected by John A. Roebling, who settled in the town of Saxonburg in Butler County, where his early workshop still stands (199 North Rebecca Street). Roebling's first bridge for Pittsburgh was an aqueduct that carried the Pennsylvania Canal over the Allegheny River, in 1845; a year later, he replaced the burned Smithfield Street Bridge with a seven-span suspension bridge; then, in 1859, Roebling constructed the suspended Sixth Street Bridge over the Allegheny, where the Roberto Clemente Bridge (1.31) stands today. None of Roebling's bridges in Pittsburgh survives, but two other world-class bridges do: one is the current Smithfield Street Bridge (1.11) of 1883, an exquisite and rare lenticular truss by Gustav Lindenthal; the other is the George Westinghouse Memorial Bridge (3.17) of 1932, which remains the longest reinforced concrete span in the United States.

The present Fort Pitt Bridge over the Monongahela (1959) and the Fort Duquesne Bridge over the Allegheny (1968) are by George Richardson of Richardson, Gordon and Associates. Both are steel arch bridges stiffened by Warren trusses that carry two-level roadways. The short stretch of highway that joins the bridges at the Point was designed by the same firm, in collaboration with architect Charles Stotz and landscape architect Ralph Griswold.

What Pittsburghers mostly love about their bridges is their beauty as well as the symbolic and effective way they tie the city together. The now-demolished Bloomfield Bridge, joining Bloomfield and Polish Hill over a deep gully, was inaugurated in 1914 by holding a wedding at its centerpoint. Seven decades later, its successor of 1986 was inaugurated in the same way.

electric streetcars in 1911, which required replacing Lindenthal's original portals with the Gothic Revival entranceways of 1915 by Stanley Roush that stand today. The current aluminum railings were installed in 1933 in conjunction with an aluminum deck—the first use of structural aluminum in a bridge. Over the years, the piers have been reinforced with concrete and decorative lighting was added to the upper arches of the trusses, to make the bridge equally distinctive at night.

1.12 PITTSBURGH MUNICIPAL COURTS FACILITY
1995, L. D. Astorino and Associates.
660 First Ave.

Though unkindly jammed between the high bulk of the Allegheny County Jail (1994, Tasso Katselas) and Liberty Bridge, the Municipal Courts Facility was conceived as a public monument, in the largeness of spirit associated with Beaux-Arts planning. Linked to the jail by a secure walkway, the structure nonetheless distances itself from the jail with a distinctive cladding in green slate and the distinctive geometry of its plan. Only fifteen feet away from the underside of Liberty Bridge at one point, the diminutive courthouse stresses the multiple tiers of penthouses on its roof to provide visual interest to the thousands of motorists who literally look down on it each day. Inside, a similar insistence on economy and articulation prevails.

Pittsburgh Municipal Courts Facility

Oxford Centre

The longer north-south axis is marked with skylights inside and pinched oriel windows outside. Courtrooms—courts are held both day and night—occupy the prominent bay that opens off the long side to the east; offices fill the corresponding bay to the west. Perhaps the only flaw in this ambitious little monument is its half-hearted historicizing references to the luxurious courthouses by Richardson (1.15) and Hornbostel (1.14) a few blocks away. But, overall, here is a building that overcame a pedestrian function, a miserable site, and a meager budget to deliver far more than the client had the right to expect.

1.13 OXFORD CENTRE
1983, Hellmuth, Obata, Kassabaum (HOK).
301 Grant St.

This mixed-use development accommodates a retail atrium at street level with an adjoining parking garage, social club, and athletic center. Over this base sit four interlocking octagons paneled in silver-painted aluminum and glass, reaching a height of forty-six stories. The stylistic flair of Oxford Centre finds no specific counterpart among the staid older buildings of Grant Street, but the geometric clarity of the octagonal towers is analogous to the more sober buildings and the generous outlay of public space at the base makes Oxford the best stylistic "good neighbor" among all the post–World War II buildings downtown.

1.14 CITY-COUNTY BUILDING
1915–1917, Henry Hornbostel for Palmer, Hornbostel & Jones, with Edward B. Lee. 414 Grant St.

Hornbostel and Lee won the competition for the City-County Building in 1913. The building serves as Pittsburgh's City Hall and accommodates additional courtrooms for the county. The detailing appears to be by Lee in a modern interpretation of classicism, while the parti almost certainly came from Hornbostel. He turned away from the most obvious elements of Richardson's Courthouse and Jail (1.15)—the elaborate towers, projecting and receding pavilions, and extravagant pointed roof—to craft a simple, hollow-rectangle plan and nine-story granite elevation that speak as much the language of business as the rhetoric of government. Decorative touches at the City-County Building are limited to the high triple-arched portico, the Doric colonnade above it, and the barrel-vaulted interior galleria. This leads from an entrance loggia with tiled vaults by Rafael

City-County Building

Guastavino and cuts axially through the light-court. It is one of the most joyous spaces of downtown: fifty-feet high and four times as long, flooded with light from all four sides and glistening with bronze columns.

1.15 ALLEGHENY COUNTY COURTHOUSE AND JAIL
1883–1888, Henry Hobson Richardson. 436 Grant St.

Along with Trinity Church in Boston (1872–1877), this complex must be accounted as the masterpiece of Richardson's standing works; it is also among the most frequently imitated buildings in the United States, along with Independence Hall in Philadelphia. This building was pivotal for Pittsburgh. Before the courthouse, Pittsburgh had neither a single monumental building nor a proper downtown, since its main streets were given over to industry. With the construction of the courthouse, everything changed. Grant Street was edged with palatial skyscrapers, industry cleared out of the downtown, and Pittsburgh's citizens had, at last, a model of great architecture on a grand scale that private patrons such as Carnegie, Frick, Heinz, and Westinghouse could emulate when they considered designs for their offices, factories, and charitable benefactions. Judge Thomas Mellon was alone in protesting the extravagance of the new courthouse.

After the Greek Revival courthouse—a decent but provincial building—burned in 1882, the Allegheny County Commissioners planned for the most modern of government buildings. They selected their architect with equal care. The short list included two prominent westerners (William W. Boyington of Chicago and Elijah E. Myers of Detroit), two prominent easterners (John Ord of Philadelphia and George Post of New York City, who ceded his place to Richardson at the last moment), and Pittsburgh architect Andrew Peebles, who failed to exhibit his drawings by the deadline of December 1883.

Richardson took the lead from the first, with elaborate photolithographs showing the proposed building in the smoky setting of downtown Pittsburgh. The design appropriated medieval sources on the outside: Salamanca Cathedral's detailing for the front tower; Venice's Campanile for those at the rear; cornice from Notre-Dame in Paris; Bridge of Sighs from Venice; and basic, hollow-rectangle massing from Palazzo Farnese in Rome. Inside, the building showed the best of the early Beaux-Arts methodology of French architects J.-N.-L. Durand and Henri Labrouste: superb circulation, inventive and economical use of space, natural illumination flooding in from the courtyard and the street, maximum efficiency for judges, juries, lawyers, police, and even decent accommodation for the accused. But the "newer" Beaux-Arts thinking was present as well, in the dramatic main staircase that recalls the one at Charles Garnier's Opera in Paris and in the courtrooms that originally were of operatic sumptuousness. Courtroom 321 was stunningly restored by UDA Architects in 1987, spurred on by architectural historian Lu Donnelly and financed by the lawyers of Allegheny County. The jail was converted by IKM Architects in 2000 to courtrooms and offices for the County's Family Courts.

Richardson's strength as a designer is also evident in the courtyard. Here he dropped all allusion to history and worked in the pure rhythmic abstraction of his walls of Massachusetts granite. It was perhaps the first design for a public building in the nation that did not draw from any one specific historical source. When the design for this courtyard facade was transformed into a street facade for his Marshall Field Wholesale Store (1885–1887) in Chicago, it had an impact on American design for decades.

Allegheny County Courthouse and Jail

Richardson also considered the relationship between the courthouse and jail with Pittsburgh's downtown. The front tower acts like a compass, with the sun lighting up first its east face (toward the Hill and Oakland), then its south face (toward South Side), and finally its west face (Grant Street, but darkened now by the Frick Building (1.16), as though it were a civic cathedral for the citizenry. The configuration of the long sides, with their brooding arches flanked by half-towers, almost surely comes from Roman city gates: to enter the courthouse is to enter the city in microcosm.

Though critical reaction has always fixated on the more dramatic jail, which now houses supplementary courtrooms, it is in the courthouse that one sees best Richardson's genius for not only extracting the required function, but also fulfilling the longing for an image presented by his clients.

1.16 FRICK BUILDING
1902, Daniel Burnham & Co.
437 Grant St.

This structure is as complex as was its patron, Henry Clay Frick. While admirable as a building, it is bizarre in motivation and regrettable in urban impact. Frick perhaps wanted this specific site so he could look down—literally—on the Carnegie Building that, until 1950, stood to its immediate west. It was in that earlier building that Frick had fought his pitched battles with Andrew Carnegie. This towering edifice was to be his revenge, but revenge was extracted at a high price to the citizenry of Pittsburgh, because Frick's twenty-story tower all but blanks out views of the facade of Richardson's courthouse. The building itself is fine: here Burnham perfected the base-shaft-cap triad of the academic skyscraper that he was to use a year later in his Flatiron Building in New York City. That was a more interesting product in shape, but it was compromised in its fuzziness

of detail. Most of the elements in the Frick Building had been in Burnham's design vocabulary for years: the alternation of columns and glass bow windows appeared in his Rookery Building in Chicago twenty years earlier.

To the design Frick contributed his near-bottomless purse, deep enough to buy the splendid woods and brass of the lobby, the bronze lions by A. P. Proctor, and a stained glass window by John La Farge. Frick's enormous financial outlay was matched by his ego, which demanded many special touches to the building. These included the beautiful public rooms on the twentieth floor, originally a private club that Frick hoped would overtake the Duquesne Club. Frick's own offices were on the nineteenth floor, complete with dressing room and the luxurious bathroom at exactly the precise angle from which—if legend is correct—he could carry out his threat to rain down on Mr. Carnegie.

Frick Building (left) and Courthouse and Jail

In 1901, Andrew Carnegie's steelworks were transferred to a consortium headed by J. P. Morgan and reemerged as the United States Steel Corporation. As a result, Carnegie became the second-wealthiest man in the world, after John D. Rockefeller; the other major beneficiary was Pittsburgh, because of Carnegie's architectural contributions to the city in Oakland and other neighborhoods. It was left to three of Carnegie's partners — Henry Oliver, Henry Phipps, and Henry Clay Frick — to make their architectural marks on the Golden Triangle, which they did in three specific baronies. For his territory, Oliver staked out the two blocks between Fifth and Sixth avenues and Wood and Smithfield streets, where, between 1903 and 1910, he and his heirs erected two notable skyscrapers: 300 Sixth Avenue Building (1902, Daniel H. Burnham) and the Oliver Building (1908–1910, Daniel H. Burnham) at 535 Smithfield Street. In the same years, Henry Phipps put up his skyscrapers on the Allegheny's riverfront, with twin buildings (one is lost) on either side of Sixth Street (1.30), facing his boyhood neighborhood on the North Side.

Henry Clay Frick was yet more ambitious. In 1901, he envisioned financing and coordinating a whole troop of skyscrapers that would stretch a half-dozen blocks down Grant Street from Richardson's Courthouse and Jail (1.15) to the new Pennsylvania Station (1.35). Of the intended buildings, Frick put up his Frick Building (1.16) and Frick Annex (1902 and 1906, respectively, with his favorite architect, Daniel Burnham), the William Penn Hotel two blocks north, in 1914–1916, and the Union Trust Building by Frederick Osterling in 1917. These structures were only a fragment of Frick's vision, to be sure, but they marked the largest one-man development of coordinated commercial buildings in the nation until superseded by Rockefeller Center (1929–1934) in New York City.

Two Mellon Bank Center (Union Trust Building)

1.17 TWO MELLON BANK CENTER (UNION TRUST BUILDING)
1915–1917, Frederick J. Osterling with Pierre A. Liesch. 501 Grant St.

This structure carries downtown's most adventuresome skyline, with two ornate, chapel-like structures crowning its elaborate Flemish Gothic roof. Urban legend holds that these are chapels, even though they are nothing more than penthouse offices and housing for mechanical services. Other legends insist that the Catholic Church obliged Henry Clay Frick to erect these pseudo-chapels as a remembrance of old St. Paul Cathedral, which had once stood on the site. The more prosaic probability is that the design conformed to the pattern of New York City's then-new Woolworth Building, which had re-popularized the Gothic Revival style and a terra cotta skin. The design had two unexpected godfathers: art dealer Joseph Duveen (later Lord Duveen), Frick's art adviser, and the Luxembourg-born Pierre Liesch, Osterling's draftsman, who worked in Pittsburgh for about a decade. For some years, Liesch and Osterling battled in court over fees and artistic paternity

of the design. Osterling advanced his claim through the styling of his studio building of 1917 at 228 Isabella Street, which still stands as a miniaturized Union Trust facade.

The interior is no disappointment: four broad corridors, basically interior streets, lead to a brilliant, eleven-story central lightwell. Until 1923, these corridors were open to the fourth floor as a shopping arcade. Shutting down the arcade was not merely an aesthetic loss: it reduced the attractiveness of downtown Pittsburgh as a retail center and abetted the fragmentation of the city into zones of specialized function—something Pittsburgh planners have fought against ever since.

1.18 WILLIAM PENN HOTEL
1914–1916, Janssen and Abbott; 1928–1929, Janssen & Cocken and Joseph Urban. 530 William Penn Pl.

Henry Clay Frick conceived of this structure (though he later withdrew from its group of promoters) as the third of three in his private row along Grant Street, which at the time was a much less elegant thoroughfare than it is today. The first part of the hotel to open was the half that overlooks what is now Mellon Square (1.22); a decade would pass before Benno Janssen returned to add the Grant Street facade. Frick intended the William Penn Hotel to compete with the Plaza in New York City, which it does in technology if not in grandeur. The exterior cladding is brick (a colonial reference to William Penn, perhaps), while Renaissance Revival prevails inside in three handsome public spaces: the Terrace restaurant, Palm Court Lobby, and Grand Ballroom.

The lobby, a multi-tiered space with conversational seating groups enclosed in a deep arcade, is especially satisfying. The star of the Grant Street annex is the Urban Room, whose punning name recalls its author, the renowned Art Deco theater and set designer Joseph Urban. The sole survivor of a series of rooms designed

One Mellon Bank Center (Dravo Building)

by Urban that existed in the Congress Hotel in Chicago and the Bossert Hotel in Brooklyn, Pittsburgh's Urban room is starkly different from the rest of the hotel. Its walls are paneled in strips of brass-bound black glass and decorated with murals. An elliptical pseudo-Persian ceiling has paintings of Urban's own design. Urban called the design "modernistic but gay," an apt summation for this Art Deco masterpiece.

1.19 ONE MELLON BANK CENTER (DRAVO BUILDING)
1983, Welton Beckett Associates.
500 Fifth Ave.

This building represents an early use of a framed steel-tube structure, whose outer walls reduce lateral sway. This was achieved by bolting quarter-inch-thick steel plates, one bay wide and three stories high, directly to the building's steel frame. Consequently, the interior columns could be relatively small and far apart, which gained the fifty-four-story tower more than eighteen inches around the perimeter of its core; this translated into an impressive additional 1.7 million square feet of rentable space. Project director David Beer declared that the primary basis for his design was to contextualize it with the pre-existing architecture of Grant Street, above all Richardson's adjacent Court-

house and Jail (1.15). This choice resulted in a melange of elements from the courthouse, the neighboring Frick Building (1.16), Union Trust (1.17), and USX Tower (1.36). The intention proved finer than the result, but there was one definite improvement over the predecessor building: the new tower was canted far back from Grant Street, giving Pittsburgh its best view of the courthouse in half a century.

1.20 MACY'S DEPARTMENT STORE (KAUFMANN'S DEPARTMENT STORE)
1898, Charles Bickel; 1913 addition
Janssen and Abbott. 400 Fifth Ave.

Founded in 1871 as a tailoring shop on the South Side by four immigrant brothers who had graduated from peddling, Kaufmann's Department Store found itself by 1885 at the best corner downtown, Smithfield Street and Fifth Avenue, where it erected a replica of the Statue of Liberty. The building that stands now as the south half of the block-long store, at Smithfield and Forbes Avenue, is a wing added in 1898 that combines Classical Revival, Romanesque

Macy's Department Store (Kaufmann's Department Store)

Revival, and Chicago School motifs. In 1913, Edgar Kaufmann, of the second generation, tore down the original 1885 store on the north half of the block and commissioned its replacement: this delicate, thirteen-story white terra cotta extension from Benno Janssen. In those same years, the store began leasing the wooded property southeast of Pittsburgh that would later host Kaufmann's weekend house, Fallingwater, by Frank Lloyd Wright.

Kaufmann's brilliance as a retailer derived in large part from his commercial exploitation of architectural and technical innovation. Janssen and Cocken's ground floor redecoration of the store in 1930 used state-of-the-art technology and contemporary design to create what architectural critics and retailing connoisseurs in the 1930s called the most beautiful store in the world. (Kaufmann had demurred on a more radical Art Deco remake from New York City's Joseph Urban.) Along with his commission of Fallingwater in 1934, Kaufmann employed Frank Lloyd Wright to design his tenth-floor private office within the store. This was acclaimed as perhaps the most noble achievement ever rendered out of plywood, but, following Kaufmann's death in 1955, the office was given to the Victoria and Albert Museum in London in 1974. The ground floor has not fared well, though Art Deco elements survive.

1.21 PARK BUILDING
1896, George B. Post. 355 Fifth Ave.

By the 1890s, the brothers David E. and William G. Park had brought their father's Black Diamond Steel Works (6.3) to world renown in specialty steel, and they sought to diversify their investments. Their goal was to put up Pittsburgh's most imposing office block, for which they chose the then-busiest corner in the city, opposite the Mellon brothers' bank and the Kaufmann brothers' giant retail store. This was the fourth steel-skeleton tower in Pittsburgh, and, at fifteen stories, it was significantly taller than the Carnegie Building (demolished) of a few years before. Today, it survives as the only downtown skyscraper of the nineteenth century. New York City architect George Post was, at the time, the pre-eminent designer of commercial buildings in the Beaux-Arts style. The novelty of the Park Building has always been the thirty telemones, or atlas figures, that bear the top cornice on their shoulders. The overall design remains an excellent material lesson in early skyscraper packaging influenced by New York City's skyscrapers (as opposed to those of Chicago), which were reluctant to sacrifice decoration to the demands of modern function and utility.

1.22 REGIONAL ENTERPRISE TOWER & MELLON SQUARE (ALCOA)
(ALCOA) 1953, Harrison & Abramovitz, with Altenhof & Bown and Mitchell and Ritchey; 1955, Mitchell and Ritchey; Simonds and Simonds, landscape architects. 425 Sixth Ave. (Mellon Square).

The ALCOA building is one of the architectural icons of post–World War II America. The integration of windows within their spandrels,

Regional Enterprise Tower (ALCOA Building)

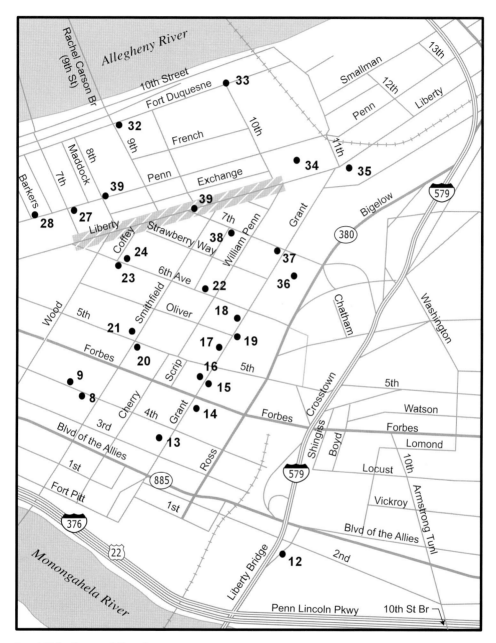

Around Mellon Square and Grant Street.
Approximate walking time: several hours to a half-day.

the simplicity of bolting the aluminum panels on their frames, the ease of cleaning the swivel windows, and the broad internal corridors that served as impromptu conference centers—these were all innovations that were supposed to change forever the art of building skyscrapers. Instead, ALCOA's influence was muted and aluminum-clad office towers remain a rarity. The ALCOA corporation itself left the building in 1998 for a low-rise of a radically different configuration on the Allegheny shore (4.1). The thirty-story tower and its striking glass-walled entrance pavilion now house a consortium of city and regional planning agencies that hope to emulate the postwar synergy of Pittsburgh's Renaissance I.

Mellon Square was conceived to highlight ALCOA, to the north, and Mellon Bank, to the south, as two crown jewels of the Mellon empire. It still bespeaks the community spiritedness of cousins Paul and Richard King Mellon, who financed the project, and the ingenuity of the architects and landscape designers in consolidating a parking garage, fringe of retail stores, cascading fountain, and ample space for lunchtime patrons.

1.23 TRINITY CATHEDRAL AND GRAVEYARD, AND FIRST PRESBYTERIAN CHURCH
(Trinity) 1872, Gordon W. Lloyd; (First Presbyterian) 1905, Theophilus P. Chandler, Jr. 328 and 320 Sixth Ave.

In 1787, the Penn family donated four lots on Sixth Avenue for the congregations of Pittsburgh. Though several different church buildings have been constructed on the plot, an Episcopalian and a Presbyterian congregation worship on the site to the present day. The Episcopalian congregation's first church, an octagonal structure, was at Sixth and Liberty avenues. The second church, designed in 1824 by John H. Hopkins, the congregation's rector, was one of the earliest Gothic Revival churches on the continent and the first in Pittsburgh.

That structure was razed in 1869 to allow for the construction of the present stone building by the English-born and trained but Detroit-based architect Lloyd. Lloyd's design derived from early fourteenth-century English Decorated Gothic precedents. Glass from the second church was incorporated into this structure, although some was replaced after a fire in 1969. Most of the rib-vaulted interior was undamaged. A notable interior addition is the pulpit of 1922 by Bertram G. Goodhue. In 1927, the church was elevated to cathedral status and became the seat of the Pittsburgh Diocese.

First Presbyterian Church, though more recent, has a longer history on the site. The Presbyterians erected a brick structure in 1802, which was rebuilt in 1812 by Benjamin H. Latrobe during his time in Pittsburgh. That structure was replaced (1851–1853) to a design by Charles F. Bartberger, which was in turn razed when the congregation sold the land for the construction (1902–1904) of the Daniel Burnham-designed building that later became the McCreery Department Store (now 300 Sixth Avenue Building). The present church dates from 1903–1905 and is a hybrid of thirteenth- and fourteenth-century English Gothic; it clothes a single large meeting hall designed for preaching. First Presbyterian's thirteen Tiffany windows are its glory, while the delight of Trinity is the old graveyard, with tombs from the eighteenth century.

1.24 DUQUESNE CLUB
1889, Longfellow, Alden, & Harlow; 1903, Rutan and Russell; 1931, Janssen and Cocken. 325 Sixth Ave.

Founded in 1873 and located on this site since 1889, the Duquesne Club's architectural setting is appropriate to its fame as the most influential businessman's club in its region. Richardsonian Romanesque was a natural choice in the year following the opening of Richardson's nearby Courthouse and Jail (1.15), and Longfellow and

Alden had apprenticed with Richardson. This commission made them one of Pittsburgh's leading design firms for two decades. The brownstone facade combines Richardson's bold materials and motifs with a more conventional classicism, which became the firm's hallmark, as it recast itself into the local equivalent of New York City's McKim, Mead, and White.

1.25 TWO PNC CENTER (EQUIBANK)
1974, Natalie DeBlois of Skidmore, Owings, and Merrill (SOM). 2 Oliver Plaza.

Oliver Plaza's three skyscrapers are shoehorned into a lackluster piazza with hardly enough breathing room for one. It was over the objections of the city planning department that the client insisted on overloading the site, but luckily SOM minimized the potential damage by creating this thirty-four-story, octagonal tower of reflective glass that nicely complements the skewed orientation of the adjacent PNC tower.

Dominion Tower (Consolidated Natural Gas Tower)

SOM's primary designer was Natalie DeBlois, who made this building the world's largest designed by a woman at that time.

1.26 DOMINION TOWER
(CONSOLIDATED NATURAL GAS TOWER)
1987, William Pedersen for Kohn Pedersen Fox Associates. 625 Liberty Ave.

The Dominion Tower is an example of the corporate lavishness of the Reagan years by a favored architectural firm of that decade. Like its Cincinnati headquarters for Procter & Gamble, Dominion is a richly detailed skyscraper carefully tailored to the shapes and sizes of neighboring buildings. An inviting plaza and pedestrian arcade outside and opulent use of traditional luxury materials inside give Dominion both distinctive character and human scale. These qualities make Dominion superior to Pittsburgh's other 1980s skyscrapers, particularly the coldness of PPG Place (1.5) a few blocks away.

Two PNC Center (Equibank)

Clad in panels of brown and pink granite, this thirty-two-story tower is meant to be seen as much from a distance as close-up. At a distance, its most obvious feature is a barrel-vaulted roof framed by arched steel trusses that mimic the nearby Sixteenth Street Bridge (4.24) over the Allegheny River. Closer, Dominion's complex massing and adroitly placed stone cornices align its bulk with the twenty-story row of older buildings to the north. On its south side, the tower scales down to a four-story segment that keeps it from overwhelming Heinz Hall (1.29) and an adjacent small park. The visual deference to Heinz Hall is appropriate, since Dominion stands on land owned by a Heinz foundation; its land rent supports the Pittsburgh Cultural Trust as the current overseer of the neighborhood.

1.27 BENEDUM CENTER FOR THE PERFORMING ARTS (STANLEY THEATER)
1928, Hoffman and Henon; 1987, restoration and addition, MacLachlan Cornelius and Filoni. 207 Seventh St.

The Pittsburgh Cultural Trust was born in the 1980s with the goal of weaning eight central blocks of downtown Pittsburgh from pornography to high culture. The blocks were demarcated by the Convention Center and Liberty Center on the east, Gateway Center on the west, the Allegheny riverfront on the north, and Liberty Avenue on the south. The success of this transformation was almost immediate in terms of improvements to the infrastructure (such as sidewalks, signage, and lighting), restoration of facades, and the new audiences and crowds of people that were attracted downtown. The area's two theaters—the Penn, now Heinz Hall (1.29), and this, the Stanley—had declined along with their surroundings.

The Stanley (now the Benedum), the third largest theater in the nation when built, was renovated as a performance space for the Pitts-

burgh Opera, Pittsburgh Ballet, Civic Light Opera, and Dance Council. To help accommodate these new functions, a new six-story backstage was added, which also includes two rehearsal halls. The old Stanley's exterior of off-white terra cotta and brick was restored to its original appearance.

1.28 THEATER SQUARE (INCORPORATING THE O'REILLY THEATER)
1999, Michael Graves. 621 Penn Ave.

The Pittsburgh Cultural Trust purchased and renovated several older structures between Liberty Avenue and the Allegheny riverfront, but Theater Square is its main venture in new construction. Consisting of a theater and parking garage by Michael Graves (an office tower remains an unfunded dream for the moment),

Theater Square (incorporating the O'Reilly Theater)

plus a small plaza designed by sculptor Louise Bourgeois and landscape architect Daniel Kiley in collaboration with Graves, the complex sits opposite Benedum Center and a block from Heinz Hall (1.29). Within a few minutes walk are the Harris Theater and the Byham Theater, also projects of the Trust. As the home of the Pittsburgh Public Theater, the O'Reilly is the key element in Theater Square. It features a thrust stage and holds 650 people on three levels. Externally, the theater is boldly articulated as a glass and concrete half-cylinder at ground level and a half-barrel-vaulted rehearsal hall above. The garage acts as an eleven-story pylon of brick and pre-cast concrete.

The innovative part of the complex is the park. Bourgeois designed a twenty-five-foot tall freeform bronze volcano through which water courses in rivulets. Spectators rest on smooth eyeball-shaped granite benches in a grove of trees.

1.29 HEINZ HALL
1927, C. W. Rapp and George Rapp; 1971, restored, Stotz, Hess, MacLachlan and Fosner. 600 Penn Ave.

Marcus Loew's Penn Theater, which opened as the "Temple of the Cinema," has the mixture of French Baroque and Rococo features that were a hallmark of the movie-theater specialists Rapp and Rapp of Chicago. The Penn was one of the first old cinema palaces in the nation to find new life as a concert hall. H. J. Heinz, II personally financed its revival, using his own favorite hall, the Vienna Opera, as guide. The Heinz endowments added the garden plaza next door as an intermission space in summer. Heinz Hall and the Benedum Center (1.27) work in easy coordination, and it is interesting to note that it is Heinz Hall, with its cream-puff renovation, that is the popular favorite, not the archaeologically correct Benedum.

1.30 RENAISSANCE PITTSBURGH HOTEL (FULTON BUILDING)
1906, Grosvenor Atterbury; 2000–2001, JG Johnson Architects, with CelliFlynnBrennan Architects and Planners. 107 Sixth St.

This is the sole survivor of a set of downtown skyscrapers erected by Henry Phipps, the most socially minded of Carnegie's partners, for both profit and social betterment. Grosvenor Atterbury, creator of innovative housing designs in Forest Hills, New York, was as progressive as his patron, although in Pittsburgh only this commercial tower (now a 300-room hotel) survives, and not his Pittsburgh bath houses, swimming pools, or subsidized housing. The Fulton's trademark was its seven-story-high arch fronting the Allegheny River, which twenty years later also became the leitmotif for the neighboring Roberto Clemente Bridge (1.31). That visual homage to the riverfront—all too rare in Pittsburgh—was made complete around 1990 when the trompe l'oeil painter Richard Haas added a bold mural about steel-making on the bare riverfront facade of the Byham (formerly Gayety) Theater (101 Sixth St.) of 1903.

1.31 ROBERTO CLEMENTE, ANDY WARHOL, AND RACHEL CARSON BRIDGES (SIXTH, SEVENTH, AND NINTH STREET BRIDGES)
1925–1928, Vernon Covell et al., engineers; Stanley Roush, architect. Sixth, Seventh, and Ninth sts. and the Allegheny River.

The only coordinated set in town, these suspension bridges are pleasing aesthetically and reminders that Pittsburgh played a major role in the history of bridge building. The "Three Sisters" bridges, as these are popularly known, were conceived in 1925 jointly by Pittsburgh's Civic Arts Commission and the Allegheny County Bureau of Bridges when the War Department

The Andy Warhol Bridge

required higher clearance on the river. These are self-anchored suspension bridges: the anchors to the suspension chains are not buried in the earth, but are visible as the box girders separating the roadway from the sidewalks. The resulting structures are light and lyrical, among the best marriages of art and engineering in the nation. Their names record three Pittsburghers who were creative in very different fields: baseball, art, and ecology.

1.32 PITTSBURGH HIGH SCHOOL FOR THE CREATIVE AND PERFORMING ARTS (CAPA)
2003, MacLachlan Cornelius and Filoni.
111 Ninth St.

Among the brightest of recent buildings designed with Pittsburgh's riverfronts in mind is this six-story half-traditional, half-outrageous,

cornerstone of the city's downtown cultural district. CAPA trains about 500 students each year. Partner in charge Albert Filoni and project architect Ken Lee produced a building that acknowledges the urban context stylistically and chromatically, and then expands on it. The long Ninth Street facade takes its cue from the old brick office building next door, six stories of which were appropriated for the new school. The shorter riverfront facade incorporates a gigantic electronic screen that presents student work and a curved six-floor-high glass wall enlivened with whimsical polychromy. The wall reflects the contemporary ALCOA center (4.1) on the opposite bank of the Allegheny.

CAPA's program was complex: laboratories, a 400-seat proscenium theater, rehearsal space, shops, and studios for dance, painting, and sculpture classes, all of which had to fit within a 175,000-square-foot structure. In addition, CAPA needed classrooms for regular academic subjects. Filoni embraced this programmatic diversity in his loose amalgam of micro-facade elements, which he quilted from white-glazed block, red brick, and glass into a strikingly polyphonic and intentionally jarring exterior.

Pittsburgh High School for the Creative and Performing Arts (CAPA)

1.33 DAVID LAWRENCE CONVENTION CENTER
2001–2003, Rafael Viñoly, with Burt Hill Kosar Rittelmann Associates. 1000 Fort Duquesne Blvd.

Pittsburgh was no more sensitive in its treatment of its riverfront than were most American cities: the rivers of interest were rivers of commerce, and the only banks Pittsburghers cared about were made of marble and housed vaults. That was true for an earlier Lawrence Convention Center from the 1980s, a forbidding box that entirely turned its back on the Allegheny River. Since then, Pittsburgh has created several new buildings that embrace and accentuate their riverside sites. The most intriguing of these is Viñoly's glazed catenary curve, which echoes three neighboring suspension bridges and eagerly thrusts its way toward the Allegheny River. The roof, held by fifteen cables, allows for unimpeded space inside and draws in cooler river air at a third-floor level, which is circulated through natural convection. Hot air rises and exits through a clerestory. Flag-topped masts externally express the building's structural tensions. The building earned a gold rating from the U.S. Green Building Council for site selection and use of non-toxic and recycled building materials.

Approximately half this complex is a parking garage, separated from the exhibition space by Tenth Street, which still carries traffic through an arcade in the building. The upper part of the Tenth Street arcade becomes a festive observation deck overlooking the river; the lower part is a ramp leading down to the water itself. The complex seems to reflect an awareness of its role as a historic nexus in American transportation history: here John Roebling's suspended aqueduct carried the barges of the old Pennsylvania Canal into the city 150 years before, and the main rail line between New York City and Chicago still snakes around the Eleventh Street end of the new building.

1.34 THE FEDERATED BUILDING (LIBERTY CENTER)
1985–1987, The Architects Collaborative, UDA Architects, and Burt Hill Kosar Rittelmann Associates. 1000 Penn Ave.

The primary function of Liberty Center was to provide a 600-room hotel (Westin Convention Center Hotel) immediately adjacent to the Lawrence Convention Center (1.33). This was expanded to encompass a twenty-seven-story office tower (Federated Investors Office Tower) and a perimeter of shops. The floor-to-ceiling

David Lawrence Convention Center

The Pennsylvanian Apartments (Pennsylvania Station, Union Station)

glazed storefronts are strategically placed between the two towers, with two-story lobbies as transition points at both ends. Nonetheless, they have yet to create a draw between the retail attractions in the Golden Triangle to the west and the popular wholesalers in The Strip to the east.

1.35 THE PENNSYLVANIAN APARTMENTS (PENNSYLVANIA STATION, UNION STATION)
1900–1902, Daniel H. Burnham and Co.
1100 Liberty Ave.

The northern apex to the Golden Triangle had already served as terminus of the Pennsylvania Canal and home to three successive railroad stations when Alexander Cassatt commissioned Burnham for this stirring rail portal to Pittsburgh. It was Cassatt, a native Pittsburgher and brother of the Impressionist painter Mary Cassatt, who oversaw Burnham's later Union Station in Washington, DC, and New York City's Pennsylvania Station from McKim, Mead and White. In 1900, Burnham was still riding his national fame as chief architect of the World's Columbian Exposition of 1893 in Chicago. In Pittsburgh, he was primarily remembered for his Exposition buildings of 1895 at the Point. Among Burnham's surviving Pittsburgh buildings are the Frick Building and Frick Annex (1.16), Highland Building (1910; 121 S. Highland Ave.), the original Union Trust Building on Fourth Avenue (1898; 337 Fourth Ave.), and the Oliver Building (1910) on Mellon Square.

At the last minute, what had been planned as a four-story building was expanded into a twelve-story edifice. The impetus for the design change probably came from Cassatt, but one suspects also the hand of Henry Clay Frick, who was about to become the Pennsylvania's largest stockholder. The basic parti of the shelved plan later resurfaced as the key element in Burnham's Union Station. Here the tower is fronted by an elegant, domed cab shelter, one of whose pendentive ornaments recall the twenty-year period (1891–1911) when Pittsburgh's name was spelled without a final "h."

Burnham manipulated standard Beaux-Arts stylistic devices for the main building and the rotunda, but employed them with restraint so as not to compromise function. The brown brick and terra cotta facade has a smooth, even texture. The main block sits on a high basement, the better to provide more bulk for its vista down Liberty Avenue. Curved entrance ramps give extra majesty to the low arches of the rotunda, which is often accounted as the most captivating architectural element in Pittsburgh.

Preservation of so large and functionally specific a building was not easy. The Pennsylvania Railroad intended to tear down the station in 1966 as part of its 148-acre Penn Park redevelopment; then, four years later, the merged Pennsylvania and New York Central railroads declared bankruptcy, imperiling the terminal a second time. The rotunda and office block now house a large apartment complex, while rail passengers catch their trains from a modest depot at the rear.

USX Tower (United States Steel Building)

vertical steel columns, each set three feet outside the curtain wall, such that columns and curtain wall connect at every third floor. The columns of Cor-Ten steel are self-oxidizing; hence they are free of any further rust. Every column circulates coolant inside, so, should the tower ever be engulfed in flames, it would keep cool for four hours before surrendering to the heat.

1.36 USX TOWER
(UNITED STATES STEEL BUILDING)
1967–1971, Harrison and Abramovitz and Abbe Architects. 600 Grant St.

At sixty-four stories and 841 feet, the USX Tower is the tallest structure in downtown Pittsburgh and symbolic of the city both in its triangular shape and its structural innovations in steel. The exterior features eighteen exposed

1.37 KOPPERS BUILDING
1927–1929, Graham, Anderson, Probst and White. 436 Seventh Ave.

The relocation of the Pennsylvania Railroad's freight yards in 1927 gave new life to what, for generations, had been the blighted corner of Grant Street and Seventh Avenue. In the space of five years, Andrew Mellon masterminded the construction of four key buildings at the corner: Koppers; the Art Deco building for the Pittsburgh branch of the Federal Reserve Bank of Cleveland (1930–1931, Walker and Weeks with Hornbostel and Wood); the forty-four-story Gulf Building (1930–1932, Trowbridge and Livingston), and the massive U.S. Post Office and Federal Courthouse (1930–1932, also by Trowbridge and Livingston) on the remaining corner of the block.

Mellon could pull off this pharaonic-scaled patronage because he and his brother, R. B. Mellon, were chief shareholders in Koppers and Gulf, while he was at the same time U.S. Secretary of the Treasury. To keep everything securely in the family, Mellon used his nephew Edward P. Mellon as supervising architect for the Koppers Building and the family's Mellon-Stuart construction firm to build it. Mellon was probably also remembering the architectural ambitions of his friend Henry Clay Frick, who, in the previous decade, had begun to line Grant Street with office towers. Even the choice of the architects was meaningful: the firm of Graham, Anderson, Probst, & White was the direct successor to Daniel Burnham, Frick's favorite architect.

But times had changed since Frick was building. In 1927, Art Deco, not Beaux-Arts, was the reigning style, so Koppers took on an appropriately streamlined image. Rising thirty-five stories with two setbacks, the first three stories of Koppers are polished gray granite, while the tower is Indiana limestone. Plain gray ribs exaggerate the building's height, and the spandrels sparkle with low-relief geometric designs. The final luster comes from a chateauesque copper roof that is spotlighted at night in a dramatic green glow. The interior, too, is a jewel. The three-story lobby has cream-colored Italian marble walls veined in pale brown with a greenish tint, and a parquet floor in pink and gray Tennessee marble. A flower-like design in cast bronze unifies elevator doors, directory panels, clocks, and balcony railings throughout

the building. In the manner of the times, the cast-bronze mailbox is a miniature of the building, roof and all.

1.38 VERIZON BUILDING (BELL TELEPHONE OF PENNSYLVANIA BUILDING)
1890, Frederick J. Osterling.
416–420 Seventh Ave.

This Romanesque Revival style switching hall is one of the earliest corporate buildings downtown and may be the oldest telecommunication facility still in use in the nation. It shows Osterling, who, as far as we know, never met Richardson, in the thrall of his work. Even the pier monogram imitates Richardson's on the Courthouse capitals. At seven stories, this was one of the taller buildings in the Golden Triangle, but the tremendous depth of the brick walls (as the windows reveal) shows that Osterling, or perhaps his client, was not yet ready to build in steel.

Verizon Building (Bell Telephone of Pennsylvania Building)

1.39 LOFT BUILDINGS

1870–1927. 800–900 blocks Penn Ave. and 700–900 blocks Liberty Ave.

These two blocks were important as wholesale stores for manufactured goods and produce in the second half of the nineteenth century. The street was both marketplace and thoroughfare; until 1905, the Pennsylvania Railroad ran freight cars right down the middle. Three generations of loft buildings survive: the earliest, at 805–807 (which bear the foundry mark of the Pittsburgh firm of Anderson & Phillips), 927–929, and 951–953 Liberty, have cast-iron Italianate facades and date from soon after the Civil War. Stores of this time often employed Gothic detailing, as does the store of 1881 at 820 Liberty. Most dramatic of all are the Richardsonian Romanesque lofts, such as the nine-story Ewart Building (1891) by Charles Bickel at 921–925 Liberty and the towering McGinnis Building (1891) at number 915. Equivalent tall buildings, generally more subdued in architectural detailing, survive on Penn Avenue.

CHAPTER 2:
OAKLAND

The Oakland plateau consists of several hundred acres at a much higher elevation than the Golden Triangle and three miles removed from it, to the east. This plateau, crowded now by buildings for the University of Pittsburgh and the UPMC medical center, lay virtually fallow until 1890, as part of a tract of several thousand acres that once stretched from Lawrenceville to Squirrel Hill. The land belonged to a single absentee owner, the London-based heiress Mary Schenley, who had inherited it from her two Revolutionary-era grandfathers, James O'Hara and George Croghan. Schenley's land was topographically erratic, with a steep hill to the north and two gullies—the St. Pierre Ravine and Junction Hollow—cutting it from the south. In 1890, Schenley gave about 400 of her acres for the making of Schenley Park (pages 48-49), but Andrew Carnegie siphoned off the best twenty acres for the new library (2.14) that he proposed to build between the two gullies.

No other part of Pittsburgh needed such dramatic changes to its natural topography before it could be settled. Between 1897 and 1915, the city artificially banked up the picturesque Flagstaff Hill in Schenley Park, bridged Junction Hollow once to carry an elegant drive into the park, then bridged it a second time to carry Forbes Avenue from the expanded Carnegie Institute to another of Carnegie's major benefactions, the Carnegie Technical Schools, now Carnegie Mellon University (2.16-2.19). (Carnegie was expediently named an executor to Schenley's estate when she died in 1903.) The city obligingly filled in the St. Pierre Ravine to render Schenley Plaza a proper entrance to Carnegie's library; it also rerouted Bellefield Avenue to funnel visitors to Carnegie Museum's new main entrance.

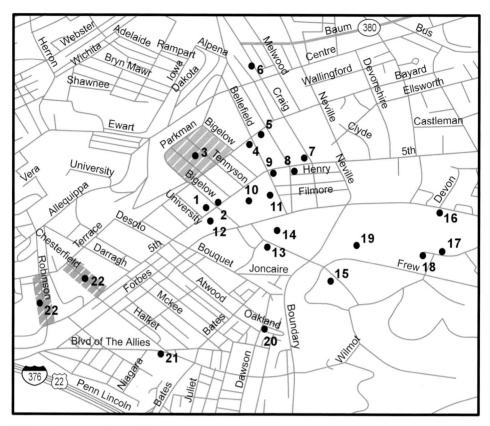

Oakland. Approximate walking and driving time: one extended half-day.

If Carnegie provided the money, then local land speculator, realtor, and developer Franklin Felix Nicola (1860–1938) provided the inspired vision for Oakland (the name derives from the estate of the glassmaker William Eichbaum, German for oak tree). Nicola, who also owned a lumber company, dreamed of building a fine residential area adjacent to a civic center. He either lured institutions to build in Oakland—the University of Pittsburgh being his biggest catch—or he invented them. The result, in an inspired partnership with the Paris-trained designer Henry Hornbostel, was block after block of one of the more harmonious City Beautiful environments in the nation.

The interiors of Oakland's grand institutional buildings provide special delights as well. Not to be missed are Phipps Conservatory (2.15); the Carnegie Library (2.14) and museums; the University of Pittsburgh's Cathedral of Learning (2.10), Heinz Chapel (2.11), and Frick Fine Arts Building (2.13); Carnegie Mellon's Research Institute (2.9) and College of Fine Arts (2.18); two excellent churches and a synagogue; and the flamboyant Soldiers and Sailors Memorial Hall (2.1). The statuary, landscaping, and visual linkage among Oakland's monuments are of the same high quality as the interiors.

There is, inevitably, a downside to all this magnificence. Decades before Carnegie fixed his eyes on Schenley's land, Oakland had provided thousands of modest homes for the ironworkers in the nearby Eliza Furnaces of Jones and Laughlin. The grand institutions and the modest residential neighborhoods have historically clashed in many a pitched battle, with the common citizen almost always on the losing side. The worst of the excesses came with the University of Pittsburgh's medical center, which by any measure is now overcrowded and overbuilt. There has been some recent improvement in Oakland's livability. Schenley Plaza redeemed itself by converting a mammoth parking lot into a lovely greensward, and bit by bit some hospitals are leaving Oakland: Children's has relocated to Lawrenceville and other research centers have moved to Shadyside and Bloomfield. "People's Oakland" (as one advocacy group calls itself) is finally asserting itself.

2.1 SOLDIERS' AND SAILORS' NATIONAL MILITARY MUSEUM AND MEMORIAL HALL (ALLEGHENY COUNTY SOLDIERS' AND SAILORS' MEMORIAL)
1907–1910, Palmer and Hornbostel.
4141 Fifth Ave.

In 1903, in the largest real estate transaction in Pittsburgh history to that point, Cleveland-born Franklin Nicola purchased a 103-acre enclave at the base of Oakland hill from the estate of Mary Schenley. This long-delayed tribute to local veterans of the Civil War stands on part of that land. After Henry Hornbostel, as the local favorite, won the competition against the much more senior Cass Gilbert, John Russell Pope, and Ernest Flagg, he faced a second hurdle: the siting. The building was to have faced east, toward Bigelow Boulevard, but Hornbostel convinced the county commissioners to rotate the plan, so it now faces south, fronted by a great lawn to Fifth Avenue.

The sandstone memorial, an adaptation of the Mausoleum of Halicarnassus, stands on a high concave podium, with meeting rooms set at the corners of the base. Engaged Doric columns and a triplex of doorways give a heroic scale to the three main facades, but more

Soldiers' and Sailors' National Military Museum and Memorial Hall (Allegheny County Soldiers' and Sailors' Memorial)

Pittsburgh Athletic Association (left) and the former Masonic Temple

prominent still is the cast concrete pyramidal roof. The cornice is the best in Pittsburgh, its linked eagles furthering the memorial's historicizing aura with the Roman symbol for military power. Charles Keck's bronze statue of America stands above the main entrance.

2.2 PITTSBURGH ATHLETIC ASSOCIATION
1909–1911, Janssen and Abbott.
4215 Fifth Ave.

This structure jump-started Oakland's civic center and Benno Janssen's lucrative career as a Pittsburgh society architect. Architectural critic Montgomery Schuyler deemed the Pittsburgh Athletic Association (PAA) one of Pittsburgh's outstanding buildings and Janssen its best architect, when he wrote about the city in *Architectural Record* in 1911. Janssen produced this made-up Venetian Renaissance palace, with its learned quotes from Italian Renaissance precedents, as the first in a series of clubhouses envisioned by the land speculator and developer Franklin Nicola. A member of the New York Athletic Club, Nicola invented the PAA in 1908 as its Pittsburgh equivalent. For the limestone and terra cotta clubhouse facade, Janssen used

stacked Corinthian orders: double-height paired pilasters for the lower floors and paired columns for the upper floors, each level set off by a prominent modillioned cornice. The rooms inside are triumphs of the same sophisticated historicism, not copies but stirring emulations of Medieval and Renaissance interiors.

The PAA spawned numerous other commissions for Janssen, some literally in its sight. The Masonic Temple (now the University of Pittsburgh's Alumni Hall) went up next door in 1914 as a somber but stately foil; design cues from classical antiquity appropriately portray remoteness and secrecy, as the massive, Hellenistic side-gable temple coolly hovers above its exaggerated basement story. In 1916, Janssen produced an elaborate scheme for Henry Clay Frick of hundreds of apartments grouped around courtyards in the manner of the Palais Royale in Paris. This was to have occupied Frick's fourteen acres opposite the PAA, where the Cathedral of Learning (2.10) now stands, but nothing came of it. In 1924, Janssen designed the Young Men and Women's Hebrew Association (now the University of Pittsburgh's Bellefield Hall) on the eastern border of those same acres, at 315 Bellefield Avenue. An eclectic mix of Italian Renaissance and colonial Virginia, it works as well as the PAA on its modest budget. In the 1930s, Janssen was still designing for the same neighborhood, this time rebuilding the Twentieth Century Club (4201 Bigelow Boulevard) in a recollection of Michelangelo's Palazzo del Senatore in Rome. He also created several house designs for Schenley Farms (2.3), the Mellon Institute (2.9) a few blocks to the east, and Eberly Hall (formerly Alumni Hall) on the hillside portion of the University of Pittsburgh campus. A richer or more varied production by a single architect for a single neighborhood can hardly be imagined.

2.3 SCHENLEY FARMS
1905–1920, various architects. Bounded by Bigelow Blvd. and Parkman, Lytton, and Tennyson aves.

This housing development is another product of Franklin Nicola's purchase of much of the Mary Schenley estate. In 1898, Nicola had already built the ten-story Schenley Hotel (2.12), today the University of Pittsburgh's student union, on one corner of that eccentric heiress's idle farmland while Schenley was yet alive. In 1906, Nicola sold a separate forty-five acres for the university's upper campus. But the core of his vision was to transform this large patch of farmland into the best inner-city neighborhood in the nation. After an initial investment of $2.5 million, Nicola's Schenley Farms Company spent an additional $1.5 million to lay out streets, plant shade trees, landscape, and lay underground utility conduits—this last nearly unheard-of anywhere else in the city. Nicola hired a dozen leading Pittsburgh architects to design eleven sample houses by 1906.

Mostly Tudor Revival and Colonial Revival in style, the homes contained such luxuries as thirteen-inch-deep brick walls with insulating air pockets, brass pipes, hardwood floors, finished basements, under-window radiators, vacuum ducts, telephones, elaborate woodwork, and stained glass. Today, these homes would be prohibitively expensive to replicate. Forty-five more houses were completed by 1909 and a total of ninety-six by 1920. Around 1913, another forty homes, smaller but equally good in design and finish, were constructed in the adjoining Schenley Farms Terrace on Centre Avenue by the design firm of Janssen and Abbott.

Nicola never revealed the source of his vision for Schenley Farms, but connections to similar improvements elsewhere are likely. The Cleveland suburbs of Euclid Heights and Shaker Heights, parallel developments with the same detailed planning, had begun taking shape around 1892 and 1904, respectively. Nicola resided in Cleveland in 1892 and was still in close touch with that city in 1904. Another contemporary of Schenley Farms was the Sage Foundation's Forest Hills Gardens in Queens, New York, which possibly gave Nicola the idea of naming his streets after English writers. Schenley Farms is smaller than these three neighborhoods but, unlike its possible precedents, it contributed population to the host city rather than drawing residents to the suburbs. Nicola's vision was the city integrated, not segregated. He promoted Schenley Farms for the easy access it gave to good music, art, books, and companionship in the schools, concert halls, libraries, and clubs nearby. Nicola attempted to lure the City of Pittsburgh to build a convention center on part of his Oakland holdings, but the city politicians demurred. Like so many urban visionaries of great design, Nicola died nearly bankrupt.

2.4 FIRST BAPTIST CHURCH
1909–1912, Bertram Grosvenor Goodhue for Cram, Goodhue & Ferguson. 159 North Bellefield Ave.

Forced to sell its downtown property (1.14) to make way for the City-County Building in 1909, the congregation relocated to this corner overlooking Oakland's emerging civic center. Until the Cathedral of Learning (2.10) changed Oakland's scale, First Baptist could be seen across the neighborhood. First Baptist reveals Goodhue's skill in manipulating traditional Gothic elements into a modern idiom for the specific needs of a Baptist meeting house. The church's cruciform plan accentuates the verticality of the elevations for an effect of uplift without intimidation. The four-bay nave is articulated externally by prominent buttresses between the stained-glass windows, while a 182-foot filigreed copper spire rises from the crossing. The two-story wing toward Bayard Street houses Sunday School rooms that can be opened to view the pulpit, and an elegant portal to the south once served as a bride's entrance. Inside, finely worked limestone arches alternate with Guastavino vaults in an unbroken space. As always in a Goodhue building, the carving and furnishings are rich and impeccable.

First Baptist has never attracted the attention it deserves, due to Oakland's radical shifts in scale and social context. Time has been equally unkind to the double house Goodhue created in 1921 for the Myler family, prominent members of First Baptist Church and patrons of its pulpit. His pseudo-timber-framed Colonial Revival house still stands in the Murdoch Farms area of Squirrel Hill, but is now split into two separate buildings, at 1331 and 1333 Bennington Avenue.

2.5 THE ORATORY
(RYAN CATHOLIC NEWMAN CENTER)
1997, David Vater. 4450 Bayard St.

A suave piece of contextual infill, this red-brick Tudor Revival center for Catholic students is an offshoot of the University of Pittsburgh campus, but it exudes a more collegiate image than many of the college buildings themselves. Yet there is nothing here of the postmodern clichés this structure might so easily have become: the design seamlessly inserts itself into the Gothic

Revival idiom of the 1920s, as though the succeeding seventy years had never happened. The gables, irregular massing, and diapered brick walls of the block-long center constitute a gem of craftsmanship in a construction world so often squeezed between high costs and declining aesthetic expectations.

2.6 ARTHUR LUBETZ ARCHITECTURAL OFFICE
1982, Arthur Lubetz Associates.
357 N. Craig St.

Lubetz gained a steady national reputation in the 1980s and 1990s from an architectural philosophy that he defined as "active, interactive, and ongoing." Not lost on his clients is Lubetz's ability to fashion a workable program from the interface of low-budget materials and elegantly conceived designs. The 12,500-square-foot Lubetz studio reflects the designer's quirky style that does not compromise functionality. The offices group in the center of the plan, creating a building-inside-a-building effect that supplies privacy inside and whimsy outside. The exterior of this former garage is adorned with stucco, concrete, and glass, a distinctive but not haughty neighbor to a workaday city street. Especially beguiling is the set of miniaturized pavilions that greet visitors as they emerge from the parking lot on the side.

A near neighbor to the Lubetz office is his firm's William S. Moorhead Tower (1981, 375 North Craig St.) for the blind and disabled. A triumph of functionality, the apartment block uses varied materials, natural lighting, and air movement to lead its residents through the halls. The focal point of the structure is the sequence of terraced roofs, which distribute light and air more broadly through their clerestory windows than would a traditional flat roof. The superficial Postmodernism of these two buildings will not mislead, for it is clear that they are among the more thoughtful designs in the city.

2.7 ST. PAUL CATHEDRAL
*1906, Egan and Prindeville. Fifth Ave. and
N. Craig St.*

This third version of St. Paul Cathedral (the
other two were downtown, on Grant Street) is
more than a single building: with its adjoining
synod house and rectory and two neighboring
schools, it constitutes a medieval grouping unto
itself. The Chicago-based architects specialized
in Catholic churches of a historicizing character. Here they were inspired by the Cologne
Cathedral's twin spires for the exterior and its
five-aisled nave for the interior. The interior's
impressively tall nave, with its pointed-arched
arcade and rib vaulting, is imposing rather than
alluring, and the best element is the immense
pipe organ donated by Andrew Carnegie.

2.8 SOFTWARE ENGINEERING INSTITUTE
*1987, Bohlin Powell Larkin Cywinski,
and Burt Hill Kosar Rittelmann.
4500 Fifth Ave.*

A joint venture between Carnegie Mellon University and the U.S. Department of Defense,
the Software Engineering Institute (SEI) was
among the first buildings in Pittsburgh specifically designed for high-tech research. The program called for a high-security environment,
which dictated the building's three core elements: a public entry pavilion, controlled-access
restricted office and laboratory block, and parking garage. Masking its impenetrability, SEI is
somewhat too eager to play the role of friendly
neighbor to Mellon Institute (2.9) to the west
and St. Paul Cathedral (2.7) across Fifth Avenue
to the north. An exedra carved out of its facade
picks up the axis of St. Paul Cathedral, whose
pseudo-flying buttresses perhaps also inspired
the aluminum struts on the SEI facade. The
cathedral is reflected in SEI's glass curtain wall,
whose two-tone vertical bands establish a secondary visual linkage with the giant colonnade
of Mellon Institute. But there are limits to how

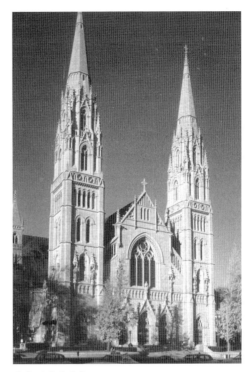

St. Paul Cathedral

self-effacing a large building can be, and SEI
ultimately provides a cautionary tale of over-
contextualization.

2.9 CARNEGIE MELLON RESEARCH INSTITUTE
(MELLON INSTITUTE FOR INDUSTRIAL
RESEARCH)
*1931–1937, Janssen & Cocken.
4400 Fifth Ave.*

Founded in 1913 by the brothers Andrew W.
and Richard B. Mellon, the Institute was one of
the world's first centers for applied research in
the natural sciences and industry. It became part
of Carnegie Mellon University in 1967. This is
its third site; an earlier home still exists on the
University of Pittsburgh campus as Allen Hall.

Planning for the building began in 1927,
with the Mellons emphasizing the classical tradition and the vague wish to create a structure
that would link science past with science

Carnegie Mellon Research Institute (Mellon Institute for Industrial Research)

present and future. The selected site also had to harmonize with two late Gothic Revival monuments: the Mellon-financed Cathedral of Learning (2.10), then under construction to the east, and St. Paul Cathedral (2.7) across the street. The Mellons' architect Benno Janssen proposed a severe Greek design that combined a grandeur appropriate to Oakland as the city's cultural center with a rational simplicity appropriate for a home of science.

The building's rectangular massing and imposing colonnade recall Robert Mills's Treasury Building in Washington, DC, while the detailing echoes the small temple of Nike Apteros on the Acropolis in Athens often pictured on Greek pots. The fruit of this hybridization looks unlike any known Greek structure, yet the impact of that tradition is clearly perceptible. The exterior is made memorable by the sixty-two peripteral monolithic columns of Indiana limestone, each of which measures about six feet in diameter at its base and five feet at the neck. Their thirty-six foot height is impressive in itself, but the fact that these are monolithic—even over the loading docks at the back—makes the Mellon Institute columns among the most remarkable ever erected.

The Mellon Institute faithfully adheres to its trapezoidal plot plan, roughly 300 feet long on each side, subdivided internally into a center core and four connecting wings. This creates four interior courts, which are lined with glazed ivory terra cotta and windows that illuminate the interior offices and laboratories. Only by

standing at the bottom of the interior courts does a visitor comprehend the vast dimensions of the building.

Three of the building's nine stories were placed below ground to minimize vibration for sensitive laboratory equipment. The marble entrance lobby mediates between the monumental exterior and the utilitarian interior. Fourteen different kinds of marble were used in construction, but Janssen, a traditionalist always intrigued by modernism, also used more aluminum in this building—for window frames, window grilles, doors, stair rails—than had been used before in the United States, no doubt at the request of the Mellons, whose Pittsburgh-based ALCOA dominated the world market. Janssen also insinuated Art Deco design into the pervasive Greek-inspired decor: pedestals in each corner of the lobby represent the traditional torches of science, while a marble bas-relief depicts the creation of scientific knowledge, beginning with the birth of the goddess Athena. Finely polished Slavonian and English oak, satinwood, and ebony provide accents to the library and main conference rooms. Anyone touring this sumptuous building must pause in its restrooms, where black Carrara glass walls and gilded faucets embellish some of the most luxurious public bathrooms in the nation.

2.10 CATHEDRAL OF LEARNING
1925–1937, Charles Klauder for Klauder and Day. Bounded by Bigelow Blvd., Forbes and Fifth aves., and Bellefield St.

The University of Pittsburgh traces its origins to the Western Academy, established downtown in 1787. One hundred years later, it moved to a hilltop on the North Side. Realizing that the move was too isolated demographically and geographically, the university relocated twenty years later to Oakland Hill on land purchased from the developer Franklin Nicola.

Henry Hornbostel's plan of 1906 for an academic Acropolis (Fig. I.3) was transposed from

Frederick Law Olmsted's plan for the World's Columbian Exposition of 1893 in Chicago—one of several points of impact of the Exposition on Oakland. The top of Oakland Hill, where the Veteran's Administration Hospital has stood since the 1950s, was to have repeated the Court of Honor, the Chicago Exposition's centerpiece, but without the lagoon. Building layout on the slopes of Oakland Hill would have been more informal, in an S-shaped curve that approximated the informal lagoon setting in Chicago. Another precedent was the hillside pilgrimage plan that won the Prix de Rome in 1897 at the Ecole des Beaux-Arts in Paris when Hornbostel was studying there. What remains of Hornbostel's hillside campus today are Allen, Old Engineering, Eberly, and Thaw halls; several of the university's early buildings were demolished in the 1990s.

As enthusiasm waned for the vision of a Pittsburgh Acropolis, the nationally prominent campus architect Charles Klauder of Philadelphia was hired to craft a skyscraper that would incorporate all academic departments of the University and create a symbolic rival to the downtown business interests. The program

Cathedral of Learning

called for a kind of academic ark: 87 classrooms, 184 laboratories, 23 lecture rooms, 19 libraries, 80 conference rooms, and 60 professors' offices. Klauder and Chancellor John Bowman briefly toyed with the idea of erecting the world's tallest skyscraper, but settled for a forty-two-story, 535-foot Gothic Revival tower of a type repopularized by the Tribune tower then going up in Chicago. Mixed with the Gothic is plenty of Art Deco streamlining. In its basic external wall massing there is little to distinguish the Cathedral of Learning from the contemporary Rockefeller Center in New York City.

The Gothic fantasy does work, however, in the Commons Room, a truly cathedral-like space of soaring vaults, brilliant sculptural detail, and some of Samuel Yellin's best ironwork. On the perimeter of the Commons Room, and also on the third floor, are nearly three dozen Nationality Rooms, many of them capturing the Arts and Crafts interests that had also come back into fashion in the 1930s.

The Cathedral of Learning is Pittsburgh's most successful building propagandistically. It was meant to broadcast the importance of education to the entire citizenry of Pittsburgh, and this it does with a 360-degree visibility that makes it a dominant, though benign, visual presence in every corner of the city.

The construction site was not ideal: a fourteen-acre trapezoid created by four streets that were oriented at four different angles and lying at four different levels. Even more disheartening, by the time architect Charles Klauder was brought in, around 1924, the intended site was ringed by architectural prima donnas, ranging from Carnegie's library and museum to the lordly institutional temples ranged along Fifth and Bellefield avenues. To design a capstone for this prominent but heterogeneous group was no simple challenge.

Klauder responded with a tower that would dominate Oakland and reach out to the whole city through its sightlines. He placed the Cathedral on the line that Forbes Avenue was planned to have taken until, around 1890, it was given a sharp curve that determined its current axis. That is why the Cathedral rises as something gigantic in front of anyone driving into Oakland from downtown, with a sheer rise of forty stories broken by just two setbacks. This was the Cathedral's "business" face, no doubt made to demand attention from Pittsburgh's business community. Then Klauder calculated four additional corner views that were all Gothic spires and pinnacles, which conversely presented the Cathedral as a guardian of spiritual values. The building's north and west corners pointed to the new medical and new apartment districts going up in the 1920s; the south corner charmed the thousands of people looking up from old Forbes Field baseball stadium—a thrilling view that still greets anyone emerging from its successor, Posvar Hall.

Why was Klauder's most exquisite corner set to point east? The Cathedral's major donors, Andrew and Richard Mellon both lived in Squirrel Hill, to the east, and they would have been delighted by their view of the Cathedral as their limousines took them downtown. Yet, the outstanding Cathedral view comes not from any street but within the mall on the rival campus of Carnegie Mellon. What dominates any photograph of that campus mall are not the Carnegie Mellon buildings but the University of Pittsburgh's Cathedral of Learning—a reminder that, in architectural propaganda, sightlines are everything.

2.11 HEINZ CHAPEL
1934–1938, Charles Klauder. Fifth and S. Bellefield aves.

Heinz Chapel stands next to the towering Cathedral of Learning (2.10), but is not overshadowed by it—a tribute to Klauder's suave editing of Paris's Sainte-Chapelle into a nondenominational worship space. The exterior, which also alludes to Mont-St.-Michel and St.-Maclou in Rouen, is complemented by an inte-

Heinz Chapel

rior of stained-glass windows by Charles Connick, who lived in Pittsburgh before moving to Boston. With the completion by 1940 of the Cathedral of Learning's tower, Heinz Chapel, and the nearby Stephen Foster Memorial, the University of Pittsburgh had given its campus an entirely new visual focus.

2.12 WILLIAM PITT STUDENT UNION (SCHENLEY HOTEL)
1898, Rutan & Russell; 1983 renovation, Williams, Trebilcock, and Whitehead. Fifth Ave. and Bigelow Blvd.

The Schenley Hotel was a key element in Franklin Nicola's vision of Oakland as Pittsburgh's cultural and social center. In 1898, when it opened, Mary Schenley was still alive, and the eleven-story, steel-framed building towered over what remained of her farmland. Carnegie Institute was the sole neighbor in a rural setting only three miles distant from downtown Pittsburgh.

For decades, the Schenley Hotel served as a social center for Pittsburgh's monied class. Presidents from Taft to Eisenhower were among the celebrities who stayed there, and the fabled actress Eleanora Duse died in a fifth-floor suite in 1924. A snapshot catches Andy Warhol, then a student at Carnegie Mellon, lounging in the generous shade of one of its porches. The hotel was also popular with the major-league baseball players who played during the glory days of nearby Forbes Field. The University of Pittsburgh converted the hotel into a student center in 1956, but its renovation came three decades later. The lobby was returned to its original French Renaissance styling, with vaulted ceiling, mirrored walls, chandeliers, and detailed moldings. Postmodern touches included an invented classical colonnade on Forbes Avenue (to articulate the new basement rooms there) and slipped keystones at several minor entrances. The suites upstairs provide office space for student organizations and university administration.

2.13 HENRY CLAY FRICK FINE ARTS BUILDING
1965, B[urton] Kenneth Johnstone.
Schenley Plaza.

This attractive replica of an Italian Renaissance palace is a serious contender should the Guiness Book of Records open a category of contemporary buildings with the longest gestation. Financed in 1925 by Helen Clay Frick as a memorial to her father, who had died six years before, the building opened only in May 1965. The grueling forty-year design review process that caused this wait involved the imperious Helen Frick and three different sites, five different teams of architects, and about fifty separate design schemes. Styles for the proposed building included Baroque, Arts and Crafts, Beaux-Arts, Gothic Revival, and Italian Renaissance, though an outside review team suggested Colonial Revival as well. As it now stands, it is a basic restatement of Ammannati and Vignola's Villa Giulia in Rome.

Almost as surprising as the architectural transformations through which this design

Henry Clay Frick Fine Arts Building

passed is its context. In 1962, Max Abramovitz produced a futuristic design for a research megastructure to fit inside Junction Hollow, a 150-foot-deep ravine that the University of Pittsburgh deliberately misnamed Panther Hollow. Abramovitz called in as collaborators the New York City firm of Eggers and Higgins, whose Gateway Center (1.2) had been such an important milestone in the rebuilding of downtown Pittsburgh. These architects saw the Frick building as the traditionalist tip for their modernist iceberg in the valley below. Otto Eggers and Daniel Higgins, who were both Beaux-Arts designers, nearly succeeded in satisfying Helen Frick's requirements for a showplace for her paintings and art books, but they ultimately withdrew in frustration. What we see now is a scandalously close reworking of the Eggers and Higgins design by B. Kenneth Johnstone, a Pittsburgh modernist who was also Dean of the College of Fine Arts at Carnegie Institute of Technology from 1945–1953.

Though the design process was tortured, the building (for the most part) is not. It functions well as the penultimate gasp of the Beaux-Arts tradition in the city; the ultimate gasp is the Frick Art Museum of 1970 created by Helen Frick in Point Breeze (6.21). Travertine walls, Italian Renaissance fresco reproductions, Vermont marble floors, cherry wood paneling, and noble proportions mark its public spaces, though artists, scholars, and students work in concrete-block cubicles behind the scenes.

In the front of the Fine Arts Building is the Mary Schenley Memorial Fountain of 1918, titled *A Song to Nature*. Its siting is somewhat accidental, a byproduct of the filling up of St. Pierre's Ravine to create Schenley Plaza, around 1915. The Plaza became a parking lot for years, and in 2006, Sasaki Associates of Boston re-landscaped it, creating seating, food kiosks, and a carousel in season. With the ravine gone, the heavy stone bridge over it became superfluous, and the city recycled it into an invisible base for this stunning monument to

the donor of Schenley Park. The work is a collaboration between H. Van Buren Magonigle, an important designer of Beaux-Arts civic monuments, and Victor D. Brenner, who also designed the Lincoln-head penny. The large, costly bronze, a stylistic cross between Art Nouveau and Art Deco, represents the sleeping earth god Pan being awakened by Harmony, who serenades him with his stolen lyre. Water pours from the mouths of four bronze turtles into Magonigle's granite basin below.

2.14 CARNEGIE INSTITUTE AND CARNEGIE LIBRARY
1892–1895, Longfellow, Alden & Harlow; 1899–1907, Alden & Harlow; (Carnegie Museum of Art) 1974, Edward Larabee Barnes; (Heinz Architectural Center) 1993, Cicognani Kalla Architects. 4400 Forbes Ave., bounded by Schenley Dr. and Schenley Plaza.

Along with Charles Klauder's Cathedral of Learning (2.10) and H. H. Richardson's Courthouse and Jail (1.15), this sprawling complex is irreplaceable in Pittsburgh. The core of Carnegie's twelve-acre library and museum was a Richardsonian Romanesque structure that included twin towers (now gone) that replicated those on the Courthouse—a mark of loyalty by Longfellow and Alden, who came directly from Richardson's office. But other design influences were already at work even on the first component, which fronted on Schenley Plaza rather than on Forbes Avenue. Although designed only four years after the triumphant reception of the Courthouse, the first block (today Carnegie Library and Carnegie Music Hall) reflects the country's avid reception of the Beaux-Arts style, grandly announced by 1889 by McKim, Mead, and White's design for the Boston Public Library. Alfred Harlow, one of the principal architects here, had formerly worked for McKim, Mead, and White; it was probably he who led the way

Carnegie Institute and Carnegie Library

to making the Carnegie complex an amalgam of the two styles.

When two of the three partners returned a decade later to expand the museums of Art and Natural History along Forbes Avenue, the transition to Beaux-Arts style was complete, having become a national fixation after the World's Columbian Exposition in Chicago in 1893. The scale and detailing of the 1895 building—particularly the delicate interiors of the library and music hall—are beguiling, but the corresponding effects in this extension overwhelm with their lavishness. The building offers an exalted architectural experience. Five spaces are especially fine: the Early-Renaissance interior of the Music Hall; the flood of gold leaf and various marbles in the adjoining Foyer; the vast Hall of Architecture, housing a large collection of plaster casts of building fragments; the Hall of Sculpture, a replica of the Parthenon interior,

complete with marble cut from the same quarries; and Andrew Carnegie's personal reception space in the exquisitely gilded Founder's Room.

The Carnegie complex was extended seventy years later with the addition of a new wing for the art museum on Forbes Avenue. This severe though grandly proportioned wing transforms the classicism of the main block into the abstraction of the late International Style.

The newest architectural elements at Carnegie Institute have been carved out with care in the Heinz Architectural Center. Here an old gallery on the second floor was transformed first into cold abstraction by Barnes, in 1974, and two decades later in unexpected warmth and intimacy by Pietro Cicognani and Ann Kalla. Working in a mere forty by 100-feet footprint, they shoehorned three full floors of exhibition, storage, and office space beneath the old skylights. Their architectural inspiration draws from such diverse sources as the neighboring Hall of Sculpture and from John Soane's house (now Museum) in London. But the architectural unity of the center is highly personalized in the eccentric mix of saturated colors, cork floors, and mottled textures that pull the disparate elements together.

At the base of the Carnegie Library's steps stands the gray granite stele of 1908 commemorating Christopher L. Magee, the local Republican party boss whose machinations enabled Andrew Carnegie to take over this corner of Mary Schenley's new park. Henry Bacon (architect of the Lincoln Memorial) set up an unobtrusive marble enclosure for a pool of water, behind which rises the stele with Augustus Saint-Gaudens's bronze bas relief. The relief represents Abundance or Charity, who holds an overfilled cornucopia below the branches of an oak.

2.15 PHIPPS CONSERVATORY
1893, Lord and Burnham; (Welcome Center) 2005, IKM Architects. One Schenley Park Dr.

This is the most prominent of a number of socially useful gifts made to Pittsburgh by Carnegie's partner, Henry Phipps. This greenhouse, slightly earlier than the Enid A. Haupt Conservatory at the New York Botanical Gardens, is by the same Irvington-on-Hudson

firm. It is located adjacent to Panther Hollow in Schenley Park.

The Phipps consists of a series of domed glass pavilions for tropical and desert plants, ferns, flowers, orchids, and palm trees. The palms grow in the central and largest room of the conservatory, which reaches sixty-five feet in height, is sixty feet wide, and 450 feet long. There are thirteen interior display gardens, two courtyards, an outdoor garden, two aquatic gardens, and a rose garden. The only loss to this otherwise perfectly preserved environment was the original Richardsonian Romanesque entry, which, in the 1960s, was supplanted by one in the International Style. That insensitive intrusion was itself replaced in 2005, and a dramatic glass-domed welcome center and café was put in its place.

2.16 CARNEGIE MELLON UNIVERSITY (CARNEGIE INSTITUTE OF TECHNOLOGY)
1905–2000, Henry Hornbostel, and others. Bounded by Forbes Ave., Margaret Morrison, Tech and Frew sts.

Conceived as Carnegie Technical Schools in 1900 by Andrew Carnegie, the institution was renamed Carnegie Institute of Technology, when it opened in 1906, and was renamed Carnegie Mellon University in 1968. The campus of some forty acres has been triply blessed:

Phipps Conservatory

Carnegie Mellon University (Carnegie Institute of Technology)

by the natural topography of the site itself, isolated from the rest of Pittsburgh by the Junction Hollow gully on the west, Schenley Park on the south, and the steep rise of Squirrel Hill on the east; by Hornbostel's refined Beaux-Arts plan; and by astute choices in its later expansion.

Hornbostel won the competition for the Carnegie Technical Schools with a scheme that featured a pronounced axial quadrangle accentuated by technology at the west, with arts on a slight rise to the east. His work was essentially done by 1930, at which point the campus froze for seventy years, with new construction limited to benignly concrete Wean Hall (1968–1971, Deeter Ritchey Sippel) to plug a gap in the quadrangle and a few half-hearted buildings to strike a third north-south axis (an equally long mall known as the "Cut") from the original quadrangle to Forbes Avenue.

This architectural lethargy ended overnight with the adoption of a new master plan in 1987,

including the striking of a third axis, east-west this time, by urbanist Leon Krier that points to the intersection of Forbes Avenue and Margaret Morrison Street, and cuts the second axis at ninety degrees. Krier's axis became the centerline for the East Campus (1987–1990, Michael Dennis for Dennis, Clark and Associates/ TAMS), which is a new quadrangle in its own right. An athletic field follows the east-west axis, with a linked range of dormitories on the south and a garage with attached stadium seating on the north. These buildings repeat the Hornbostel idiom of yellow factory brick. Here the brick is variegated in color, but laid with the same care as the old work. The buildings are crisp in wall texture and detailing.

The University Center (1989–1996) strengthens the "Cut" as the campus's north-south axis. Designed by Michael Dennis and Associates and UDA Architects, this center for student life is a look-alike in factory brick to the Uffizi Gallery in Florence, and it includes spaces for sports, lectures, a chapel, other student activities, and dining. These conflicting functions occasionally intersect, not always to the pleasure of the users who often find them randomly juxtaposed. The Purnell Center for the Arts (1991–2000, Michael Dennis and Associates and Damianos + Anthony) mirrors the University Center on the west side of the "Cut," but with a simpler program.

2.17 MARGARET MORRISON CARNEGIE HALL (MARGARET MORRISON CARNEGIE SCHOOL FOR WOMEN)
1906–1907, 1913, Henry Hornbostel; 1990– 1996, Bohlen Cywinksi Jackson, with Pierre Zoelly. Margaret Morrison and Tech sts.

Margaret Morrison Carnegie Hall, the former women's college named for the benefactor's mother, is one of the oldest buildings on the campus complex, and it was set by Hornbostel on a divergent northeast axis from the main quadrangle. The Beaux-Arts style building is

If you wish to see a monument to Edward Manning Bigelow, Pittsburgh's visionary Director of Public Works from 1888 to 1906, Schenley Park offers two: a bronze portrait statue (1895, Giuseppe Moretti) that stands on Schenley Drive opposite Phipps Conservatory (2.15), and the 465-acre Schenley Park. The fact that Bigelow got a monumental bronze statue in his own lifetime hints at his ambition and his dictatorial reign as Pittsburgh's most memorable public servant.

Bigelow was the great force behind Pittsburgh's park system, and he put his faith in the City Beautiful and back-to-nature movements, envisioning arcadian oases that would uplift the working masses and remedy the smoky image of the city. Coaxed out of the rugged terrain straddling Oakland and Squirrel Hill, Schenley Park was, ironically, the main factor in Oakland's loss of its semi-rural character. Construction of the park, with Carnegie Institute at its entrance, initiated the metamorphosis of Oakland from rural refuge into civic center. The park contributed to the development of Squirrel Hill as well, increasing land values and bringing the public transportation that ended the district's isolation.

Work on the park began shortly after 1889, when Bigelow persuaded Mary Schenley to donate a 300-acre tract and sell 100 adjoining acres to the city. By 1896, the park's major roads were complete, and Junction and Panther hollows, two gorges slicing through the park, were crossed by the two stone and steel-deck truss bridges that H. B. Rust built in 1897–1898. The Schenley Park and Panther Hollow bridges still give easy access to the park today.

William Falconer, appointed Park Superintendent in 1896, transformed these acres through a massive program of planting and grading. Further improvements were made by Falconer's successor George Burke, including several picturesque bridges of tufa stone at Panther Hollow's base. The result was a superb romantic park in the Olmsted tradition, complete with dramatic vistas and shadowy woodland paths, contrasted by gently rolling pastures and quiet waterways.

In addition to the bronze portrait sculpture of Bigelow, Schenley Park includes other fine sculptural works. It was Bigelow who convinced the academic sculptor Giuseppe Moretti to leave Italy and create ornaments for both Schenley and Highland parks. Moretti's four marble panthers (more prosaically mountain lions) on the Panther Hollow Bridge of 1897 commemorate the animals that roamed these grounds well into the nineteenth century. With their powerful muscles, sleek coats, and true-to-life strength, the panthers capture the essence of European academic realism.

A latecomer to the Beaux-Arts monuments of Schenley Park, but akin in spirit, is the fine memorial of 1930 to George Westinghouse a few hundred yards from Phipps Conservatory (2.15). This costly memorial to Pittsburgh's heroic inventor was made possible through small contributions from more than 60,000 Westinghouse employees worldwide. Henry Hornbostel and Eric F. Wood designed a semicircular exedra with integrated pond and black Norwegian granite benches, then planted a large weeping willow tree. On the exedra are Paul Fjelde's large reliefs of Westinghouse's main inventions and Daniel Chester French's medallion bust of Westinghouse. Opposite the medallion stands French's life-sized bronze statue of a schoolboy with books in hand. He stares at Westinghouse, as if looking for inspiration.

The park contains one reminder of this area's early history in the Robert Neill log house built c. 1787 (reconstructed with mostly new wood in 1969) on Serpentine Drive adjacent to the park's public golf course. The house, which measures a mere nineteen by twenty-five feet, has a loft and two side-by-side fireplaces, the smaller one probably used to heat the house at night.

Margaret Morrison Carnegie Hall (Margaret Morrison Carnegie School for Women)

fronted by a magnificent, semicircular Doric portico that encloses an oval-shaped courtyard. The recent expansion, a vertical addition called The Intelligent Workplace, is a shimmering 7,000-square-foot glass penthouse. The offices and research labs sit in a cybernetic cocoon that is a living laboratory of futuristic office architecture and technology.

2.18 COLLEGE OF FINE ARTS
1912–1916, Henry Hornbostel. East end of Main Quadrangle.

Set on a slight rise at the eastern end of the main quadrangle, the College of Fine Arts was Hornbostel's tribute to his own classical but interdisciplinary education at the Ecole des Beaux-Arts in Paris. Named in cartouches atop the cream-brick facade are the five arts-related subjects originally taught. The structure also provided budding architects with three pedagogical displays: five facade niches exemplify in

bold relief the major stylistic periods from Egyptian to Renaissance. Inside, five inlaid marble floor designs recall other great monuments of the past, and murals overhead depict more recent design achievements, not forgetting Hornbostel's design for Hell's Gate Bridge in New York City.

2.19 HAMERSCHLAG HALL
1912, Henry Hornbostel. East end of Main Quadrangle.

Machinery Hall, renamed Hamerschlag for the school's first director, is an architectural silk purse made of a sow's ear. The building program demanded little more than a boiler plant below and workshops above, but Hornbostel decked it out in the guise of Leonbattista Alberti's S. Andrea at Mantua, with a high temple pediment surmounting an enormous ceremonial entrance arch. The crowning touch was the most poetic (and risqué) smokestack in the nation: an industrial-brick cylindrical Temple of Venus penetrated by a circular brick chimney, the whole further enriched by helical stairs recalling the spiral minaret of the Great Mosque of Samarra.

The most neglected part of the campus had always been the slide into Junction Hollow, behind Hamerschlag, but this changed in 1987 with the addition of the volumetrically complex Physical Plant Building by IKM Architects, which gives access to neighboring buildings at several different levels and compass orientations. In deference to Hornbostel, the architects employ the same yellow brick. Next door, the George A Roberts Engineering Hall (1993–1997, Payette Associates) was hung on the escarpment between the railroad tracks and the high exposed podium of Hamerschlag Hall. The resulting visual prospect either diminishes or enhances the old structure above, depending on one's purist or populist point of view.

2.20 OAKLAND SQUARE
1889–1890. Bounded by Dawson St., Parkview Ave., and Oakland Pl.

The uniform street scenes of old Paris or Boston were not for Pittsburgh, but an exception was made in this peaceful setting of a wooded park ringed by twenty-six frame and brick single and double houses. Charles Chance, chairman of the Oakland Board of Trade, developed the houses on a shapeless parcel belonging to land speculator Eugene O'Neil. In creating Oakland Square, Chance seized on three incidents: the establishment of the Jones and Laughlin blast furnace a half-mile away in 1859, the inauguration of Oakland's cable-car service to downtown in 1888, and the establishment of Schenley Park in 1889. Chance also turned the property's main defect—its sharp fall-off into Junction Hollow—into a theatrical view of Schenley Park. Today, trees limit the impressive view to wintertime, though

Oakland Square

from the right vantage points glimpses of Panther Hollow and the Charles Anderson bridges are still rewarding.

Oakland Square's architectural style draws on the exaggerated architectural forms associated with Frank Furness, as seen in the oversized dormers that sweep high above the rooflines. Unfortunately, the wrap-around porches that once animated the corner houses are now lost as are the steps and terraces down the bluff that permitted the neighborhood children—Andy Warhol among them—to easily explore the park.

2.21 UPMC MAGEE WOMEN'S HOSPITAL ADMINISTRATIVE OFFICES (ISALY'S DAIRY)
1930, The McCormick Co.
3380 Blvd. of the Allies.

This three-story Art Deco monument of buff brick and cream-colored terra cotta is situated at a strategic bend in the then-newly built boulevard. Its visibility was an important asset to what was essentially a glorified ice-cream stand and ice-cream factory for a chain of several local stores. Here were made and sold three essential

elements of the old Pittsburgh diet: Klondike ice-cream bars (later distributed nationally), skyscraper cones, and chipped ham. The building was converted into offices in the early 1990s.

2.22 CHESTERFIELD RD., ROBINSON, AND DUNSEITH STS.
c. 1904–1930. Bounded by Fifth Ave., Aliquippa and Terrace sts.

These long hilly streets (two blocks of Robinson and one block of Chesterfield) constitute an urban oasis. Both are early twentieth-century developments of modest wood-frame houses probably erected for steelworkers at the Jones and Laughlin steel mill at the base of Oakland. Despite high-density encroachments by the University of Pittsburgh, the Oakland medical complex, and large public housing projects, the streets retain their remarkable cohesiveness as a middle-class African-American neighborhood. The hardiness of these streets is partly architectural, reflecting the basic quality of their design, and partly social, in the presence of Breech-Menders, a local advocacy group that mends literal and metaphoric breaks in the street scene.

Dunseith Street

Pittsburgh Technology Center

2.23 PITTSBURGH TECHNOLOGY CENTER (8 BUILDINGS)

1990–2002. Technology Drive, between Second Ave. and the Monongahela River.

University of Pittsburgh Center for Biotechnology and Bioengineering. 1990–1993, Bohlin Powell Larkin Cywinski

Carnegie Mellon Research Institute. 1991–1994; and Aristech Chemical Corporation. 1997, Bohlin Cywinski Jackson

Union Switch & Signal Systems and Research Center. 1993–1995, The Design Alliance Architects

Technology Center Parking Garage. 1995; and 2000 Technology Drive office building. 1996, WTW Architects

TelCove Office Building. 1999–2001, Burt Hill Kosar Rittelmann Associates

Bridgeside Point Office Building. 2002, Burt Hill Architects. 100 Technology Dr.

The office and research buildings on this forty-eight-acre site were harbingers of new things when they were built in the early 1990s. Their symbolism was almost palpable, since the shiny new structures were going up where the Eliza Furnaces of Jones and Laughlin had stood for almost a century and a half. The complex remains significant and growing, in tribute to the competent manner in which Pittsburgh's Urban Redevelopment Authority (URA, a city-county agency) has nourished it. True to their high-tech functions, the buildings look sleek and efficient with exterior surface materials that include glass and metal panels. Still, to many Pittsburghers, the smoke-belching mills were a thrilling sight in contrast to the structures that replaced them. A Peter Eisenman design from the mid-1980s was originally intended for this site, but Eisenmen's deconstructivist recollection of the old J & L mills had spaces that were too eccentric to be rentable.

One important remnant of the river's industrial past near the Pittsburgh Technology Center (adjacent to Second Ave. and Bates St.) is the Hot Metal Bridge (c. 1887), which actually is two bridges with similar profiles sharing a set of stone piers. The upstream side held two tracks of the Monongahela Connecting Railroad; it was adapted in 2000 for automobile traffic. The downstream side held a single track underlain with metal plates protecting its wooden ties from sparks and the molten metal being shipped between the former steel-making plant on one side of the river and the fabricating plant on the other.

CHAPTER 3:
SOUTH SIDE AND THE
MONONGAHELA VALLEY

Pittsburgh's South Side, occupying an extensive floodplain on the south bank of the Monongahela River, directly across from the Golden Triangle, offers a completely different visual experience from the glitz of the nearby downtown or the flashy new sports stadia and office parks of Pittsburgh's North Side on the opposite bank of the Allegheny River.

An old Revolutionary-era farm turned workhouse, South Side was first named Birmingham, in the obvious hope that industry would flourish here as it had in Birmingham, England. The town was settled around 1810 and reached its peak population of some 45,000 around World War I. By then, East Carson Street, its main spine, stretched for almost two miles with a continuous line of stores and apartments. Today, broken in only a few spots, East Carson remains a fascinating thoroughfare. Streets could be laid in a more regimented manner over this floodplain than in most of Pittsburgh, which made it the most cohesive of the city's neighborhoods. This physical cohesion was then augmented by ethnic links (first Germans, then Poles, then immigrants from Eastern and Southern Europe) and an expressive architectural and visual collectivity.

The attraction of the South Side was work, in a multitude of jobs in its glassworks, ironworks, foundries, and crucibles, a critical component of ironmaking, that may be the perfect metaphor for this district of modest houses and ethnic churches and clubs. The Jones and Laughlin (J & L) steelworks were the biggest draw. Everything east of the Birmingham Bridge and most of the opposite shore from the Birmingham to the Glenwood bridges was occupied by the J & L sheds and blast furnaces until the mid-1980s, when the economy and steelmaking fortunes changed.

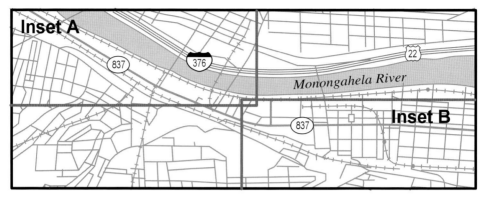

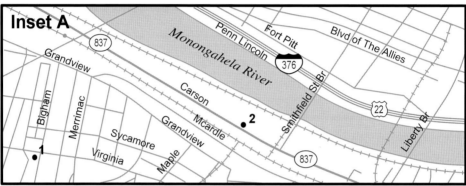

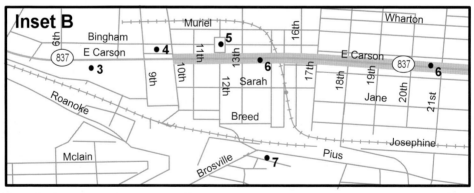

The South Side. Approximate driving time: several hours.

A mill district such as South Side was effectively a company town that was devastated by the closing of the glasshouses and steelworks; by the 1980s and 1990s, its population had dropped to slightly more than 10,000 compared to double that in World War II. An eventual economic upturn came in the 1990s not from any revival of industry, but from the South Side's hundreds of lively nineteenth-century storefronts. Bars turned into gourmet restaurants, and mom-and-pop food shops resurfaced as antique stores, clothing boutiques, and nightclubs. Up on the slopes, there was a parallel move to rehab the wooden worker's homes into affordable housing for singles and young families. Today, South Side's economic troubles are not entirely behind it, but it has emerged as the undisputed entertainment center of Pittsburgh and moved from just preserving its architecture to expanding it in vigorous new housing by the river and office/retail complexes at both ends of the restored Hot Metal Bridge (2.23).

South Side was always a microcosm of the Monongahela Valley. Its rise foretold the later expansion of mill towns such as Homestead, Braddock, Duquesne, McKeesport, and Turtle Creek, upriver. Similarly, its fall announced their eventual fall, too, as metals processing was outsourced from Pittsburgh to overseas. Those were the true company towns, and they lack South Side's diversification and nearness to the metropolis. Here and there one sees revitalization, particularly in historic preservation, but the new dawn of the Monongahela Valley mill towns seems a long way off.

Chatham Village

3.1 CHATHAM VILLAGE
*1932, 1936, 1956, Clarence S. Stein and
Henry Wright, planners; Ingham and Boyd,
architects; Ralph Griswold and Theodore
Kohankie, landscape architects. 412 Bingham
St., bounded by Bingham, Virginia, Olympia,
and Pennridge rds.*

The Buhl Foundation, in its brochure for the
project, promoted this for-profit housing as
the "First large scale, planned, residential community built from the ground up in one operation to be retained in single ownership and
managed as a long-term investment." Chatham
Village always had a national, and even international, impact out of proportion to its rather
modest dimensions, deriving in part from the
names of Clarence S. Stein and Henry Wright,
the acclaimed planners of Sunnyside Gardens
in Queens, New York, and Radburn, New Jersey. More notable than its successful adaptation
of those suburban designs is the complex's
highly irregular contour; rarely had low-cost
housing dealt so successfully with steep-slope
topography. Helping its fame also was the
decade in which Chatham Village went up; in
the 1930s, governments everywhere in the
nation were contemplating public-assistance
housing. Chatham Village became a model for
schemes across the nation.

The complex fits 216 families on sixteen
acres: 129 rowhouses date from 1932, sixty-
eight from 1936, and a three-story, nineteen-
unit apartment building went up in 1956. The
planners left four acres for playgrounds and
commons, plus twenty-six adjoining acres of
untouched woodland. Rented from the Buhl
Foundation until 1960, the homes then became
a cooperative and were privatized. Nonetheless,
the complex retains strict restrictions on upkeep
and changes.

The Greek Revival former Thomas James
Bigham mansion of 1849 is a community center
named Chatham Hall. Its original owner and
builder was an avid abolitionist, newspaper publisher, and politician, and his house was used as
part of the Underground Railroad.

3.2 STATION SQUARE
(PITTSBURGH & LAKE ERIE RR TERMINAL)
*1901, William George Burns; 1976
renovation, Landmarks Design Associates.
Bounded by the Smithfield St. Bridge, West
Carson St., and the Monongahela River.*

This forty-acre rehabilitation of Beaux-Arts and
industrial buildings constituted Pittsburgh's first
recycling of an integrated complex of buildings.
Initiated by the Pittsburgh History and Landmarks Foundation, the renovation and adaptive
reuse had a profound effect on the revitalization
of the whole of South Side.

The centerpiece remains the old seven-story
passenger terminal of the P&LE Railroad,
which, though it made most of its revenue
hauling iron ore and coal, lavished considerable

Station Square (Pittsburgh & Lake Erie Railroad Terminal)

Seventeen inclines (inclined planes) once operated on the hillsides of Pittsburgh. The two that survive today are technically funiculars that are pulled by cables, rather than San Francisco-type cable cars with their cables suspended below ground. Born out of pure necessity, the inclines long ago became a crucial part of Pittsburgh's urban environment. In 1869, John Endres of Cincinnati teamed with Budapest-born Samuel Diescher to construct the Monongahela Incline, the first in the city, to lift its passengers 640 feet up Mount Washington. The wire cable was furnished by John Roebling, an early landmark in a career that culminated in his Brooklyn Bridge.

The Monongahela Incline operates all day between West Carson Street and Grandview Avenue, directly above Station Square. The Duquesne Heights Incline, farther down West Carson Street toward the Ohio River, also reaches up to Grandview Avenue, opposite Oneida Street. Built in 1877 and rebuilt a decade later, this was the fourth of Pittsburgh's inclines. Diescher was again the engineer, this time operating with a track 793 feet long. The system is operated by the nonprofit Society for the Preservation of the Duquesne Heights Incline, which also oversees a collection of memorabilia in the upper station. The original hoisting drum and wooden drive gear are still in use, set at a ninety-degree angle from the incline to save space. The cars on both inclines are the originals, or nearly so, but the rails were early on converted from wood to iron and the power source was switched from steam to electric power in the 1930s. Neither incline has ever had a major accident.

expense on the waiting room. This elaborate space under a barrel-vaulted stained-glass skylight was among America's more dramatic railroad station interiors. It was restored c. 1980 for use as a restaurant, which works well in that ceremonial space.

The adjoining office building, freight terminal, and warehouse also found new uses as office and retail space, in the process bringing thousands of suburbanites back into the city for work or entertainment.

3.3 ST. JOHN THE BAPTIST UKRAINIAN CATHOLIC CHURCH
1895, 1917. 109 S. Seventh St.

This grand monument at the western end of the East Carson Street commercial district is the most striking reminder of Eastern European heritage in South Side life. In 1895, the congregation, affiliated with the Catholic—not the Orthodox—church, began to meet in the red-orange-colored brick narthex, the only part of the church then built. The maroon-hued brick main hall in a traditional Ukrainian cross-in-square configuration was added in

St. John the Baptist Ukrainian Catholic Church

1917. The church is surmounted by six onion-shaped domes and the central dome, with its covering of gold-leaf, shines brilliantly. The two front domes fit less well on their towers, and were perhaps added as afterthoughts to reinforce the Eastern European appearance of the church.

3.4 BEDFORD SCHOOL APARTMENTS
1850; 1997 renovation, EDGE studio.
910 Bingham St.

This three-story Greek Revival schoolhouse from 1850 was retrofitted in 1997 with a dozen light-filled apartments, several with the original chalkboards still on the walls. The old school is a key element in stabilizing a neighborhood of rich architectural heritage that is under considerable pressures from a growing population in the newly trendy South Side.

3.5 BEDFORD SQUARE
c. 1820–1893. Bingham and S. Twelfth sts.

This is a relic of Nathaniel Bedford's plan for his settlement of Birmingham, drawn up in 1811. Evidently a copy of the Golden Triangle's Market Square (created in 1784 in George Wood's plan of Pittsburgh), it works as a squared roundabout for the four arteries (two segments of Bingham Street and two of South Twelfth Street) that would otherwise intersect here. Unlike Market Square in the Golden Triangle, Bedford Square retains its market house, South Side Market. The first market on the site went up in 1813, when Bedford laid out the settlement. The current structure is a simplified 1915 reconstruction of Charles Bickel's original market of 1893, which was destroyed by fire. It currently houses a drop-in center for the elderly. The tiny homes and shops on the perimeter of the square, some in wood and others in brick, preserve the general Greek Revival massing if not the specific structures of the early nineteenth century, which makes this the oldest intact housing group in Pittsburgh.

3.6 EAST CARSON STREET STOREFRONTS
Mid- to late-nineteenth century. Between Tenth and Twenty-Seventh sts.

When Nathaniel Bedford laid out East Carson Street as the commercial spine of his borough of Birmingham in 1811, its future prosperity was assured. Connected to downtown Pittsburgh in 1816 by the first of the three Smithfield Street bridges, the street also functioned as a feeder road to the Washington Pike and National Road (now U.S. 40), both south of the city.

East Carson Street's great boost came with ironmaking. By 1860, the Clinton Furnace (Station Square today) at its western terminus was balanced on the east by Jones and Laughlin's American Iron Works around Twenty-fifth Street. (The J & L company store survives as a Goodwill store.) When the South Side became a mecca for immigrant steelworkers from western and later central and eastern Europe, East Carson was stamped with their numerous churches and fraternal halls. The multi-domed St. John the Baptist Ukrainian Catholic Church (3.3) is the most grandiloquent of the group, while the smaller onion-domed former Cleaves Temple (1913) at 1005 East Carson (now a café) is the most affecting.

The central mile of East Carson offers one of the best collections of nineteenth-century commercial architecture in the United States. Generally two to four stories in height, most of the standout storefronts are either Italianate or Second Empire in style or have such late-nineteenth-century features as segmental arches and bracketed corbel tables, as does the Ukrainian Home at number 1113. The Pittsburgh National Bank of 1902 at number 1736, a Beaux-Arts study in contrasting yellow-gray sandstone and red brick, shows that a limited amount of capital investment came in the twentieth century too. Rare and precious are examples of Art Deco, the last of South Side's period styles: two of the best are Siegel's Jewelers at 1510 and Dotula's Cafe at 1605 East Carson. While most stores on the street had their lower

East Carson Street storefronts

stories altered over time, a community revitalization project in the late 1960s, coupled with a current design review process, returned many storefronts to historical accuracy.

3.7 ANGEL'S ARMS CONDOMINIUMS (ST. MICHAEL'S PARISH COMPLEX)
1861–1890s, Charles F. Bartberger, and others; 2000–2006, Hanson Design Group.
1 Pius St.

This complex of Romanesque Revival buildings served the parish of St. Michael's (now amalgamated into Prince of Peace parish) on the slopes above the South Side. The first church of 1848 was demolished a decade later to make room for the current St. Michael's designed by Bartberger and completed in 1861. It is a stern and handsome red brick German-style Romanesque Revival building with a tall square entrance tower. Several impressive support buildings added over the decades include the Rectory at the corner of Pius and Clinton Street (1889, Frederick Sauer), several school buildings, and a parish house known as the Casino. All are in variants of the Romanesque Revival idiom. In the early twenty-first century, almost everything in this complex, church included, was turned into condominiums, though exterior changes were minimal.

Higher still on Mt. Washington is Bartberger's St. Paul of the Cross Monastery (143 Monastery St.) of 1853, again in Romanesque Revival. This Passionist priory served the German-immigrant workers who erected the hundreds of tiny frame houses that cover the hillside. St. Michael's Cemetery on South Eighteenth Street lies at the brow of Mt. Washington. This

Angel's Arms Condominiums (St. Michael's Parish Complex)

windswept slope represents Pittsburgh's industrial melancholy at its best. The gravestones, mainly chiseled in German, are evocative, but unforgettable is the view across the Monongahela River into Oakland, the Bluff, and the Golden Triangle. On a slope too daunting to be turned to industrial profit, the skilled German craft-workers rest in the harshness of their adopted land.

3.8 JOHN WOODS HOUSE
1792. 4604 Monongahela St.

This three-bay, two-story farmhouse of random-cut sandstone has interior end chimneys and a wooden entrance hall. The builder was either George Woods, who prepared the plan for the Golden Triangle, or his lawyer son, John. Located high on Hazelwood Hill, the house once enjoyed a view of the wooded Monongahela shore before this succumbed to the later Hazelwood coke works.

3.9 EPISCOPAL CHURCH OF THE GOOD SHEPHERD
1891, William Halsey Wood.
Second and Johnston aves.

This church is a masterful demonstration of the power of a medieval idiom freely interpreted. The high Episcopalian faithful who first met on this site in 1870 were probably summer residents

of Hazelwood in its bucolic pre-industrial days. By the time the existing church was replaced with this structure, Hazelwood was in the throes of industrialization. Nonetheless the site itself remains verdant; and, in conjunction with Wood's choice of varied and highly textured materials—stone, brick, and shingles—and its louvered tower, the church beautifully captures the rustic feel that the congregation must have requested. There is little that is specifically medieval here, yet a definite and tangible spirituality emerges in the tradition of the free interpretations by such British designers as William Morris or Philip Webb.

3.10 GEORGE AND PERLE MESTA HOUSE
c. 1890. 540 Doyle Ave.

This two-story clapboarded Colonial Revival mansion, with a finely detailed single-story ballroom added later for Perle Mesta, who gained international fame as a political hostess, testifies to the no-nonsense outlook of the early industrialists. No more than a five-minute walk from the Mesta factory, famed for its tools and dyes, the house is only marginally grander than the homes of the other factory managers on this secluded hillside. Later, when the Mestas became enormously rich, they were obliged by social convention to leave this worker town and move to Squirrel Hill. The factory lingers on, downsized, but the core firm of the Mesta empire has recycled itself into software.

3.11 ST. MICHAEL THE ARCHANGEL CHURCH
1927, Comes, Perry and McMullen.
E. Ninth Ave. and Library Pl.

Few Pittsburgh architects around World War I were busier than John Comes, as a dozen local Roman Catholic churches and an additional score around the United States testify. A handsome home at 3242 Beechwood Boulevard in Squirrel Hill documents the profitability of his practice.

Episcopal Church of the Good Shepherd

The majority of American cities were born of their rivers but later turned their backs on them. This was poignantly true in Pittsburgh, which by the mid-nineteenth century choked its riverbanks with docks and rail lines and, by 1958, with expressways. That sour fate changed only in 1976, when Station Square became Pittsburgh's first major reuse of a historic complex of buildings and, simultaneously, the first project to embrace a riverfront.

A decade passed before that riverside development was echoed in the North Shore Center and Allegheny Landing Park in 1984 (4.2). Development of the north bank of the Allegheny returned with vigor when the Carnegie Science Center (4.4) rose on the east bank of the Ohio River between 1988 and 1991. Two significant developments dating from the 1990s were the ALCOA (4.1) center and its residential neighbor, Lincoln at North Shore. Shortly after, the two separate development zones were linked by two sports stadiums and an office park that is still underway. (By contrast, the old Three Rivers Stadium of the 1970s failed to engender any development beyond a sea of parking lots.) Important input came from urban visionaries, too. The Three Rivers Heritage Trail doggedly forged what will eventually become nearly forty miles of delightful walking/biking paths along the six riverbanks of the Allegheny, Ohio, and Monongahela. The Riverlife Task Force also hopes to beautify at least the mile of the Ohio River that flows from the Point to the West End Bridge.

What initially turned Pittsburgh's attention to its rivers was not some sudden conversion to urban generosity, but the chance to make money from the vast brownfields opening up with the collapse of Big Steel. This cynical observation can be verified in downtown Pittsburgh, which had no industrial installations to take over and, in consequence, has put up only two recent river-focused buildings: the Convention Center (1.33) and the Pittsburgh High School for Creative Arts (CAPA) (1.32).

The brownfields presented, and present, the toughest redevelopment challenges. The two pioneers here, both in the 1990s, were the Pittsburgh Technology Center (2.23), with its eight office buildings replacing the Eliza Furnaces of Jones and

Laughlin, and Washington's Landing (4.28), with several-score townhouses and some light-industry facilities. Both initiatives were good economically, but the designs were bland suburban look-alikes.

At the end of 2006, three huge riverside zones were well under redevelopment. The gaunt factories in the Strip, that unfortunately named but delightful floodplain on the south bank of the Allegheny, are coming alive as apartments and condominiums. But progress can be maddeningly slow. The immense Armstrong Cork Factory sat vacant and vandalized for forty years before rehabilitation began. The Heinz Lofts (4.25) are effecting the same alchemy on the Allegheny's north bank.

Four current and massive developments are transforming the two banks of the Monongahela, too, in quite different ways. The Waterfront in Homestead represents the old school, tearing down the historic U.S. Steel mills there, and replacing them with a suburban retail mall that could be Anyplace U.S.A. Closer to town, the South Side Works is proceeding in more adroit fashion. This complex, on a thirty-acre site at East Carson Street, has tightly linked itself to the old South Side both visually and functionally, with equal emphasis on retail, food, and entertainment and on working and living places. In both instances, unfortunately, the closeness to the river has been slighted, though not entirely overlooked. Downstream at Rankin, the Steel Valley Taskforce has preserved part of the Carrie Furnaces for interpretive display, and, in Hazelwood, the Almono Project — a consortium of foundations — has purchased the old Jones and Laughlin Coke Works, where it hopes to develop a mixed-use project, including research space and housing on the 178-acre site. The Hazelwood Coke Works ceased production in 1999, ending the last element of the manufacture of steel within the borders of Pittsburgh.

Meanwhile, the biggest water-based redevelopment factor of all goes begging: some mode of transportation that will get Pittsburghers around on the water itself.

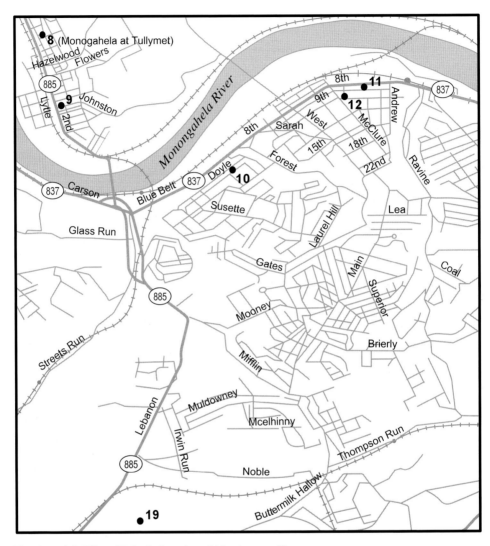

The Monongahola Valley at Pittsburgh. Approximate driving time: several hours.

Comes began his career at the turn of the twentieth century with several important projects for himself or for larger firms: St. Augustine's and St. John the Baptist churches in Lawrenceville (the latter now a brewpub), Epiphany Church on the Hill, St. Agnes in Oakland, and St. Anthony's in Millvale—all Romanesque Revival variants. Comes died in 1922, but the firm of Comes, Perry and McMullen continued to put up such highly coloristic Gothic Revival works as the convent attached to St. Mary's Church in McKees Rocks and St. Bernard's in Mt. Lebanon (8.5). Along the way were occasional forays into Modernism, such as St. Josaphat's Church of 1909–1916 at 2314 Mission Street, a kind of

St. Michael the Archangel Church

Polish folk-modern, or this church in Munhall known as Kostol St. Michael to the Slovak community. The gabled-fronted church is a stylized and modernized Italian Romanesque Revival style constructed of factory-style brick and brightened by hundreds of color tile inserts. The memorably tall, square bell tower is topped with Frank Vittor's aluminum statue of St. Joseph the Worker (1966), which depicts the father of Jesus not as a carpenter but as a steelworker.

3.12 NATIONAL CARPATHO-RUSYN CENTER (ST. JOHN THE BAPTIST GREEK CATHOLIC CATHEDRAL)
1903, Titus de Bobula. 427 E. Tenth Ave.

In their 1940s heyday, Homestead and neighboring Munhall were home to more than fifty churches (about thirty survive), of which the former St. John the Baptist Cathedral remains the most distinctive. It is that rarity in American architecture: a true Art Nouveau building, though of a peculiarly Central European variety.

Located on the hill that characterizes much of Munhall, St. John's towers above the scores of worker houses in which its Carpatho-Rusyn parishioners lived. The facade of St. John's begins in walls of stone and brick on a raised stone basement, then soars into twin towers that have tall narrow windows under exaggerated sandstone voussoirs. The verticality of the towers is checked midway by the horizontal of a loggia in the center of the facade. The towers end in columned tholoi surmounted by Greek crosses. De Bobula created stunning textural discordances through jumps between smooth and rough-hewn stones. He overscaled the egg-and-dart molding and small modillion blocks under the eaves and cornices, to the point that a visitor eyes the whole church warily, as though it cannot be trusted. The architect's blend of historic styles is echoed in the adjacent, two-story brick rectory, which incorporates fluted Corinthian columns and a cornice ornamented with acanthus leaves.

Long after de Bobula left Hungary, where his father and brother were well-known conservative architects, he maintained contact with the old country. In two of his surviving buildings, First Hungarian Reformed Church of 1903 at 221 Johnston Street in Hazelwood and Sts. Peter and Paul Ukrainian Orthodox Greek Catholic Church of 1906 at 200 Walnut Street in the suburb of Carnegie, as well as in a dozen sketches published in Pittsburgh, de Bobula quoted liberally from Art Nouveau and such Viennese pioneer architects as Otto Wagner. De Bobula is the most original force to have emerged from the many immigrants who enriched Pittsburgh with their artistic heritages.

3.13 KENNYWOOD PARK
1898, George S. Davidson, engineer. 4800 Kennywood Blvd.

Sprawling across forty acres along the west bank of the Monongahela River on the periphery of what was once a thriving milltown, Kennywood Park survived the Depression, two World Wars, and several financial panics to become one of the leading trolley parks from late-nineteenth-century America.

In 1818, the site was the farm and coalfield of Charles F. Kenny. As early as the Civil War, its groves of oaks and maple were a popular picnic area. By the time the Monongahela Street Railway Company extended out from Pittsburgh to reach the farm in the 1890s, the site was widely and popularly known as "Kenny's Grove." Soon after, the railway leased part of the land for a trolley park named Kennywood. Davidson, chief engineer of the Railway, was appointed the park's first manager, and he provided the first layout.

When the park opened to the public, its only built attractions were a cafeteria, dance pavilion, and small bandstand surrounding a shallow lake. Kennywood's distinction among enthusiasts as "Roller Coaster Capital of the World" came only later, with the creation of the Racer, the Thunderbolt, the Jack Rabbit, and the Steel Phantom—once clocked as the world's fastest roller coaster. Today, the park maintains a good deal of its original landscape, including a lake and such early buildings as the Casino and Pagoda.

Historic preservation has long been a concern at the park, whose latest component is Lost Kennywood, a recreation of amusement parks of the past whose decorative arched entrance reproduces the arch of Pittsburgh's Luna Park of 1905, now demolished.

3.14 CHARLES SCHWAB HOUSE
1889, Frederick J. Osterling.
541 Jones Ave.

Charles Schwab was Carnegie's most flamboyant associate. Beginning work as a common laborer, he became superintendent at Carnegie's Braddock works, then at his Homestead works, and finally president of Bethlehem Steel. Schwab's mansion, built when he was only twenty-seven years old, sits high on a hill above the dreary streets of Braddock, the mills, and the Monongahela. The house, like Schwab's own persona, suggests a prince among the people. It preceded Frick's rebuilding of "Clayton" (6.21) by three years, but Frick's aristocratic lifestyle was Schwab's probable model. A handsome house with compact massing, varied stonework, steep gables, towers, and spires, it seems to speak to the mill workers of the glorious possibilities of labor and hard work. The house has been meticulously restored: the mahogany beams glow again, the stained glass windows sparkle, and a century of soot from the Edgar Thomson blast furnaces has been dislodged.

3.15 CARNEGIE LIBRARY OF BRADDOCK
1888, William Halsey Wood; 1893 music hall, Longfellow, Alden & Harlow.
419 Library St.

A few minutes walk from his Edgar Thomson steel plant, this is the first library Andrew Carnegie donated in the United States, though he built it solely for his workers, not the general public. Lively in design and elegantly executed inside with costly woodwork, this library with adjoining music hall, gym, pool, and baths is programmatically part of the mills.

The library is designed in Pittsburgh's ever-popular Richardsonian Romanesque, but it departs from the majesty of the downtown Courthouse and presents instead a picturesque and variegated silhouette marked by the two squat towers flanking the entrance and a taller tower rising above the roofline. One imagines that Wood, in choosing the light gray stone of the structure, envisioned the effect the then ever-present dust and smoke would have. After years of neglect, the library has been tended back to life by volunteers.

Carnegie Library of Braddock

3.16 UNITED STATES STEEL EDGAR THOMSON WORKS
1873, Alexander Holley, engineer; rebuilt many times. Thirteenth St. and Braddock Ave.

When Andrew Carnegie proposed construction of a Bessemer steel mill in 1872, his mentor William Coleman suggested as an ideal location the riverside meadow where General Edward Braddock met defeat at the hands of the French and Indians in 1755. Situated eight miles southeast of Pittsburgh, the land was cheap and traversed by both Baltimore & Ohio and Pennsylvania Railroad lines. It was perfect for bringing raw materials on the Monongahela

and not far downstream of the Youghiogheny River, along which rail lines carried Connellsville coal and coke to the area.

Carnegie undertook the project with his customary enthusiasm, which did not flag even in the financial panic of 1873. To plan the works, he hired Holley, a preeminent mill designer who brought with him the legendary Captain William Jones to help build and later manage the mill. Production of steel rails began in August 1875 and hung on through the mill closings of the 1980s to remain the last steel producer in the Pittsburgh area.

Edgar Thomson is best viewed at night, perhaps from a vantage point in nearby Rankin or atop one of the thrill rides in Kennywood Park

(3.13), when the huge glowing plant, smoky and noisy and belching fire, evokes the grit and power of Pittsburgh a century ago.

3.17 WESTINGHOUSE MEMORIAL BRIDGE
1931–1932, Vernon Covell and George S. Richardson, engineers, with Stanley Roush, architect. US 30 over Turtle Creek Valley.

From this bridge one sees the two most innovative industrial engines of Pittsburgh: Andrew Carnegie's Edgar Thomson Works (3.16) by the Monongahela River and George Westinghouse's immense electric works of 1894 (today an incubator for startup businesses), about a mile inland. The bridge itself is noteworthy, with its elegantly proportioned piers and the seeming effortlessness of the semi-elliptical arches. It is the masterpiece of Richardson's half-century of bridge construction for Allegheny County. The five reinforced-concrete spans range in length from 200 to nearly 500 feet, and the center span was for decades the longest of its type in the world. From the road-way—part of the pioneering national Lincoln highway—the excitement of the industrial landscape is heightened by the heroic severity of Frank Vittor's Art Deco reliefs on the bridge's four entrance pylons. Carved between 1934 and 1936, the scenes depict the development of Turtle Creek Valley and commemorate Westinghouse's contributions to industry. From the valley floor, the five semi-elliptical arches perfectly echo the natural drama of the valley itself.

3.18 WESTINGHOUSE AIR-BRAKE COMPANY COMPLEX, AND THE WILMERDING PLAN
1889, attributed to Frederick J. Osterling. 325 Commerce St.

It was his need for a new air-brake plant that induced George Westinghouse to purchase 500 acres of land in Turtle Creek in 1888, a few miles from Carnegie's mill at Braddock. Both corporations enjoyed spectacular success over the next century, and their ultimate decline was a staggering blow to the region.

Westinghouse Memorial Bridge

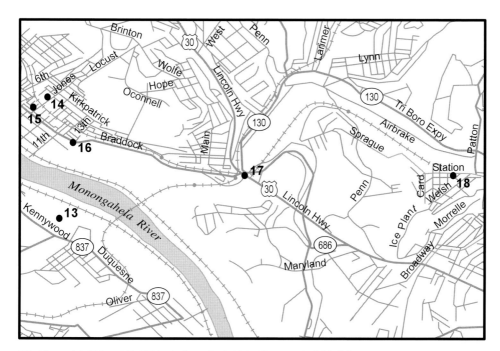

The Monongaheh Valley outside Pittsburgh. Approximate driving time: an extended half-day.

Westinghouse, the consummate inventor, earned his first patent at the age of fifteen; over the course of his career he would win some 360 more. He introduced the alternating-current system of generating and transmitting electricity and developed a compressed-air braking system for railroads. A patent for the latter was issued in 1869, and the Westinghouse Air-Brake Company was incorporated a few months later. Established first in the Strip, where its old factory still stands (6.2), the facility moved to an old cotton mill in Allegheny City. When he outgrew those facilities, Westinghouse looked to a sparsely populated area on the main line of the Pennsylvania Railroad and, in 1889, began construction of a plant here.

Wilmerding, named for Joanna Wilmerding Negley, whose family had owned the land and whose husband sold it to Westinghouse; lies on the floor of a valley shaped by Turtle Creek.

The plant was built on an island formed when the creek forked (one branch was later diverted). What remains of the original plant is the handsome Machine Shop, some drawings for which bear the signature of Frederick Osterling. This tripartite structure sets gable roofs on either end of a squared-off facade. Brick corbels climb to the apex of each gable, while pairs of windows with segmental-arched lintels extend across the first floor. The Foundry stood to the east, perpendicular to the Machine Shop. Here were housed Westinghouse's innovative "traveling tables," the direct precursors of Henry Ford's assembly line, in that product components were carried to workers, and not vice-versa.

Since only four homes stood in the area at the time of the land's acquisition, Westinghouse formed the East Pittsburgh Improvement Company to construct worker housing while the plant was going up. Initial plans for the company town called for three types of houses to be built on the south side of Turtle Creek, facing the plant. The most elaborate had electricity and eight rooms, plus a cellar and bath. The houses on Marguerite and Walsh avenues, though now clad in aluminum siding and typically remodeled, retain their initial high quality. The least expensive had five rooms and lacked indoor plumbing, but all were relatively well-constructed and all eventually could be purchased at cost over a ten-year period. A second phase of construction took place from 1898 to 1900 on the hillside facing the plant. Airbrake Avenue, parallel to Turtle Creek, consists of brick duplexes in the guise of large single-family residences. Least pretentious of all are the red brick row houses with double-height porches, above and behind the creek on Middle Street.

While the plant is the focal point of the town, the Westinghouse Air-Brake Company General Office Building, situated midway up the southern hillside, is Wilmerding's dominant building. Probably modeled after Carnegie's Braddock Library (3.15), Library Hall (popularly known as the Castle) opened in 1890 with a swimming pool, bowling alley, reading rooms, and public baths. Unlike Carnegie's steelworkers, Westinghouse employees were given free half-days on Saturdays; they were among the first workers in the nation to do so. Hence, they had time to use these facilities. Osterling seems to have designed the original building as well as its 1896 replacement after a fire. By then the library had become the administration offices, to which Janssen and Cocken added an east wing in 1926. Today, the building houses the George Westinghouse Museum and the Education and Research foundation of the American Production and Inventory Control Society.

Westinghouse Air Brake Company complex

Allegheny County Airport (Allegheny County Municipal Airport)

3.19 ALLEGHENY COUNTY AIRPORT (ALLEGHENY COUNTY MUNICIPAL AIRPORT)
1929–1931, Stanley Roush; 1936, additions, Henry Hornbostel. Lebanon Church Rd. at PA 885.

Being so involved in solutions to mechanical problems, Pittsburgh also took an early lead in American aviation: the first transcontinental plane was built here in 1910. As early as 1915, amateur pilots were taking off from the old race-track in Schenley Park and Pittsburgh Airways had regular commercial service by 1920. Early airfields, usually no more than grassy fields with steel hangars, were distributed all around town. Though boasting the first hard-surface runways in the United States, Allegheny County Airport was relatively primitive in function. Nonetheless, by 1937 the airport handled 70,000 passengers a year on Trans World Airlines (TWA) and the local Pennsylvania Central Airlines.

Architecturally, the airport marks a cautious essay in Modernism by two Beaux-Arts designers who made clear where their real design loyalties lay. Published sketches for the airport show that Roush, the Allegheny County architect, was first thinking of something considerably more streamlined, akin to Erich Mendelsohn's widely published department stores in the 1920s in Germany. In the end, a more comfortable Art Deco triumphed. The airport makes no secret of its affinity for the Beaux-Arts, however. The architectural historian James Van Trump has likened it to a small Baroque country palace, with its horticultural allees turned into a starburst of runways.

For the exterior of a building devoted to so futuristic a function, Roush chose Art Deco, nationally popular in the 1920s and 1930s for transportation terminals of all types. In a field of glazed white bricks are Mayan-style zig-zag friezes in rich earth tones that tie the building to the land and the sky. The vivid green and black terra cotta pots at the entranceway also represent the earth's clay, though the decoration on them represents banks of stylized planes. The building's taller central section, surmounted by the control tower, is symmetrically flanked by lower wings. The airport survives today as a notable instance of an Art Deco building almost unchanged physically or programmatically. Still busy, the airport is now restricted to corporate jets and private planes.

CHAPTER 4:
NORTH SIDE AND
THE ALLEGHENY VALLEY

Immediately opposite downtown Pittsburgh, on the north bank of the Allegheny River, is the district called North Side. (Local city planners are attempting to substitute the loftier "North Shore," but to date the new term has not stuck.) This was originally Allegheny City, the most ambitious settlement of the early days of western Pennsylvania. Some correspondence survives between the surveyor David Redick, on the site, and Benjamin Franklin in Philadelphia, but why Redick based his 1788 design on a New England model is not documented. The urban grafting worked surprisingly well, however, and the basic square-doughnut shape of Redick's town can still be made out. The central square carries institutional buildings as Redick planned, among them the Children's Museum (4.16) and a Carnegie Library. The surrounding eastern, northern, and western strips of common grazing ground are still verdant as small parks, and the housing stock in the outlying blocks remains, for the most part, intact. Just the southern strip of green on the riverside is lost. Its fate was sealed when the Pennsylvania Canal cut its right-of-way immediately south of Allegheny in 1832; when the canal ceased operations after 1852, the Pennsylvania Railroad laid its tracks on the same alignment.

Allegheny City provides a cautionary tale against the advancement of metropolitan government. As the settlement prospered, it annexed Manchester and other contiguous towns. Then, in 1907, the comeuppance: it was itself ensnared by Pittsburgh and then decayed for three-quarters of a century. What saved the North Side was historic preservation of residential and commercial properties in the dozen blocks newly designated as the Mexican War Streets (4.18). Along with its many handsome streets and hundreds of the best middle-class homes in Pittsburgh, the North Side is now a museum mecca. The Children's Museum (4.16), Carnegie Science Center (4.4), and National Aviary

(4.15) present traditional museum fare, and the Andy Warhol Museum (4.3) and the Mattress Factory (4.20) exult in the contemporary and experimental. Upriver on the Allegheny is a mixed and fascinating landscape of raw industrial satellites (Millvale and Etna), boating marinas, and the leafy suburbs of Evergreen Hamlet, Fox Chapel, and Oakmont.

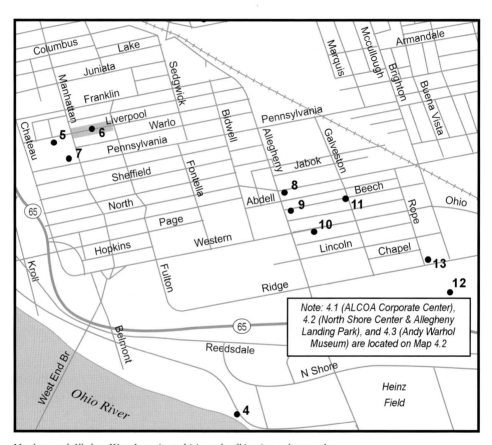

Manchester and Allegheny West. Approximate driving and walking time: at least two hours.

4.1 ALCOA CORPORATE CENTER

1994–1998, The Design Alliance and Rusli Associates, architectural design consultant. 201 Isabella St.

ALCOA's 1953 downtown home (1.22) was an epochal corporate headquarters, but at thirty-

two stories and 475,000 square feet it no longer corresponded to corporate needs of the 1990s. This replacement downsized ALCOA to 340,000 square feet in a radically different configuration of just six stories.

The new ALCOA helps restore to the north bank of the Allegheny River the visual coherence lost after World War II through piecemeal destruction and construction. West of ALCOA stands the North Shore Center office park; east of it rises (rather awkwardly) Lincoln at North Shore, a maze of apartments and townhouses from 1997. Behind ALCOA, at 100 Sandusky Street, is the elegant headquarters of SMS Demag (1994, UDA Architects). These are all important parts of the emerging urban fabric of the North Shore, but it is the wave-like ALCOA that best defines the district now.

The architects worked closely with the firm's employees to program the six-story building into three segments. The first is a small entrance and reception area on its north face, away from the river. The second, also on the north side, is a boxy housing of the heating, cooling, elevators, escalators, restrooms, restaurants, and a newsstand. Some of these elements are normally located on the roof, but architect Agus Rusli sought to shield the unattractive mechanics from the view of the downtown high-rises. The third element is the block-long serpentine curve of the headquarters itself. The skeletal frame of cantilevered sunscreens is aluminum, and the curtain wall is untinted glass to maximize both natural illumination and the striking views of the river and city. The sunscreen accentuates the S-curve of the building and fractures the base geometry into countless smaller shapes. The Three Rivers Heritage Trail cuts between the river and ALCOA's purist sandstone floodwall, with path and wall together muting the structure's bend.

4.2 NORTH SHORE CENTER AND ALLEGHENY LANDING PARK
1984, UDA Architects, with R. Jackson Seay, Jr., landscape architect. Bounded by Isabella, Federal, and Sandusky sts. and the Allegheny River.

Enjoying a majestic view of downtown Pittsburgh, North Shore Center combines one of the nation's first urban sculpture parks with an early attempt to exploit the recreational benefits of the city's waterfront for a commercial development. It was also a pivotal contributor to the popular perception of the north bank of the Allegheny (the newly baptized North Shore) as an independent entity. The three-acre park is an integral part of North Shore Center, an important selling point to prospective tenants.

The sculptures—by Ned Smyth, Pittsburgh's George Danhires, George Sugarman, and Isaac Witkin—stand in or near a central plaza between the riverfront office blocks. Smyth's *Mythic Source* is inspired by Stonehenge and acts as transition to the waterfront. Metal reliefs depict ancient symbols and muscular workers to honor the building trades and the city's reliance on waterbound trade. Danhires's bronze *The Builders* presents two life-size construction workers as a specific tribute to the builders of Pittsburgh's Renaissance I and II.

The two brick office buildings encircle and cradle the circular plaza and its fountain. The gently sloping meadow between the offices and the river also functions as an amphitheater, with a stage adjacent to the water. Joggers take advantage of the Three Rivers Heritage Trail and boaters use the docking facilities and fishing access.

4.3 ANDY WARHOL MUSEUM (FRICK AND LINDSAY)
1911, William G. Wilkins Co. Ltd.; 1918 and 1922 additions, O. M. Topp; conversion to museum 1994, Richard Gluckman and Associates and UDA Architects. 117 Sandusky St.

This cream-toned terra cotta-clad warehouse was a natural choice for conversion into a showcase for Pittsburgh's Andy Warhol, making it one of the world's largest museums devoted to a single artist. Its industrial character alludes to Warhol's use of industrial sites for his studios, while the mass production involved in industry

Andy Warhol Museum (Frick and Lindsay)

reflects the mass production basis of Warhol's own work. Frick (a distant relative of the magnate) and Lindsay, the building's original owners, lavished much care on their 1911 plumbing supply warehouse, not stinting on a bounteously ornamented Beaux-Arts cornice. Long gone, the cornice was replicated for the new museum, using high-tech lightweight fiberglass. Inside, virtually all non-structural elements were removed from the seven-story building, leaving only the exterior walls, piers, and concrete floors. Gluckman then split the warehouse into nineteen galleries on six floors for rotating shows of Warhol's thousands of paintings, graphics, films, videos, and personal archives. Visitors begin a tour by taking an elevator to the top floor, then progress downwards on the staircase inserted into the old freight elevator shaft. A new addition at the rear provides administrative areas, an auditorium, and a theater for regular showings of Warhol's films. While the question "What would Andy have thought of all this?" cannot be answered, the popularity of the museum suggests that the main design decisions were solved with uncommon sensitivity.

4.4 CARNEGIE SCIENCE CENTER
1989–1991, Tasso Katselas Associates.
1 Allegheny Ave.

Blessed with a dramatic site on the Ohio River, just west of Heinz Field and prominently visible from the Point, the red and gray Carnegie Science Center stands as a guardedly populist temple to science and education. The Center is part of the Carnegie consortium, whose main library (2.14) stands in Oakland, but whose Andy Warhol Museum (4.3) lies less than a ten-minute walk away. Katselas gave the four-story building three major components: an Omnimax theater, a planetarium/auditorium space, and housing for specialized exhibits, linked by a system of ramps and staircases to provide visual and physical unity. Somewhat brooding and somber despite color touches in red, the structure's domed Omnimax theater is on the city side, and a glass-skinned atrium and science theater are at the opposite end. Between the two sits the main exhibition block. The entrance is on the landside, reached by a bridge from the parking lot. Busses use a second entrance below the bridge, which also allows direct access to the Omnimax theater.

A certain degree of disorientation seems endemic and possibly useful in science centers, and the lobby and attached atrium of this one does not disappoint, with a large and noisy gift shop, Aquabatics Fountain, and a restaurant on the lower level overlooking the river. The three upper levels are each devoted to different themes. The interior is at its best with throngs of students climbing and descending its ramps, while the grounds are at their best when peaceful. Science education continues on the Ohio River with the USS Requin, a docked World War II diesel-electric submarine.

Carnegie Science Center

4.5 ANDERSON MANOR
(JAMES ANDERSON HOUSE)
c. 1830; 1905. 1423 Liverpool St.

One of the first Pittsburgh ironmasters to strike it rich, Anderson erected this imposing home around 1830 on a knoll that afforded a fine panorama of the Ohio River. Anderson's estate was diminished almost immediately by the imposition of the Manchester street grid (4.6) in 1832, but enough remained to make him a lordly figure in Pittsburgh's industrial fraternity. Anderson's tiny public library, eagerly used by a young Andrew Carnegie, was the model for Carnegie's later worldwide library donations.

The brick house resembles a plantation in Tidewater Virginia in its basic scheme of a two-story, five-bay cube with central hall. What distinguishes it is a two-story pedimented portico, which is rare in western Pennsylvania, though a notable feature of Palladian-influenced plan-

tation houses such as Drayton Hall near Charleston, South Carolina.

In 1905, a wing was added to accommodate the house's new function as a private-care residence for the elderly, which it remains. The facade was re-bricked and the portico rebuilt, though faithful to the original design. While the delicacy of the original facade is lost, the house recalls an era of almost unimaginable calm before men such as Anderson turned the North Side into a hellfire of industrialization.

4.6 HOUSES ON LIVERPOOL STREET
(ORIGINALLY LOCUST STREET)
1880s. 1300 block Liverpool St., between Manhattan and Fulton sts.

Laid out in 1832, Manchester was already an important industrial center by the time it became part of Allegheny City in 1867, in a prelude to its annexation by Pittsburgh in 1907.

Houses on Liverpool Street (originally Locust Street)

This block is one of the most impressive in Pittsburgh and the focus of one of the largest National Register Historic Districts in the city. The 1300 block was originally settled in the 1880s by German-Jewish merchants and professionals. Edgar Kaufmann, the client for Fallingwater (9.2), was born around the corner in 1885. The rows of tall mansions, coupled with the tree-lined red brick sidewalks, create an exhilarating and sophisticated urban scene. The nine double houses on the north side of the block are identical in their Second Empire styling and were originally erected as rental properties on land owned by Letitia Robinson, a scion of Allegheny's founding family. Houses on the block's south side were put up individually by such well-known merchants as Charles Aaron and Gustave Langenheim, whose freestanding house at number 1315 is the star of the block. The neighboring houses are mixed in style, but visual unity is maintained by similar mansard roofs, flat incised stone lintels, and the repetition of such basic design elements in the dormers, windows, and porch columns.

The decline of industry and the building of PA 65, which severed Manchester from other parts of the North Side, contributed to the severe decline of the neighborhood in the twentieth century. Since the late 1960s, however, the Manchester Citizens Corporation (MCC) and Pittsburgh History and Landmarks Foundation (PHLF) have played key roles in neighborhood revitalization. PHLF rehabilitated most of the buildings on the north side of this block in the late 1960s in a program that later involved hundreds more homes throughout Manchester. MCC continues to lead Manchester's redevelopment through initiatives designed to replace the neighborhood's dilapidated public housing with new units for sale and rental and overseeing necessary social and community services.

4.7 CALLIOPE HOUSE
(WILLIAM AND MARY LEA FRAZIER HOUSE)
1875–1876. 1414 Pennsylvania Ave.

This starkly dramatic three-part Italian villa, with verandah and high tower, was built by a lumber baron whose factory on the Ohio shore was only a ten-minute walk away. In 1876, this was already an old-fashioned design, suggesting that it was inspired by a source from an earlier generation, such as Andrew Jackson Downing's *Architecture of Country Houses* of 1850. Downing—long dead by then—would have been surprised both by the enduring popularity of his illustrations and by the perversity of locating a country villa in one of the sootiest environments in the nation. The sprawling brick mansion was the founding site for the Pittsburgh Folk Music Society and today accommodates the Balmoral School of Highland Piping.

4.8 EMMANUEL EPISCOPAL CHURCH
1885–1886, Henry Hobson Richardson.
957 W. North Ave.

When the nascent Emmanuel Church in prosperous post-Civil-War Allegheny City created a building committee, it selected Malcolm Hay, a prominent Pittsburgh lawyer and politician, as its head. Hay possibly knew Richardson personally, but as an Episcopal layman he had particularly studied the designer's brilliant solution for Episcopal liturgy in his Trinity Church in Boston. The committee selected Richardson for the commission in 1883. By the time Richardson committed himself to the work, he was also planning the Allegheny County Courthouse and Jail (1.15), in which Hay seems again to have played a role.

Richardson's first plans for Emmanuel were similar to his previous churches: Romanesque Revival in style but eclectic in detail. Richardson's first design adhered to the limitations of the plot (50 feet × 100 feet) but ignored the congregation's restricted budget. At $48,972,

the projected cost was quadruple the budget, so the design was rejected. Eventually the building committee prevailed and the church was built for only $12,300. In this budget fight—and not in some independent artistic source—lies the main reason for the simplicity of the plan and its reductionism from what until then had been Richardson's characteristically ornate style.

Emmanuel, massive and unadorned compared to the eclecticism of the other styles then present in Pittsburgh, is in no way visually poorer, thanks to the richness of its red brickwork and the striking comprehensiveness of its image. Five rows of voussoirs outline the three entrance arches and the tall windows that surmount and echo the entrance. The bricks outside the voussoirs are first laid in a basket-weave pattern, then in horizontal rows, and finally as what the Dutch call "mouse-teeth" on the edges of the gable.

Neighbors have long referred to Emmanuel as the bake-oven church because of its low-pitched roof and unbroken transition to a semi-circular apse. The interior is somewhat richer but still rustic, except for a white marble Tiffany-style glass reredos that was added in 1898 by the Pittsburgh designers Leake and Greene. Richardson underestimated the thrust of the beams as well as the weight of the roof, which in just a few years gave the exterior aisle wall on Allegheny Avenue a picturesque but

Emmanuel Episcopal Church

unthreatening batter. Frank Alden of Richardson's Boston office was called in to evaluate the wall, which he found to be architecturally sound. It was Alden, in 1888, who built the adjoining parish house.

Though not an unsurpassed masterpiece, Emmanuel marks a significant turning-point in Richardson's vocabulary. Given that a famous architect was here incited to better work by a steadfast patron, Emmanuel stands as a good design lesson even beyond its local significance.

4.9 CALVARY METHODIST EPISCOPAL CHURCH
1892, Vrydaugh and Shepherd, with T. B. Wolfe. 971 Beech Ave.

The effusive academic detail of this society church contrasts markedly with Richardson's Emmanuel Episcopal church (4.8) a block away. Calvary, whose Gothic Revival facade is marked by the enlivening contrast between the two differently sized facade towers, was almost a private devotional project for the four main families that backed it. So expensive was land in 1892, when Allegheny City was at its fashionable height, that one-quarter of the budget is said to have been spent just for the site. Construction of the church cost another quarter of the budget, interior furnishings another quarter, and the last quarter went (by private subscription) into three of Louis Comfort Tiffany's best windows: the Apocalypse, Resurrection, and Ascension.

4.10 VICTORIA HOUSE BED-AND-BREAKFAST (JOSHUA AND ELIZA RHODES HOUSE)
c. 1866. 939 Western Ave.

A large post-Civil-War mansion on Western Avenue is one of the settings for Marcia Davenport's 1943 novel *The Valley of Decision*, about a family of Pittsburgh industrialists from 1873 to 1941. This house, in which the family of a traction czar lived from the 1860s through the 1920s, may have been the inspiration for that

setting; certainly it constitutes a fascinating remnant of Victorian Pittsburgh. The house is Italianate, of a simple sort that added florid hood-molds (easily purchased from mill yards, and, later, from mail-order catalogues) and brackets to its plain brick walls. The house's vibrantly colored interior with original cabinetry, its ballroom, the servant quarters in a long rambling structure to the rear, and the remnants of its vegetable garden to the left of the house make it remarkable. The ballroom is occasionally used by historic preservationists who, here, have much to celebrate.

4.11 HOUSES ON BEECH AVENUE
1860s–1900. 800–900 blocks Beech Ave., between Allegheny Ave. and Brighton Rd.

These two blocks of brick houses bisected by Galveston Avenue give a perfect idea of upper-middle class Pittsburgh life after the Civil War. The blocks, unbroken and further unified by the roof cornice, are enlivened by the overlay-

Houses on Beech Avenue

Community College of Allegheny County

ing rhythm of prominent door and window moldings and punctuated by the occasional verandah. Two of the residents here were famous not for wealth but for their literary talent. Gertrude Stein was born at 850 Beech in 1874; Mary Roberts Rinehart wrote a dozen of her mysteries in the solid house at number 954.

4.12 COMMUNITY COLLEGE OF ALLEGHENY COUNTY
1973, Tasso Katselas Associates.
255 East Ohio St.

This mega-structure of gray poured concrete and soft brown brick climbs the south slope of old Monument Hill. One of Katselas's stated objectives was to maintain the bulk of Monument Hill and not level it. The structure gently cascades in and out of the earth, in a flow of movement that is also emphasized by the angularity of the escalator system.

Like many expressionist works of the 1960s and 1970s, Community College (CCAC) reveals certain internal secrets externally, offering

viewers a glimpse into the inner workings of a building of this kind. Pipes, beams, and other internal elements become decorative as well as functional devices to offer visual movement to the viewer. Inside, the school has an open circulation and free-flowing hallways. The crisscross pattern of many of the hallways provides pedestrians with what Katselas calls a "series of discoveries," as they pass from classroom to classroom. Curving—and often looping—hallways bend through the school, providing kaleidoscopic views of the outside through the narrow slit windows cut into the walls.

Katselas sought to keep faculty and students in touch with one another by creating faculty cubicles that would be accessible and welcoming to students, while providing free zones where group interaction and discussion would foster the learning process. A design so strongly expressionistic is bound to have its detractors, and CCAC has many. Still, it succeeds in reclaiming a time when college campuses were not faceless education malls, but places of distinction and flair.

4.13 JONES HALL, COMMUNITY COLLEGE OF ALLEGHENY COUNTY (BENJAMIN JONES HOUSE)
1908, Rutan and Russell. 808 Ridge Ave.

This forty-two-room reinforced-concrete Tudor Revival pile was designed by two followers of Richardson for the heirs of Jones and Laughlin Steel, and it remains a prime document to the time when Ridge Avenue was among the most glamorous Millionaires' Rows in the nation. The house was planned before Pittsburgh annexed Allegheny City in 1907 and wealthy families began to abandon the North Side for their country estates at Sewickley. The Joneses stayed until 1931. By 1912, the nature of this demographic shift must have been evident, because Thomas Hannah built Western Theological Seminary next door in the same style and scale as the Jones house, but it was intended for institutional use from the first. Today, both buildings serve the community college across the street. Another dozen neighboring mansions on Brighton Road and Ridge and Beech avenues have been restored from flophouses to private residences.

4.14 ALLEGHENY COMMONS EAST
1974, Tasso Katselas Associates. 255 E. Ohio St.

This high-density complex of nineteen four-story brick townhouses successfully avoids most of the stereotypes associated with subsidized housing. Attractive, well-maintained, and spacious, its design parallels certain theses in Oscar Newman's *Defensible Space* of 1973. Katselas's design concept was to exploit architectural space to promote social interaction among the residents. A pedestrian street winds its way through the center of the village and leads to a large park that has a courtyard, playground, and basketball courts. Each dwelling unit has a private arched entranceway that looks onto the common space of the pedestrian street. Large windows overlook both this common space and the contiguous park, a remnant of the eighteenth-century Allegheny City commons. Lights are placed

Allegheny Commons East

The Mexican War Streets, Old Allegheny, and Fineview. Approximate driving and walking time: at least two hours.

alongside landscaped pedestrian paths, allowing residents visual control over their village by day and by night. Within easy walking distance are other parks, churches, schools, and shopping and commercial areas.

Allegheny Commons East is part of the larger seventy-nine-acre Allegheny Center urban renewal project that was completed in 1978. This controversial redevelopment was intended to reverse the economic and social decay of the North Side, but it ended up obliterating much of it instead. Allegheny Commons East was built for low- and moderate-income tenants as a social counterbalance to the upscale apartment blocks and townhouses elsewhere in Allegheny Center. In the end, the architectural quality of this subsidized complex was superior to that of its richer cousins.

4.15 THE NATIONAL AVIARY IN PITTSBURGH
1952, Lawrence Wolfe; 1967–1969, Lawrence and Anthony Wolfe; Simonds and Simonds, landscape architects; 1997, STUDIO DeLisio Architecture and Design. Allegheny Commons West in West Park.

Only three buildings have been erected in West Park in its 200-year history, and all were on the same site. From 1828 to 1887, John Haviland's Western Penitentiary, much praised by penal reformers of the times, stood here. When the jail moved, the building was replaced by Phipps Conservatory and Floral Gardens, a forerunner of Phipps's more elaborate Conservatory of 1893 across town in Schenley Park. The West Park greenhouse was destroyed in a gas explosion in 1927. In 1952, a rectangular glass-walled aviary with a Gothic-arched roof was built on the site. Parallel to this structure, and more square in shape, is the addition of 1969. This cage of

trusswork with glass walls tripled the aviary's space. A large glass dome, added in 1997, crests the juncture of the two building parts. The interconnected pavilions house a humid interior for 200 species of birds in their natural habitats as well as several free-flight rooms. The Pittsburgh Aviary became the National Aviary in 1993, one of a few such specialized facilities in the world.

4.16 CHILDREN'S MUSEUM OF PITTSBURGH (OLD POST OFFICE MUSEUM AND BUHL PLANETARIUM AND INSTITUTE OF POPULAR SCIENCE)
(Post Office) 1894–1897, William Martin Aiken. (Buhl) 1939, Ingham & Boyd; addition 2000–2004, Konig Eizenberg Architecture and Perkins Eastman. 10 Children's Way.

When the Buhl planetarium opened in 1939, it was the largest of the five planetaria in the

Children's Museum of Pittsburgh, incorporating the Allegheny Post Office and Buhl Planetarium

United States. It occupies the site once occupied by Allegheny City's Italianate city hall, which became redundant after the city's forced merger with Pittsburgh. The Buhl Foundation, its donor, also had links to the site: the Boggs and Buhl Department Store stood diagonally opposite the planetarium until the 1950s.

The Buhl Planetarium's science exhibits, rooftop observatory, astronomy workshops, and planetarium drew many visitors. Supplanted in 1993 by the Carnegie Science Center (4.4), the Buhl was given to the Children's Museum, which in the previous decade had taken over the Allegheny City Post Office.

The Buhl's exterior stripped classical walls, clad in gray limestone, hint at streamlining in their stylized quoins, and bold astronomy-themed Art Deco reliefs by Sidney Waugh provide a foretaste of the stylishly decorated interior. In 2004, an addition linked the domed Buhl to its neighbor, the former post office, to give convenient access between the two parts of the museum. The glass addition is sheltered by a gossamer-like screen of plastic petals that ruffle in the wind, yet allow light to enter the newly created space. A wind sculpture by Ned Kahn stands in the forecourt. Inside the museum is a replica of Mr. Rogers's Neighborhood House and puppets from his famous children's show on public television.

Carnegie Library of Pittsburgh, Allegheny Branch

4.17 CARNEGIE LIBRARY OF PITTSBURGH, ALLEGHENY BRANCH

1889, Smithmeyer and Pelz. 5 Allegheny Sq.

This library enjoys the technical distinction of being the first Carnegie public library in the United States, since Carnegie's library in Braddock (3.15) was a proprietary gift to his steelworkers at his nearby plant. Carnegie made the gift offer in 1886 to Allegheny City, "the city which was my first American home." The national competition for the library was handily won by Smithmeyer and Pelz, who had just

finished the Library of Congress in Washington, DC. Taking no chances, they adhered closely to the detail and massing of H. H. Richardson's Courthouse and Jail (1.15), especially in the massive square tower that anchors the corner. The library included spaces for an art gallery, lecture hall, and concert auditorium to accommodate an audience of 1,200. The library remains today, but the other components have disappeared, and the auditorium serves now as a theater. In front of the library stands the central portion of Daniel Chester French's monument (1904, Henry Bacon) to James Anderson (4.5), which Carnegie commissioned in memory of the man who, before him, made books available to a working public. The monument was dispersed during the urban renewal of the 1960s, but was reassembled thirty years later.

Mexican War Streets Houses

4.18 MEXICAN WAR STREETS HOUSES
c. 1850–c. 1870s. Bounded by Jacksonia and Federal sts., W. North Ave., and Brighton Rd.

This core district of the North Side constitutes the largest area of development in uniform architectural style in the city. With its brick herringbone sidewalks and new trees, it is also one of the most pleasing neighborhoods visually. The developer, William Robinson, Jr., was the first mayor (in 1840) of Allegheny City. Around 1850, he subdivided a portion of his inherited land just north of Allegheny Commons Park into approximately 300 lots on twelve city blocks. Having just returned from military service in the Mexican War, Robinson named the streets after battles and generals of that conflict: Monterey, Palo Alto, Sherman, Taylor, and Resaca. Building followed, beginning in the 1850s with Greek Revival houses (mixed with some Italianate detailing) around Arch Street at the east and ending in the 1870s in Richardsonian Romanesque around Brighton Road at the west. Unlike contemporary developments in Philadelphia or Baltimore, these houses were put up one by one, not in rows. They are of similar size (generally twenty feet in width and two stories in height) and material (nearly always brick, though with a few standouts in wood frame or brownstone). There are some rare breaks between the homes.

By the early twentieth century, middle- and upper-class residents had left these homes, and they became rental and boarding houses. By the 1950s, the buildings had fallen into disrepair, and the neighborhood was unsafe. Very few homes were torn down, however, as there was simply no economic incentive to do so. In the 1970s, these streets became one of Pittsburgh's earliest ventures into the historic preservation of a complete neighborhood, spurred by the new Pittsburgh History and Landmarks Foundation (PHLF). Today one of the premier preservation groups in the nation, PHLF buys homes for resale, either restored or as-is, and it also assists landlords in maintaining their rental units. The result is, for the most part, an avoidance of the phenomenon of gentrification. The Mexican War Streets today have a growing and heterogeneous population, all concerned with preserving this gem of a neighborhood.

4.19 RENAISSANCE APARTMENTS (ORPHAN ASYLUM OF PITTSBURGH AND ALLEGHENY)
1838, John Chislett; 1873, additions; rehabilitation, 1984 and 2006, Landmark Design Associates. 308 and 310–322 N. Taylor Ave.

This is the North Side's oldest institutional building, built for an orphan asylum and located on land donated by William Robinson, Jr., developer of the area. Pittsburgh's second professional architect, John Chislett, designed the brick main structure in severe Greek Revival, five bays wide and three stories high, with a central pediment. In 1866, the by-then-vacant building was purchased by the Allegheny Ladies' Relief Society to house Civil War widows and was renamed the Allegheny Widow's Home. When North Taylor Avenue was extended to meet Sherman Street in 1872, a section of the building had to be removed. In compensation, rows of housing were added, one house deep, around a central courtyard on North Taylor and Sampsonia Way. Today, as the Renaissance Apartments, the complex serves as federally subsidized housing for the elderly.

4.20 THE MATTRESS FACTORY
c. 1870; 1991 interior renovation, Joel Kranich; 2003 addition, Landmark Design Associates. 500 Sampsonia Way.

This brick, six-story former factory, which for about a century produced mattresses, was converted into a leading site for installation art in 1977, though the interior was not materially changed until a renovation in the 1990s. The ceilings and windows are high, the interior

The Mattress Factory

volumes capacious, and the galleries numerous enough that whole rooms can be dedicated to certain installations for decades. As well as its changing exhibitions featuring experimental artists, it has a growing permanent collection, including work by James Turrell. The gallery was expanded with an addition in 2003. A mesmerizing visual experience of art and architecture inside, the Mattress Factory also created an interesting ruins-garden outside, using the foundations of homes and outbuildings that once stood next door.

4.21 HEATHSIDE COTTAGE
(COLONEL JAMES ANDREWS HOUSE)
c. 1864–1865, attributed to Joseph Kerr.
416 Catoma St.

This brick Gothic Revival cottage in the Fineview neighborhood (formerly Nunnery Hill) makes an extraordinary visual impact with just

Heathside Cottage (Colonel James Andrews House)

a half-dozen rooms. It was commissioned at the end of the Civil War by James Andrews, a Scottish stonemason and self-taught engineer who built the piers for the Eads Bridge in St. Louis. Around 1846, Andrews served as masonry contractor for the Pittsburgh Custom House and Post Office on Smithfield Street, downtown, which brought him into close collaboration with the architect Joseph Kerr. The expert wood detailing of Heathside Cottage bespeaks a master's touch; hence, the family tradition that Kerr designed this house for his old collaborator, most likely in the 1860s. A poem in the Andrews family archive indicates a courtship between Andrew Carnegie and one of Andrews's daughters. This came to naught, but Carnegie remained a family friend and business colleague, adding to the Andrews's standing in the community. Andrews's growing family lived in this small cottage for about six years before buying a larger lot down the street and constructing Ingleside (demolished). Nearby are two other Gothic Revival residences dating to c. 1860, the ten-room stone Henderson House (1516 Warren St.) and a board-and-batten cottage (1521 Warren St.).

4.22 ALLEGHENY GENERAL HOSPITAL
1929–1936, York and Sawyer.
320 East N. Ave.

The seventeen-story Art Deco tower of this 1,200-room hospital building is topped by a penthouse in the guise of a Greek temple. Illuminated at night, it can be seen from many parts of town—Liberty Avenue in Bloomfield is the best viewing point—as a floating mirage. The same talent for combining function and fantasy emerges in the vaulted, Byzantine-influenced entrance portico internally, which is supported on slender red and gray alternating granite columns with terra cotta capitals. The numerous arches of the brick corbel table are filled with sculpted reliefs of major figures in the history of medicine.

Allegheny General Hospital

4.23 THE PRIORY AND GRAND HALL
(ST. MARY'S ROMAN CATHOLIC CHURCH)
1853–1854, church; 1906, vestibule, Sidney
Heckert; 1888, priory, Henry Moser.
614 Pressley St.

Father John Stibiel, second pastor for this parish of German immigrants, is the architect of record for this brick church. Externally, the twin-towered church is a melange of neoclassical features, but the interior betrays a far greater architectural talent. There, high barrel vaults held on four crossing columns intersect below a beautifully lit umbrella vault and skylight. Similar interior boldness marks Charles F. Bartberger's contemporary St. Paul of the Cross Monastery (3.7) (148 Monastery Ave.), and St. Mary's may be his work as well. The church serves now as a busy banqueting hall; the Romanesque Revival priory next door is the first of a handful of boutique hotels that Pittsburgh carved out of its Victorian white elephants at the end of the twentieth century.

4.24 SIXTEENTH STREET BRIDGE
1923, Warren & Wetmore; James Chalfant,
engineer. Sixteenth St. and the Allegheny
River.

Like the "Three Sisters" bridges (1.31), the design of this span was overseen by Pittsburgh's Civic Arts Commission, which demanded a monumental aspect to what was the third bridge on this site. The New York City architects had recently completed Grand Central Terminal in Manhattan, and here, too, they employed outsized sculptures—in this case, giant bronze horses and globes by Leo Lentelli—to render the bridge a true civic monument. Two steel side arches flank a 437-foot center span, creating what has been described by bridge historian Steven Fenves as "an indeterminate hybrid, part trussed arch and part full-depth truss." The abutments consist of high stone piers carrying Lentelli's horses and globes.

4.25 HEINZ LOFTS
(J. HEINZ COMPANY FACTORIES)
1889, attributed to Frederick J. Osterling;
various dates for additions, Robert Maurice
Trimble, Albert Kahn, and Skidmore,
Owings and Merrill; 2003–2005, loft
conversions, Sandvick Architects and
Developers. 300 Heinz St.

From this riverside site, Henry J. Heinz staged a revolution in food-processing and packaging techniques, ultimately building his food and condiment business into a global operation. The brand began modestly in 1869, with Heinz selling horseradish out of his family's house in Sharpsburg, three miles up the Allegheny. Twenty years later, Heinz consolidated his offices and plants in this model industrial complex, which grew to thirty-two buildings. Still standing are fine examples of late-nineteenth-century industrial buildings and noteworthy newer additions.

Riverview Park's 251-acres were deeded to Pittsburgh in 1894 by the pioneer Watson family, whose early-nineteenth century log cabin still stands in what was for a century its private land. The park's terrain is steep, with multiple views over the Ohio Valley and deep furrows on the west leading down to the now-dry valley of Woods Run. The Park is maintained as unmanaged woodlands, with only minimal roads and trails cut through.

The Observatory sits in the middle of the park. Its godfathers were Samuel Pierpont Langley (1834–1906) and John Alfred Brashear (1840–1920). Langley served as Director of the Observatory in its earlier home from 1867 to 1887, when he moved to Washington, D.C., to serve as Secretary of the Smithsonian Institution. He encouraged Brashear and helped him find sponsors. Brashear, one of the great astronomers in the nation and one of several self-taught geniuses to emerge from industrial Pittsburgh, gained fame for the accuracy of the lenses he ground in a small workshop that still stands, virtually in ruins, at 2016 Perrysville Avenue. Brashear arranged the donation of land and funding for the building of a new observatory. David Park, the co-founder of Crucible Steel, donated 200 acres in 1894 for a park and observatory on the highest hill in Allegheny County. Henry Clay Frick, the Mellons, George Westinghouse, and railroad magnate William Thaw co-sponsored the enterprise. Construction proceeded slowly between 1900 and 1912, although Andrew Carnegie rushed the building to partial completion in 1910 so that he could observe Halley's Comet through its telescopes.

The Observatory (for many years a research branch of the University of Pittsburgh) featured three telescopes, one of which was turned from visual to photographic recording as early as the 1920s. In the 1980s, the Observatory succeeded in computer-aided measuring of the solar system. The floors below two of the telescopes rotate, but each stands on an independent foundation of bedrock.

The Observatory's architect, Swedish immigrant Thorsten Billquist, arrived in Pittsburgh around 1893 after serving an apprenticeship with McKim, Mead and White in New York City. The buff-brick building is Greek Revival in style, with fluted Ionic columns outlining the dome and an entrance marked with a pedimented portico. This is an enchanting and somewhat mysterious place, serving science and art equally well. Brashear, his wife Phoebe, and James E. Keeler, director (1891–1898), and his son Henry are buried in a crypt at the observatory's core. The telescopes are open for public use on select evenings.

Heinz began life as a brick worker, and these marvelous brick walls show the patron's understanding of the craft. Indeed, the old man caught his death of cold in 1919 while inspecting construction of a brick wall in this complex. Nearly everything that went up during his lifetime was in Romanesque Revival, probably designed by the local master of that style, Frederick Osterling. Utilitarian buildings executed in brick with stone trim, the structures feature corner spires, pronounced corbelling, and Roman arches, some structural and some decorative. Among the best-preserved older structures are the Bottling Building (1896, with 1905 additions), Bean Building (1912), and Maurice Trimble's Meat Products Building (1920).

Two of the early Heinz buildings depart from the Romanesque Revival idiom. Outside the complex, on East Ohio Street, stands the Tudor Revival Sarah Heinz House designed by Trimble in 1913, a neighborhood youth center.

H. J. Heinz Company Factories (now Heinz Lofts)

And at the heart of the complex stands the five-story reinforced concrete Administration Building (1906), by the pioneer industrial architect Albert Kahn. Its neoclassical lines, rusticated Gouveneur granite facing, and white terra cotta piers underscore its status as the seat of managerial power.

Kahn returned to the complex to add the four-story Employee Service Building, in close conformity with the earlier Romanesque Revival units. This housed dining facilities, an auditorium, and other amenities for Heinz workers. Seeking to avoid the labor unrest that bedeviled other Pittsburgh industries, Heinz established benign but firmly paternalistic policies to encourage productivity among his employees. Kahn's other structure, an annex of 1930 to the Administration Building, shows a clear stylistic break; it is a severe industrial block of light-colored brick, devoid of ornamentation.

In 1949, the company demolished seven obsolete buildings and commissioned Gordon Bunshaft of Skidmore, Owings and Merrill to erect a Vinegar Works and a central storage warehouse. The blue-colored glass curtain wall of the Vinegar Works marked not only the first use of the International Style among Pittsburgh corporations, but also an early and bold use of uncompromising Modernism for industrial use anywhere in the nation. While food processing continues in some parts of the complex, the former Shipping, Meat, Bean, Cereal, and Reservoir buildings were converted to housing units between 2003 and 2005.

4.26 PENN BREWERY
(EBERHARDT & OBER BREWERY COMPANY)
1894, Brewhouse, Joseph Stillburg.
800 Vinial St.

Penn Brewery hugs the base of Troy Hill immediately across PA 28 from the Heinz plant (4.25). After the Civil War, German workers

Penn Brewery (Eberhardt and Ober Brewery Company)

from the tanneries, breweries, and meat packing industries gravitated to Troy Hill. In 1870, two brothers-in-law from Troy Hill, John Ober and William Eberhardt, took over this site in the hollow of the hill, where beer had been brewed since the 1840s, and built their brewery. It joined the Pittsburgh Brewing Company in 1899 and remained in operation until 1952, after which the buildings deteriorated.

In 1986, the North Side Civic Development Council initiated a program to revitalize the area's economy, using a mix of public and private funding. Part of the old brewery was restored for Penn Brewery and part was recycled into offices for the Brewery Innovation Center, an incubator of small startup companies. The squat-towered brewhouse houses a restaurant and microbrewery, while some thirty tenant companies and their common support services use the brick office building (1897) next door. The Romanesque Revival-styled bottling building across Vinial Street is now independent of the brewery.

4.27 ST. ANTHONY OF PADUA SHRINE
1880; 1890–1891 addition, Suibertus G. Mollinger. 1700 Harpster St.

In the late 1870s, Suibertus G. Mollinger, the Belgian-born pastor of Most Holy Name of Jesus Church in Troy Hill, faced a unique problem: he had to house the thousands of relics that he and his agents in Europe had acquired. In 1880, Mollinger used his personal inheritance to build St. Anthony's Chapel, a small twin-towered structure. It attracted such throngs of pilgrims that it was enlarged in 1890 to its present size.

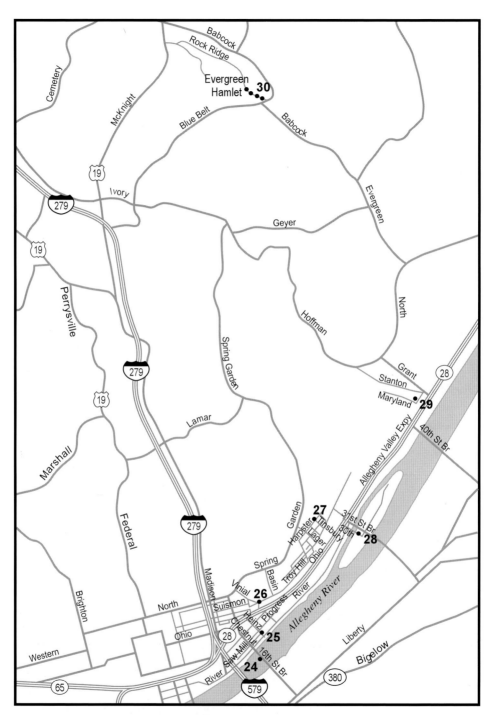

From Troy Hill to Millvale and Evergreen Hamlet. Approximate driving time: an extended half-day.

The chapel's brick-and-sandstone walls and twin square towers are a German version of Romanesque Revival popular earlier in the nineteenth century. Both the roof and octagonal spires are of slate-covered timber. The church fits comfortably in the neighborhood; it is attractive, solid, and substantial, if not spectacular. In contrast, the interior is flamboyant in a dazzling Baroque explosion of gold leaf and stained glass windows, with yet more gold in the monstrances and reliquaries. Life-sized figures of the Stations of the Cross, imported from Munich, line the walls of the chapel. Behind and to the sides of the altar stand massive walnut cabinets, fashioned by local craftsmen, to house more reliquaries.

After World War II, the numbers of pilgrims declined, and by the 1970s the shrine had fallen into disrepair. Restored and refurbished in 1977, the shrine attracts a swelling number of visitors, with a catalogue of the relics now on a computer database.

4.28 WASHINGTON'S LANDING
(HERR'S ISLAND)
1989–1999, Urban Redevelopment Authority of Pittsburgh, City of Pittsburgh Department of City Planning, and Environmental Planning and Design, master planners; LaQuatra Bonci Associates, landscape architects; Bohlin Cywinski Jackson, site planners; Montgomery and Rust, developers. (Commercial structures), Damianos Brown Andrews; The Design Alliance; and Kingsland, Scott, Bauer, Havekotte Associates. (Housing), Donald Montgomery and Bob Worsing. Allegheny River, from Twenty-ninth to Thirty-fourth sts.

The forty-two acres of Herr's Island, two miles upstream from the Golden Triangle, entered history in 1753 when George Washington nearly drowned near here. A century later, Benjamin Herr made a fitful start at developing the island into a village of tree-lined streets, homes, shops, and recreational areas. But Herr's village was taken over by industry in the 1850s and given its first stockyards by the tanner James Callery in 1885. In 1903, the Pennsylvania Railroad erected huge, metal-roofed livestock pens on half of the island, turning it into one of the key livestock and slaughterhouse complexes in the nation. The railroad and food processors abandoned Herr's Island in the 1960s, leaving behind a scrap yard, slaughterhouse, livestock auction house, soap works, rendering plant, and 100 empty cattle pens.

After rusting for thirty years, the old installations were torn out as planners re-baptized the island Washington's Landing. The intent was to use neo-traditional town planning to create a multi-use walkable urban village with adjacent areas for offices, light industry, and recreation. Millions of dollars of public and private funds and intense collaboration among public and private planners and developers combined to create such a village fifteen years later. Traditional house types and materials give a consistent architectural continuity to the sycamore-lined streets of the village at the southern end of the island, with its ninety townhouses of brick and clapboard siding. The usual rows of identical townhouses have been eliminated here by "clusters" of homes that are identified by distinctive bay windows, columned porches, and gabled roofs with cupolas.

Though Washington's Landing resembles such neo-traditional projects as Duany and Plater-Zyberk's town of Seaside, Florida, it differs from them by being located inside a major city and being a true multi-use plan. Its commercial tenants were attracted to the island by its recreational facilities, and the homeowners—mainly ex-suburbanites or newcomers to Pittsburgh—extol their five-minute walks to work, or boating and rowing. The island's seven-acre public park provides bike paths and jogging trails, which, in turn, link to the North Shore and the Three Rivers Heritage Trail by a converted nineteenth-century railroad bridge.

St. Nicholas Church

4.29 ST. NICHOLAS CHURCH
1901, 1922, Frederick Sauer.
24 Maryland Ave.

This yellow brick church's Colonial Revival exterior with its twin towers (added by Sauer in 1922) gives no hint of the congregation's Croatian heritage, but inside lies an unforgettable portrayal of their former homeland in Maximilian Vanka's 1937 mural cycle. It depicts the Croatian experience in the New and Old Worlds in an eye-catching mix of Byzantine forms and social realist imagery in the manner of the then-dominant Mexican muralists Jose Orozco and Diego Rivera. Characteristic is the scene of a Pittsburgh millionaire, deathly-pale, dining at a table outfitted with a stock ticker.

4.30 EVERGREEN HAMLET
1851–1852, Joseph W. Kerr; Heastings and Preiser, landscape architects. Rock Ridge Rd., just north of intersection of Babcock Blvd. and Evergreen and People's Plank rds.

This is one of America's first "romantic" suburbs, a few years before Alexander Jackson Davis's better-known Llewelyn Park in West Orange, New Jersey. Six families compacted to build on this hilltop five miles north of downtown Pittsburgh, in what must have been a reflection of the glorification and advantages of rural life espoused by Henry David Thoreau. In the end, only five houses rose on the eighty-five-acre site, and four remain, built for William Hill, William Shinn, Robert Sellers, and Wade Hampton. The Hampton (102 Rock Ridge Rd.) and Sellers (161 Rock Ridge Rd.) homes are boxy in shape with their walls laid in shiplapped siding. Hill's House (164 Rock Ridge Rd.) is more recognizably Gothic Revival in its gabled front and vaguely Tyrolean porch design—an amalgam of rural cottage designs found in Andrew Jackson Downing's three books on architecture and landscaping published between 1841 and 1851. Inside, the T-shaped disposition of the main rooms is more dynamic without being in any literal way Gothic. Only the cottage of the colony's founder, William Shinn (168 Rock Ridge Rd.), fully complies with the ethos, style, and environmental concerns of Downing. It is cruciform-shaped, the walls laid in

Pittsburghers — even those who live in its suburbs — still think of their city as the cohesive unit it was before railroad lines and expressways fragmented it into the 130 municipalities that currently make up Allegheny County. The reality is substantially different, with Pittsburgh's sprawl now rated as one of the worst in the nation, since it keeps expanding in area but declining in population.

Suburbanization in Pittsburgh is little different from elsewhere across the nation. The settlers who sought refuge in Evergreen Hamlet (4.30) in 1851 were innovative in hitching their utopia to the new railroad line coming into town. The railroad speeded up the adoption of the commuter lifestyle in the hills west of downtown (today Sewickley Heights) where, between the Civil War and World War I, summer bungalows gave way to year-round houses. After World War I, the automobile made permanent commuter communities out of Fox Chapel and Oakmont, on opposite banks of the Allegheny.

It is instructive to follow the changing urban and architectural patterns in a flourishing interwar and postwar suburb such as Mt. Lebanon (8.4), where the early tracts were linked to the trolley lines and the later ones to the highways. Sometimes, suburbanization fails or is flawed. In Pittsburgh, the prime candidate for success is Swan Acres in Ross Township, part of Pittsburgh's so-called North Hills. This little colony of modernistic homes was designed by Quentin S. Beck and Harry C.

Clepper in 1936, and survives, incomplete, off Babcock Boulevard, northeast of the intersection of U.S. 19 and Three Degree Road.

The November 1937 issue of *Architectural Forum* heralded Swan Acres's first five homes as the beginning of America's first modern tract housing. Two of the original seven units, of stucco over concrete block, still sit relatively unchanged on the original thirty-five acres, but they are now joined by unrelated post-World War II homes. The beguiling colony provides a fascinating mix of such 1930s stylistic currents as rounded corners, corner windows, and glass block, as well as some clear sidelong glances at Le Corbusier's and Frank Lloyd Wright's work.

Evergreen Hamlet

board-and-batten sidings, and the bargeboards beautifully cut in intricate curves. Coming up to it on the deliberately winding road from below, one would be well prepared to meet a recluse such as Thoreau.

4.31 FREDERICK SAUER HOUSES
1904–1930s, Frederick Sauer.
615–627 Center Ave.

These houses are a private fantasy by the otherwise restrained designer of a dozen staid Gothic and Classical Revival Roman Catholic churches around Pittsburgh. Though trained as an architect in Stuttgart, Sauer's hometown was Heidelberg, which was the likely model for this rugged and rambling group with their curved and angular forms, picturesque rubble walls, turrets, and chimneys. (One of the units bears the name "Heidelberg".) The six rental properties in brick and random stone were built by Sauer with his own hands, and they share something of the idiosyncratic glory (though none of the height) of Simon Rodia's contemporary Watts Tower in Los Angeles. This being Pittsburgh, Sauer's collection of fantastic shapes was, and is, commercially viable.

4.32 SHADY SIDE ACADEMY
1922 and later, Edward P. Mellon, and others. (Senior School), 423 Fox Chapel Rd.; (Middle School), 500 Squaw Run Rd. East.

The Academy was founded in 1883 as one of two distinguished offshoots (the other was Chatham College) of Shadyside Presbyterian Church (6.38). The Academy's Junior School is still in the Point Breeze neighborhood in Pittsburgh proper, but the Middle and Senior schools moved to this 125-acre campus in 1922. This move corresponded to a wider relocation of many of Pittsburgh's East End residents and their institutions to the Fox Chapel community in the 1920s, just as much of the North Side, in the preceding decades, had migrated farther northwest to Sewickley. The first institution to come to Fox Chapel, in 1915, was the Pittsburgh Field Club, followed seven years later by Shady Side Academy, Fox Chapel Golf Club, and the Pittsburgh Hunt Club in the mid-1920s. Edward Mellon laid out the core of the campus as a quadrangle of six Georgian Revival brick structures. Decades later, additional buildings were added that are mostly

Frederick Sauer Houses

Revival mansion on a sixty-acre estate that was designed around 1930 by Maximilian Nirdlinger, a pupil of Frank Furness.

The other institutional homes in Fox Chapel are distinguished products of the 1920s academic revivals, too. The best of these are by Brandon Smith, who designed the Colonial Revival Fox Chapel Episcopal Church (c. 1928) at 630 Squaw Run Road East, which was originally a house. In 1931, he laid out the Fox Chapel Golf Club clubhouse in the same style, near the intersection of Fox Chapel and Squaw Run roads. A half-dozen of his homes dot the wooded streets nearby.

4.33 LA TOURELLE (EDGAR AND LILIANE KAUFMANN HOUSE)
1924–1925, Benno Janssen.
8 La Tourelle Ln.

sympathetic in style, scale, and materials. About half a mile north is the Middle School, the former James Edward Lewis house, a Tudor

This exquisite eighteen-room fantasy seems more a monastery or clubhouse than a private residence, and not without reason. At least one of Janssen's sketches refers to La Tourelle as a country house, which it may as well be, given

La Tourelle (Edgar and Liliane Kaufmann House)

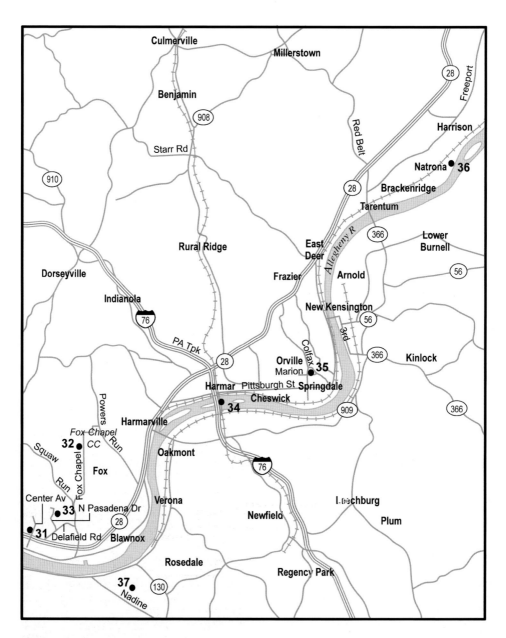

From Fox Chapel to Natrona. Approximate driving time: less than three hours.

its total isolation in spirit, if not in mileage, from Pittsburgh. The client was Edgar Kaufmann, an outsider to the Pittsburgh elite for whom Janssen was designing mansions and clubhouses in the same years. Janssen's Longue Vue Club (4.37) stands a few miles away on the opposite bank of the Allegheny, and La Tourelle can best be understood as a private Longue Vue. The roofs have the same high pitch and narrow gabled dormers as Longue Vue, and they are covered in the same Vermont slate. And though the walls here are brick, not sandstone, Janssen gives the massing the same artistic visual fragmentation, juxtaposing the turreted entrance—the estate's namesake—with the main house, the servants' wing, and the equally picturesque garage. Inside, the appointments were no less careful: the master ironworker Samuel Yellin forged a wealth of wrought-iron decoration for the house right in the main fireplace. La Tourelle was greatly admired through the 1930s as a consummate achievement in the Academic Revival style favored by the nation's rich, but the client's attention was by then wandering to Modernism. It was in La Tourelle's rich fake-Medieval living room, in 1934, that Kaufmann discussed with Frank Lloyd Wright the building of a radically different country house in nearby Fayette County: Fallingwater (9.2).

4.34 BESSEMER AND LAKE ERIE BRIDGE
1916–1918, H. T. Porter and C. G. E. Larsson, engineers. Freeport Rd., near I-76 and the Allegheny River.

This railroad bridge, designed by the Chief Engineer of the Bessemer and Lake Erie Railroad and the Assistant Chief Engineer of the American Bridge Company, was touted in the engineering press as "strikingly original" and represented a return to the use of the cantilever. Its span is 500 feet, and it rises 160 feet above the river. Clearly intended as a showpiece for U.S. Steel's wares and fabricated by a

U.S. Steel subsidiary, the bridge utilized a new silicon steel type for its I-bars and larger-than-usual rivets. The entire project symbolizes Andrew Carnegie's theories about vertical integration, since the bridge facilitated the delivery of Great Lakes ore to Carnegie's mills, using Carnegie's railroad. By the time the bridge was constructed, Carnegie had sold both his mills and his railroad to U.S. Steel, but this bridge, as an important aspect of the landscape of steel, allowed Carnegie's theories to live on and be tangibly present in this double track, continuous truss design.

4.35 RACHEL CARSON HOUSE
1840. 613 Marion Ave.

This modest farmhouse was Carson family property from the time that the family settled on what was then a forty-three-acre farm, a century before Rachel Carson grew up here.

Rachel Carson House

Though the dwelling is primarily of interest because of its association with the ecological scientist and author of *The Sea Around Us* (1952), *Silent Spring* (1962), and the children's book *The Sense of Wonder* (1965), the house has additional value as a survivor of a type of small wooden farmhouse no longer well represented in Pittsburgh's environs. It can be visited by appointment with the Rachel Carson Homestead Association, a foundation that educates the public about Rachel Carson's works.

4.36 PENNSYLVANIA SALT MANUFACTURING COMPANY WORKERS' HOUSING
1850–1857. Bounded by Blue Ridge, Pond, and Penn sts.

About 150 houses survive in this early company town, set between the Pennsylvania Canal (now shared by Blue Ridge Street and the Amtrak railroad bed) and the Allegheny River. The salt works was incorporated in 1850 by five Quaker entrepreneurs from Philadelphia, and the town was built in the following years. The plant made caustic soda for lye soap from the salt wells bordering the village of East Tarentum. The forty-acre town (renamed Natrona from the Greek natron, or soda) grew up around a score of industrial buildings that have since disappeared, but the company store still stands at the corner of Blue Ridge and Federal streets among the many brick row houses and detached frame cottages.

The row houses evoke the sober streets of early nineteenth-century Philadelphia, but the wooden houses on Federal Street strike an entirely different note. These two-story board-and-batten cottages (though aluminum siding long ago covered the wood) resemble "A small Cottage for a Working-man" from Andrew Jackson Downing's *The Architecture of Country Houses* of 1850. The plan consists of an all-purpose room and a bedroom on the ground floor and one or two tiny bedrooms above. Unfortunately, Pennsylvania Salt did exactly what would have horrified Downing: eliminating the eaves brackets and

Pennsylvania Salt Manufacturing Company workers' housing

the window and door ornaments that would make these homes more cheerful.

Today, only a few American company towns survive from the half-century between the New England textile mills of the 1820s and Chicago's late nineteenth-century Pullman, which makes Natrona an environmental document of the highest national importance.

4.37 LONGUE VUE CLUB
1921–1923, Janssen & Cocken; Albert D. Taylor, landscape architect. 400 Longue Vue Dr.

This complex perfectly evokes the architecture and expansive spirit of the 1920s. On an inspiring site high above a wide bend in the Allegheny River, Janssen created a miniature English-style Cotswold village of exquisite plan, profile, and materials for this golfing clubhouse. The clubhouse rests between two hills, and its second-story is carried via bridges, which allows automobiles to pass under the structure as it frames glimpses of the Allegheny River valley beyond. Though this picturesque device is certainly not restricted to Pittsburgh's buildings, it had specific Pittsburgh precedents in Richardson's Courthouse and Jail (1.15) (two bridges that were filled in around 1924) and in Hornbostel's Carnegie

Longue Vue Club

Mellon campus (2.16). The bridges at Longue Vue allowed Janssen to skew the axes of his building and to compartmentalize its functions. They also work well with the timelessness expressed by the club's hand-hewn sandstone walls and high-pitched slate roofs. The golf course was designed by Scottish golf-course architect Robert White.

CHAPTER 5:
MCKEES ROCKS AND
THE OHIO VALLEY

The Monongahela River led Pittsburghers upriver to West Virginia, and the Allegheny led them to upstate New York, but the Ohio River was their path to the larger world, via the Mississippi River to New Orleans and the Gulf of Mexico. The gateway to this prospect was McKees Rocks, the impressive hill on which Native Americans for centuries lived and buried their dead.

There are no internationally significant buildings along the Ohio's banks in Pittsburgh today, but notably intriguing environments abound. The first of these is McKees Rocks itself, the best preserved of Pittsburgh's industrial satellites. The segregation of the immigrant workforce—not only by religion, but also by ethnic origin—eventually produced an overabundance of churches here. The Roman Catholic St. Francis de Sales (810 Chartiers Avenue), designed by Marius Rousseau in 1899 as an exquisite miniature of S. Maria del Fiore in Florence, Italy, is now a banqueting hall. Nearby churches include a Russian Orthodox and a Byzantine Catholic, but the synagogue has been demolished.

Factories were the old glory of the Ohio Valley's architecture in Pittsburgh. The greatest of the region's factory complexes in extent was the miles-long Jones and Laughlin steel mill at Aliquippa, which was flattened in the 1980s as precipitously as it had gone up in 1907. Two of Pittsburgh's most striking factories survive—unloved—in McKees Rocks. One, the Pittsburgh and Lake Erie locomotive repair shop (5.3), is traditionalist and massive; the other, the old Taylor-Wilson plant (5.2), is radical and gossamer light. Both are underused and serve as little more than storage facilities.

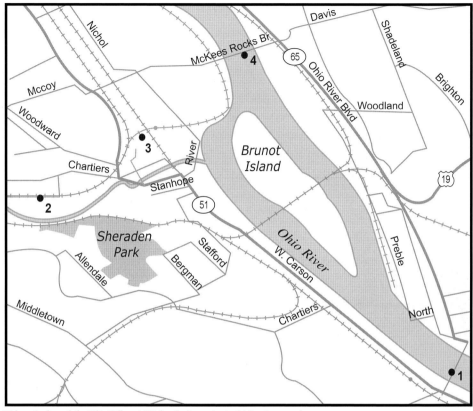

Mckees Rocks and the Ohio Valley at Pittsburgh. Approximate driving time: one hour.

5.1 WEST END BRIDGE

1930–1932, Vernon Covell and George S. Richardson, engineers. US 19 and the Ohio River.

This and the McKees Rocks Bridge (5.4) went up as part of Allegheny County's energetic interwar program of improvements to its infrastructure, especially bridges and roads. The West End Bridge capitalizes on the 755-foot clear span of its steel parabolic arch to make an unforgettable impression as it bounds over the Ohio and simultaneously frames a view of Pittsburgh's Point.

5.2 PENNSYLVANIA DRILLING COMPANY (TAYLOR-WILSON MANUFACTURING COMPANY)

1905, Robert A. Cummings, engineer. 500 Thompson Ave.

One of a handful of buildings remaining in a barren industrial strip, the former Taylor-Wilson factory is an overlooked marvel of the pioneer generation of "daylight factories" that revolutionized industrial design at the turn of the twentieth century. By 1884, engineer Ernest L. Ransome had perfected a system of reinforcing concrete with iron rods to increase its strength. This reduced the need for struc-

West End Bridge

tural support and allowed the number and size of windows in exterior walls to be increased significantly. Industrial buildings could now consist of more window than wall, and, flooded with natural light, they provided a more productive and humane environment for workers. Significantly, Ransome built his first "daylight factory" in 1902 in nearby Greensburg (Westmoreland County), and Cummings doubtless visited it. For Taylor-Wilson, Cummings followed Ransome's patented mode of construction, which allowed exterior columns to intersect with projecting floor slabs, hence countering structural forces through a framework rather than through solid masses of wall.

Cummings designed Taylor-Wilson to be cheap and fireproof and also to show artistic flair. Six bays wide, sixteen bays long, and three stories high, it encloses an enormous space (160 by 120 feet) with a gently arched roof, one-story projecting aisles, and a facade

Pennsylvania Drilling Company (Taylor-Wilson Manufacturing Company)

Pennsylvania Drilling Company (Taylor-Wilson Manufacturing Company)

dominated by a round-arched window twenty feet in height, though now boarded over. Wooden window frames were painted red to provide contrast with the intervening bands of gray concrete. Used originally for the production of custom-built machinery for heavy industry, the factory currently is used only as a storage facility.

5.3 PITTSBURGH & LAKE ERIE RAILROAD STEAM LOCOMOTIVE REPAIR SHOP
1885, with later additions. Pittsburgh & Lake Erie Railroad Yards (0.3 miles north of the intersection of Locust St. and Linden Ave.)

The Pittsburgh & Lake Erie Railroad put its locomotive maintenance and associated shops astride its tracks in McKees Rocks around 1885. Of the several buildings on this site that survive, the Erection Shop is the largest and most im-

pressive. It was constructed in 1903 after a fire involving steam-powered motors. This magnificent brick basilica is twenty-four bays in length and four bays in width. The external structure, with its round-arched windows and decorative cornice, is entirely of brick, whereas the internal trusses and columns are iron and steel. Four locomotives could sit abreast during repairs; electric motors that powered overhead cranes picked up whole locomotives to place them for rebuilding. With the conversion of the line to diesel power in the 1950s, the Erection Shop became redundant. Only onetenth of the building is used now (for an electrical reheating furnace), but this is one of the finest remaining buildings of Pittsburgh's industrial heritage, and every effort should be made to ensure its preservation. Its former companions, two huge roundhouses and a powerhouse, have been demolished.

Pittsburgh and Lake Erie Railroad steam locomotive repair shop

5.4 MCKEES ROCKS BRIDGE

1931, George S. Richardson, engineer.
Ohio River Blvd., Termon Ave., and
the Ohio River.

Standing 2.5 miles from the West End Bridge (5.1), the McKees Rocks Bridge was another product of Allegheny County's modernization program. The bridge unites five different units to achieve its length of nearly a mile over the "bottoms" of McKees Rocks and the Ohio River. The engineering solution here uses a central through-arch of steel over the river itself, with vertical stays stiffening the deck and four severe stone pylons to give appropriate structural and visual support.

5.5 WILPEN HALL

(WILLIAM PENN SNYDER HOUSE)
1898, George Orth. Bounded by Blackburn
and Water Works rds.

A steelmaker with excellent architectural taste, Snyder hired Orth to build this brownstone and shingle Queen-Anne style home first, then a Beaux-Arts townhouse that still stands at the corner of Ridge and Galveston avenues

on the North Side. By the 1920s, automobile roads were improved, and the North Side had decayed so much, that the family turned this summer retreat into their permanent home. This was the pattern as well for their neighbors, the Benjamin Franklin Jones family (4.13), whose adjacent "Fairacres" estate was even more lavish. Today, all that survives of "Fairacres" are a half-dozen servants' houses

Wilpen Hall (William Penn Snyder House)

visible from Blackburn Road and a summary notion of the once-lavish gardens.

5.6 WAY FAMILY HOUSES
c. 1810 and 1838, with later additions. Beaver Rd. at Quaker Rd. and 108 Beaver Rd.

One of two families that have prospered in Sewickley and Edgeworth for two centuries, the Ways established an inn and tavern (c. 1810) that still stand at the intersection of Beaver and Quaker roads, just inland from the Ohio River shore. John Way's home at the same intersection is a three-bay-wide brick Federal style house with a central hall. The house, rebuilt after it burned in 1841, received several additions during the nineteenth century. A block south, Abishai Way, an agent for the Harmonists, built his raised Greek Revival home in 1838 at 108 Beaver Road, giving it a pedimented portico supported on slender columns.

5.7 NEWINGTON (SHIELDS-BROOKS HOUSE)
1816; 1823; 1868 chapel, attributed to Joseph W. Kerr; c. 1870 gardens, attributed to Samuel Parsons; 1893 mausoleum, John U. Barr. Beaver Rd. at Shields Ln.

Certainly an oddity in what was an industrial region and rare in the northern parts of the United States, this estate includes a chapel and a mausoleum. The house has served a single family without breaks in ownership since the 1770s. David Shields, an agent for the nearby Harmonists, built the smaller two-story brick block in 1816 on land granted decades before to his father-in-law, the surveyor Daniel Leet. The main house, two-and-one-half stories in height, followed seven years later in a more refined Greek Revival style. The gardens are the glory of the eleven-acre estate, and they include an early-twentieth-century labyrinth, attributed to Bryant Fleming.

Newington (Shields-Brooks House)

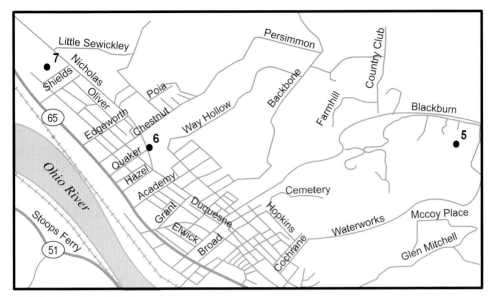

Sewickley. Approximate driving time: one hour.

5.8 MIDFIELD TERMINAL COMPLEX, PITTSBURGH INTERNATIONAL AIRPORT
1992, Tasso Katselas Associates.
Bordering PA 60.

This is one of the largest airport complexes in the nation. Aviation came to this site, then the Bell Farm, just weeks after the attack on Pearl Harbor because of the need to protect Pittsburgh's vast industrial installations. A residual military airbase still borders the airport. The terminal replaces a structure of 1952, but the airport uses the same 12,000-acre site and runways. Katselas created an ingenious and efficient solution to the problem of connecting passengers and their airplanes by creating two terminals—a landside terminal and an airside terminal—linked by an underground people-mover. Multiple ramps flanking both sides of the landside terminal speed traffic toward and away from the building, while automated sidewalks inside a vaulted shed connect passengers with their cars in the outlying parking lots.

The X-shape of the airside terminal and its total isolation from any other structure allows unimpeded taxiing to the gates, a huge economy of time and fuel. Because Pittsburgh is a major air hub for connecting flights, most visitors use only the airside terminal. Here, too, careful programming produced the first Air Mall in the nation, consisting of some 100 retail operations, concessions, and restaurants that line the corridors.

Katselas attempted to offset travel fatigue by incorporating symbolic color, illuminating the barrel vaults over the corridors with clerestories and skylights, and by placing artwork throughout both terminals, including an immense Alexander Calder mobile inherited from the 1952 terminal.

Every city in the world is a city of neighborhoods, and Pittsburgh is no different. But neighborhoods seem more distinct here, and their hold on the residents is tenacious. The city's innate conservatism accounts, in part, for the endurance of, and residential loyalty to, Pittsburgh's neighborhoods, and its topography gives the city's eighty-eight neighborhoods the hills, gullies, rivers, bridges, train tracks, and expressway traffic that create borders of striking prominence. Add to this mix Pittsburgh's traditional ethnic solidarity and the bonding that came from neighbors laboring side by side at death-defying jobs in the mills, and the result is the classic physiognomy of a Pittsburgh neighborhood.

The dozen neighborhoods presented here have visual and social cohesion and a commonality of age, architectural styles, scale, color, and building materials. Mills that dominated many of these quarters are now gone, but certain places, such as Holy Rosary Church (6.18) and the Liberty Avenue stores (6.8), continue to distill and broadcast the essence of a neighborhood. The architectural glory of Pittsburgh may ultimately rest not in its buildings, but in its neighborhoods.

THE STRIP, POLISH HILL, LAWRENCEVILLE, AND BLOOMFIELD

The Strip, Polish Hill, and Lawrenceville are three contiguous neighborhoods that are linked by topography and a shared involvement in early industry. The Strip got its name from its shape: a flat, long, narrow strip of 300 acres hemmed in by the south bank of the Allegheny River and the steep rise of the Hill. Nearby transportation routes made it an area of intense industrial activity early in Pittsburgh's history, and the plentiful

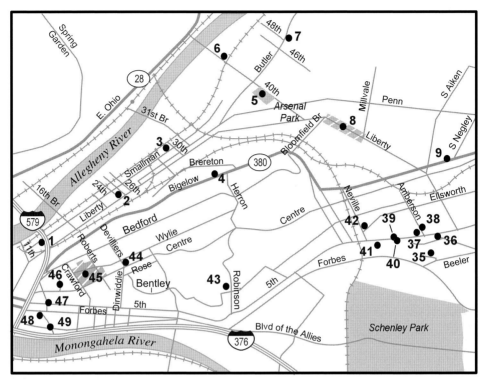

Characteristic Pittsburgh neighborhoods east of downtown and Shadyside. Approximate driving and walking time: an extended half-day.

jobs attracted immigrant workers who built row houses and churches amid the commercial buildings. Early in the twentieth century, industry outgrew the Strip's natural confines, and the district fell into a decline that lasted into the 1970s. The decline has since been halted, and now wholesalers, food markets, nightclubs, and eclectic restaurants give the Strip its vibrant early-hours and weekend street life.

If the Strip and Lawrenceville offered jobs, the isolation of Polish Hill offered domestic sanctuary to the thousands of Poles who settled here around 1885. The wood-frame homes clinging to this hillside are now attracting newcomers to settle here, though the majority of the neighborhood continues to be of Polish origin. Although Lawrenceville, upstream on the Allegheny, may be another extension of the Strip, it nonetheless has a separate character by virtue of its density along two spine roads, Butler Street and Penn Avenue, and its distinct central core in the old Allegheny Arsenal (6.5).

Like Lawrenceville, Bloomfield straddles two main thoroughfares, in its case Liberty and Penn avenues, which here rise high above the Allegheny, giving Bloomfield the aspect of a hilltown. Buildings along Liberty Avenue are superior in architectural quality, and the secret of Liberty Avenue's animation lies in its unusual width, as it passes through Bloomfield, and in its social cohesion, as the undisputed heart of the city's Italian-origin community. Italians began to arrive from the Abruzzi region in the 1880s; by World War I, they had settled in this neighborhood, which had been founded by German immigrants a half-century before.

6.1 SENATOR JOHN HEINZ PITTSBURGH REGIONAL HISTORY CENTER (CHAUTAUQUA LAKE ICE COMPANY)

1898; Frederick J. Osterling; 1993–1996, Bohlin Cywinski Jackson; 2003–2004, Astorino. 1212 Smallman St.

This former ice warehouse is a formidable, seven-story, red brick building, whose function dictated its enormous construction strength. The ground floor carries low masonry vaults between riveted steel beams, while upper-floor ceilings are of massive timber construction. Windows are narrow and recessed to protect the stored ice from sunlight. Ice blocks entered and left the building on railroad cars that ran directly into the building through the chamfered northeast corner. In 1993, the Historical Society of Western Pennsylvania chose the warehouse as a headquarters that could be equipped with galleries, archives, and meeting rooms. The remodeling presented the designers with numerous challenges. One of the most

Senator John Heinz Pittsburgh Regional History Center (Chautauqua Lake Ice Company)

significant was to provide ventilation, access, and light in a structure built to prevent those things. Inner cagework was removed to form a seven-story atrium, which is topped by a new roof structure and partial clerestory. To the west, an elevator tower, clad in copper and steel and terminating in a lattice-like steeple shape, was added to the exterior.

In 2004, the Heinz History Center was expanded by a five-story, red brick addition of a simple rectangular shape. It was designed to meet Leadership in Energy and Environmental Design certification requirements in keeping with Pittsburgh's leadership role in environmentally sound architecture. The Center's exhibits celebrate Pittsburgh's heritage of industrial contributions and ethnic diversity—exactly the lessons visible in the streets around it.

6.2 2425 LIBERTY AVENUE (WESTINGHOUSE AIR BRAKE COMPANY)

1870–1871. 2401–2425 Liberty Ave.

The wooden-trussed, brick-faced plant is a striking memorial to George Westinghouse, one of the nation's most important inventors. The legacy of Westinghouse—second in patent acquisition only to his rival Thomas Edison—has long been neglected in his adoptive city. Westinghouse came to Pittsburgh from upstate New York in the 1860s because it offered the industrial expertise, venture capital, and climate of aggressive entrepreneurship in which he could flourish.

Though Westinghouse branched out into switches and signals, electricity, turbines, appli-

2425 Liberty Avenue (Westinghouse Air Brake Company)

ances, natural gas, and even shock absorbers, the manufacture of railroad air-brakes was his first and central concern. It was for this enterprise that he supervised construction of this factory, an amalgam of three structures that eventually reached twenty-five bays in length and covered a full city block. In less than a decade, the plant proved too small for worldwide demand for his product. He then built a larger plant on the North Side in 1881, abandoning it nine years later to create a company town at Wilmerding (3.18). This Liberty Avenue building now accommodates office spaces.

6.3 RALPH MEYER COMPANY
(PARK BROTHERS AND COMPANY, LTD.,
BLACK DIAMOND STEEL WORKS)
1880s; 1890s. 2949 Smallman St.; remnants from Twenty-eighth to Thirty-second sts.

James Park, Jr., founded Black Diamond Steel Works in 1862. By the time it was incorporated in 1884 as Park Brothers and Company, it was the largest producer of fine tool steel in the world. Around 1899, the enterprise was amalgamated with Crucible Steel (the name coming from the process of melting quality steel in cru-

cibles), later a part of Cyclops Steel. Today, the various buildings house a roofing and sheet metal service.

At its height, Black Diamond occupied both sides of Smallman Street from Twenty-eighth to Thirty-second streets, but, even so, these mills represented small-scale Pittsburgh industry, not the gigantic scale it assumed at the hands of Carnegie, Frick, and Westinghouse. Ironically, it was the abandonment of the Strip by Carnegie and his move to far-off Braddock in 1873 that opened the area to the relatively small-scale operations such as Black Diamond.

2949 Smallman Street (Park Brothers and Company, Ltd., Black Diamond Steel Works)

Until the Civil War, this site was the Allegheny County and Western Pennsylvania Fairgrounds. Union troops occupied the fairgrounds, and only after their departure did Park begin constructing his factories there. Thirty years later, Park was still adding structures. The sheds standing on the northeast and southeast corners of Thirty-first and Smallman streets are relatively late in date, but the type predated the Civil War. The material is deep red brick, with five-foot-high clerestory windows and pilaster strips along the side walls to show the support points for the wooden trusses inside. The trusses, as many as a dozen per shed, are reinforced with vertical iron rods to create a spacious and open work area, free of posts. One block closer to the Allegheny River, on Railroad Street between Thirty-first and Thirty-second, stands the old Black Diamond Plate Mill.

Quite different and almost palatial in character is the Italianate headquarters of David and William Park (c. 1870) at 2949 Smallman. Neighborhood oldsters will misinform you that this was the mansion in which the Park brothers lived. Such proximity to the workplace might have been the case in the 1840s, but by the 1880s it was contrary to Pittsburgh convention; more likely, the fine building served as their office and counting house.

6.4 IMMACULATE HEART OF MARY ROMAN CATHOLIC CHURCH
1904–1905, William P. Ginther.
3058 Brereton St.

This church enjoys the best scenographic placement of any in the city, but not without cost. Its location high on Polish Hill affords it prominence both from Bigelow Boulevard above and from a wide sweep of the Allegheny below; but had the church burrowed headlong into the hillside, as it appears to, its apse would have been shrouded in darkness. Instead, Ginther set the church parallel to the hillside and designed a fake facade for one of the building's long sides. The moment worshippers cross the threshold, they must make a ninety-degree turn to enter the nave.

The original church was a small wooden frame structure at the base of Polish Hill near the railroad tracks. In 1899, Polish immigrant mill workers gathered $10,300 to purchase

Immaculate Heart of Mary Roman Catholic Church

property at the crest of Brereton and Dobson streets, just below the newly announced site of Bigelow Boulevard. Having resolved the problem of straddling the church across the brow of Polish Hill, architect Ginther, of Akron, Ohio, appropriated various European precedents for his design. Borromini's S. Agnese on Piazza Navona in Rome appears to have contributed the high domed towers and the central dome (reaching almost 100 feet in height on the interior), while the high attic with its prominent square windows with their flared moldings—so important for the dramatic effect on motorists on Bigelow Boulevard—is closely patterned after Michelangelo's St. Peter's in Rome.

6.5 ALLEGHENY ARSENAL
1814–1860s, Benjamin H. Latrobe and others. Penn Ave. at Fortieth St.

Although the Arsenal functioned until 1926, little survives of the buildings that once stood in the thirty-seven acres that stretch above and below Butler Street. Arsenal Park preserves the main vestige: an L-shaped powder magazine with cyclopean vault, half buried in the sloping ground. The more important buildings were those that stood for almost a century and a half and were systematically destroyed by their then-owner, a food distributor.

The layout of U.S. Allegheny Arsenal was based on designs by the English immigrant Latrobe, the first professionally trained architect and engineer to practice in the United States. He came to Pittsburgh in 1812 to design and build steamships. When Congress voted funds (eventually $300,000) for a Pittsburgh arsenal, Latrobe drew up the required plot plans and details in a set of drawings that are today preserved in the Library of Congress. It appears, however, that neither Latrobe nor his protégé, Thomas Pope, stayed long enough in Pittsburgh to supervise construction of the buildings. But Latrobe's severe neoclassical imprint was unmistakable both at the Arsenal and in the neighboring Greek Revival houses built for the munitions workforce. One of the best houses on the Arsenal grounds is on Thirty-ninth Street, between Foster Street and the river: a three-story brick home with fanlight attic windows at both gable ends. The brick house at 257 Fortieth Street, opposite the powder mag-

Allegheny Arsenal

azine, probably dates from the mid-nineteenth century, but keeps the severe forms and simplicity of proportions set by Latrobe. Other notable surviving outbuildings or worker houses stand on Thirty-eighth, Carnegie and Home streets, McCandless Avenue, and Modoc Alley.

The Allegheny Arsenal was among the first and most extensive of the nation's arsenals, a result of the federal government's concern for a permanent system of defense and supply that preceded the War of 1812 and was then much invigorated by that conflict. Pittsburgh was deemed a strategic locale for manufacture and storage of ordinance, because of its established iron industry and its superior water access to military posts from Canada to the Gulf of Mexico.

The Arsenal used one of the first steam engines in western Pennsylvania to manufacture ammunition, infantry and horse equipment, caissons, and gun carriages through the Civil War. Latrobe's layout drew on the quadrangle format of fort architecture, but it also reflects his proposal of 1800 for a national military academy that he sent to Vice President Thomas Jefferson. Latrobe's quadrangle here, roughly 600 feet in length on each side, was located between Butler Street and the river with the entrance facing the street. This range included a three-story manufacturing building of stone, flanked by long carriage sheds, and officers' and commandant's quarters at the corners. The latter were massive, plain buildings of carefully dressed stone blocks with heavy architraves and window surrounds, fronted by Doric porches.

Brick barracks for non-commissioned officers along the east and west ranges featured first-floor arcades whose rhythms were echoed by the windows above. The north range included carriage, machine and paint shops, and a smithy. A canalized river landing and at least one temple-shaped machine shop stood outside the quadrangle, near the river. The latter was truncated for construction of the Fortieth Street Bridge in the 1920s; it was demolished in 1990. The powder magazine was located well away

from the main site, in what since 1907 has been Arsenal Park. After 1868, the installation served as storage, and by 1926 the government had sold the last remnants. Portions of the Arsenal's perimeter wall and several of the stone piers from which iron gates once hung are visible along Thirty-ninth Street, and nearby are some post-Civil War brick utility buildings.

6.6 NATIONAL ROBOTICS ENGINEERING CONSORTIUM (EPPING-CARPENTER COMPANY)
1898, Samuel Diescher; 1994–1996, adaptive reuse, Burt Hill Kosar Rittelmann. 10 Fortieth St.

Situated on five acres beside the Allegheny River, the Consortium is a joint venture undertaken by NASA, Carnegie Mellon University's Field Robotics Center, and private corporations to develop robotic technology applicable to industries ranging from mining to space exploration. The Consortium occupies 100,000 square feet in a rehabilitated steel-framed brick basilica that civil engineer Diescher built in 1898 for the Epping-Carpenter Company. In 1925, the Pittsburgh Piping and Equipment Company added a four-bay pipe shop and shipping area facing the river.

When Pittsburgh's Urban Redevelopment Authority purchased the facility in 1993, it was structurally sound, but its interior was unsuitable for high-tech endeavors. The interior was gutted, mechanical systems were overhauled, and half of the addition of 1925 was demolished

National Robotics Engineering Consortium (Epping-Carpenter Company)

for parking and outdoor testing grounds. Diescher's original brick walls were fitted with thick, semi-opaque windows for maximum heat retention, and the original wooden roof was cleaned and re-insulated, giving the interior a striking rusticity for so futuristic an environment. The principal facade, facing the bridge on the west, was replaced with a glass curtain wall. Diescher's east facade on Forty-third Street now has large plate-glass windows illusorily fitted with small panes and set tightly in the wall plane.

6.7 ALLEGHENY CEMETERY

1844, John Chislett, landscape architect; 1848, Butler Street Gatehouse, John Chislett, and 1868–1870, Barr and Moser; 1887, Penn Avenue Gatehouse, Macomb and Dull; 1903, William Falconer. 4734 Butler St. and 4715 Penn Ave.

Allegheny Cemetery is one of the earliest garden cemeteries in the United States. Chislett laid out the grounds, designed the first structures, and then remained for some years as superintendent. Inspired by Mount Auburn

Cemetery (1831) in Cambridge, Massachusetts, Chislett, along with Dr. James Speer and merchant Charles Avery, had promoted the idea of a "romantic" cemetery as early as 1834. The goal was to alleviate overcrowding in Pittsburgh's graveyards and to create a park for a city that had none. The city now surrounds the 300-acre cemetery, but the sense of an oasis is in no way diminished.

Chislett carved the original 100 acres from John Shoenberger's country estate. Superintendent William Falconer (creator of Schenley Park) landscaped the expanded acreage around 1903, augmenting the picturesque qualities of the natural topography with artificial lakes and new planting. The cemetery's architecture is just as rich. The Butler Street gatehouse is in Tudor Revival, the towered chapel behind it is Gothic Revival, and the huge gatehouse on Penn Avenue is Richardsonian Romanesque. The first burial took place in 1845. Among the more memorable monuments are the Gothic Revival, chapel-like mausoleum with stained glass windows for James Moorhead, designed by Louis Morgenroth in 1862, and a granite tree

Allegheny Cemetery

commemorating members of the Wilkins family. The songwriter-composer Stephen Collins Foster, who grew up in Lawrenceville, and actress Lillian Russell Moore are among those who rest here.

6.8 COMMERCIAL BUILDINGS IN BLOOMFIELD
Late nineteenth century. 4400–4800 blocks Liberty Ave.

This is one of the best nineteenth-century streets in the city in its combination of architectural quality, social amenities, and liveliness. Although Bloomfield's Liberty Avenue storefronts were constructed for German-origin merchants, as is evident from the name-plaques on their gables, it was the later Italian community that gave the street its incomparable urban spirit. One secret of its animation lies in its unusual width. These Gothic and Romanesque Revival storefronts remain in a generally good state of repair, and the restaurants, art galleries, bakeries, insurance offices, professional offices, and shops that use these old buildings are respectful but creative in their adaptations. The best of them is at 4722 Liberty, where a care-

Commercial buildings in Bloomfield

fully recreated exterior leads to a dramatically galleried interior that acts as a microcosm of the bustling streets outside.

EAST LIBERTY AND HIGHLAND PARK

Two Pittsburgh neighborhoods that could be said to live in a symbiotic relationship are East Liberty and Highland Park. Highland Park was being farmed before the American Revolution, but was given its street patterns only after the Civil War. East Liberty was already a flourishing transportation and commercial nexus early in the nineteenth century. By mid-century, it was a piketown on the turnpike to Philadelphia and the prime crossroads for Pittsburgh's East End—a status augmented by the introduction of horse-cars in 1859. By the early twentieth century, East Liberty was Pennsylvania's third most important commercial core, after downtown Philadelphia and downtown Pittsburgh. In the relationship of the two neighborhoods, East Liberty sold goods and Highland Park bought them, and the prosperity of the one was always dependent on the other.

Then, in the 1960s, East Liberty was hit hard by urban renewal of the most rigid ideology. Its rabbit warren of streets and loading docks was bulldozed into a kind of suburban mall surrounded by a ring of high-rise subsidized housing projects that left it isolated. The decline of East Liberty badly afflicted Highland Park. Demolition of the worst of the decayed buildings left gaping holes, which turned out to be big enough for a half-dozen big-box retail chains to move in, giving East Liberty a new hold on life as a kind of inner-city suburb.

6.9 BAUM BOULEVARD DODGE
(CHRYSLER SALES AND SERVICE BUILDING)
1933–1934, Albert Kahn. 5625 Baum Blvd.

Since its creation in the mid-nineteenth century, the two-mile length of Baum Boulevard has served as a modest but useful connector road between the Oakland and East Liberty neighborhoods. Around 1910, it became the regional center for the emerging automobile industry; a Ford assembly building still stands at the corner of Morewood Avenue. Dozens more gas stations and car dealerships emerged on Baum in the next decades. Kahn's Chrysler showroom—one of many he designed in the nation—is a three-story modernist composition of finely cut stone and concrete with a high-ceilinged showroom lit by plate glass windows. The dealership's distinguishing characteristic is its corner cylindrical tower, a recurring motif in Kahn's work for Chrysler. The building is marred only superficially by some gaudy signage. Its blueprints are in the Architectural Archives at Carnegie Mellon University.

Baum Boulevard Dodge (Chrysler Sales and Service Building)

Motor Square Garden/AAA East Central (Liberty Market)

6.10 MOTOR SQUARE GARDEN/
AAA EAST CENTRAL (LIBERTY MARKET)
1898, Peabody and Stearns. 5900 Baum Blvd.

This is one of just two survivors of the dozen markets that once served Pittsburgh; the other is in the South Side (3.5). Its circular dome of metal, timber, and glass rises above a block of light and dark yellow bricks, colored terra cotta, and geometric ornament, while enormous round-arched windows in gabled wall dormers on all four elevations illuminate the interior. It ceased functioning as a market in 1916 and since then has been used for various purposes, including an exhibition space.

6.11 EAST LIBERTY PRESBYTERIAN CHURCH
1931–1935, Cram and Ferguson.
116 S. Highland Ave.

This immense church is visually and socially impressive. The congregation first assembled in a rural schoolhouse on this block in 1819, then built a succession of five different structures on the site. The wealthy congregation, the Negley and Mellon families being among its members, could afford a generous budget, so the church is luxuriously furnished with rib vaults, stained

East Liberty Presbyterian Church

glass, a marble bas-relief of the Last Supper, a towering reredos of ivory-colored stone, and an elaborately carved pulpit.

Although Ralph Adams Cram believed that no other church in the nation achieved such completeness of utility and art, the design lacks the élan of his earlier (though scarcely much bigger) St. John the Divine in New York City. East Liberty works best as part of the urban fabric: its Spanish Gothic Revival crossing tower, a 300-foot massive tower of steel and concrete, dominates the East End as a pendant to the Mellon-backed Cathedral of Learning in Oakland (2.10).

6.12 ALPHA TERRACE
1880s–1890s; attributed to James T. Steen.
700 block of N. Beatty St.

These two dozen row houses create a kind of private green between Stanton and Hayes avenues. The houses on the east side are in the Queen Anne style of stone and wood, and those on the west side are Romanesque Revival of stone. On both sides, the uniform height is punctuated and enlivened by spires, miniature towers, and large gables. A building permit was granted to the house-builders Murphy and Hamilton for the west side of the terrace in June 1894, by which time the east side had stood for half a decade. Steen is traditionally regarded as having designed both sides. Uniform terraces

like this were once fairly common in the East End, and this survivor is still effective as a visual and social anchor to the neighborhood.

6.13 BAYWOOD
(ALEXANDER AND CORDELIA KING HOUSE)
1880s. 1251 N. Negley Ave.

Baywood sits on land that the Virginian William Heth sold to Jacob Negley (ancestor to the Mellon family) in 1799. In 1856, it became the estate of Alexander King (grandfather to Richard King Mellon), who introduced soda ash to the glass manufacturing industry. When the house that Negley built burned in 1879, King replaced it with this two-and-one-half-story brick structure in a somewhat stiff Second Empire style, with a mansard roof, single- and double-arched dormer windows, and tall square tower. A greenhouse verandah across the front allowed Cordelia King to raise exotic plants and butterflies. Unfortunately, the two subsequent generations of the family who occupied the house allowed its lush planted terraces to go to ruin. Deeded in 1954 to the city of Pittsburgh as a cultural center, the mansion was sold in 1994 and was restored as a single-family dwelling.

6.14 VILSACK ROW
1912, Frederick G. Scheibler, Jr.
1659–1693 Jancey St.

Scheibler was Pittsburgh's local prophet of Modernism: a designer unschooled in architecture who apprenticed to the local Barr and Moser firm and worked in traditional styles until he established his own firm in 1901. None of Scheibler's works are as uncompromising in their horizontality, absence of decoration, and singleness of focus as this terrace of eighteen attached apartments. Unfortunately, these units were subject to unsympathetic additions over the years. The tacked-on porches especially becloud what was once a clear dialogue of projecting solids of the stair towers and the receding

Vilsack Row

voids of window walls. Popular legend in Pittsburgh has Frank Lloyd Wright being inspired by Scheibler, which is untrue but significant as an attempt to understand how Scheibler, who never left Pittsburgh, had traveled so far and so fast stylistically.

6.15 HIGHLAND PARK AND THE ZOO
1889 and later, Berthold Froesch, landscape architect. Bounded by Antietam, Bunker Hill, and Butler sts. and Washington Blvd.

Highland Park is both a park and a city neighborhood of the same name that stretches a mile from East Liberty to the Allegheny River. Park and neighborhood both illustrate the profound influence Edward Bigelow had on the urban development of Pittsburgh, a legacy that also survives in his three boulevards and in Schenley Park. Working here with the city's trolley czar, Christopher Lyman Magee, Bigelow surreptitiously bought 360 acres of hilly woodlands bordering the river and conveyed them to the city as a park in 1893. Magee developed approximately one third of the park into the Pittsburgh Zoo in 1898, then profited for years for his generosity by running trolley lines to the zoo through the newborn neighborhood.

The landscape architect was probably the German-born Berthold Froesch. Bigelow was always careful to adorn his development projects with both fine plantings and good sculpture. Here, as at Schenley Park, his collaborator was Giuseppe Moretti, whose heroically scaled statuary in bronze and granite greets visitors at the Highland and Stanton avenue entrances to the park. These were restored in 2000 for the park's centenary.

Highland Park and the Pittsburgh Zoo

In 2000, the PPG Aquarium (Indovina Associates Architects) opened in its splendid new 45,000-square-foot facility, a glass-faced rectangle with a curvy roofline that enlarged the original aquarium of 1967. The same architects designed Water's Edge (2006–2007) for polar bears, walruses, and other animals.

6.16 LINCOLN-LARIMER FIRE STATION (LEMINGTON ENGINE HOUSE NO. 38)
1908, Kiehnel and Elliott. Lemington Ave. at Missouri St.

Just before World War I, the firm of Kiehnel and Elliott was challenging Pittsburgh's orthodoxies in public architecture just as architect Frederick Scheibler (see 6.14, 6.19, and 6.27) was challenging the city's orthodoxies in housing. German-born Richard Kiehnel came to Pittsburgh from Cleveland, but he had worked in Chicago during the early years of the Prairie School. He joined in partnership with Pittsburgher John Elliott in 1906. This simple fire station, with minimalist brick walls set off by exaggerated dark stone cornices, shows the influence of Frank Lloyd Wright. The placement of the windows on the main facade seems almost lifted from Unity Temple, a Chicago masterpiece of which Kiehnel was surely aware.

6.17 LEMINGTON ELEMENTARY SCHOOL
1937, Marion M. Steen and Edward J. Weber. 7060 Lemington Ave.

This is the most successful of a number of Art Deco schools designed by Weber during Steen's tenure as Superintendent of Buildings. The building's rather severe classical massing and factory brick is enlivened with vividly colored terra cotta ornament representing the five races of man. With Weber, Steen also designed Schiller School in 1939 (1018 Peralta St.). The three most successfully resolved Art Deco public monuments in Pittsburgh are Lemington Elementary School, the New Granada Theater (6.44), and the Allegheny County Airport (3.19).

Lincoln-Larimer Fire Station (Lemington Engine House No. 38)

6.18 HOLY ROSARY CHURCH
1928, Ralph Adams Cram, for Cram and Ferguson. 7160 Kelly St.

This is the most inventive of Cram's three churches in Pittsburgh, with a powerful and idiosyncratic Spanish-inspired design for a congregation originally of German and Irish extraction and now African-American. The surrounding blocks of identical frame houses are dwarfed by the church's tall and spiky spire. The numerous pinnacles on the sides and the crocketed spires on the facade make the vibrancy of this Iberian fantasy—a restatement of the cathedral of Burgos in northern Spain—all the more powerful. Inside, Catalan Gothic provided Cram's precedent for a forest of slender columns and ribbed vaults that create the most dramatic nave in Pittsburgh. As the Roman Catholic parish church of the Homewood neighborhood, Holy Rosary has served since the 1950s as the spiritual and visual focus for much of Pittsburgh's African-American community.

Old Heidelberg Apartments

6.19 OLD HEIDELBERG APARTMENTS
1905 and 1908, Frederick G. Scheibler, Jr. 401–423 South Braddock Ave.

Probably the most admired of Scheibler's many houses and apartments in the city, Old Heidelberg is a twelve-unit, three-story, concrete apartment block with cottage wings, strongly akin to his nearby Linwood Apartments (1907) at McPherson Boulevard and North Linwood Avenue and the Whitehall (1906) at East End Avenue and Tuscarora Street. Although Scheibler is seen today as a pioneer Modernist, his tendency here was a more decorative treatment of openings and surfaces. The starkness of the white walls and the dramatic back-and-forth massing of the apartment volumes are resolutely modern, but the effect is rendered ambiguous by the pseudo-thatched profile of the massive, brooding roofs.

6.20 HOMEWOOD CEMETERY
1878; 1923 entrance buildings, Colbert T. A. MacClure and Albert H. Spahr. 1599 S. Dallas Ave., bounded by Forbes and Braddock aves.

Founded in 1878, Homewood is named after Judge William Wilkins's estate and his Greek

Holy Rosary Church

Homewood Cemetery

Revival mansion, which stood nearby from the 1830s to the 1920s. The cemetery's 205 acres constitute about half of Wilkins's former estate, with the other half now Frick Park and residential streets in Point Breeze and Squirrel Hill. The Romanesque Revival and Beaux-Arts mausolea for the Fricks, Mellons, Heinzes, Mestas, and Rockwells constitute a true necropolis, whose visual and social order mimics the nearby streets that the industrial barons dominated when they were alive. The cluster of buildings at the entrance include a Gothic Revival chapel and Tudor Revival gatehouse and administration building.

6.21 FRICK ART & HISTORICAL CENTER ("CLAYTON" HENRY CLAY AND ADELAIDE CHILDS FRICK ESTATE)
1860s; 1892 rebuilt, Frederick J. Osterling.
7200 Penn Ave.

Following their marriage in 1880, Henry and Adelaide Frick moved into and partially rebuilt the Italian villa that still constitutes the core of this mansion. In 1890, they commissioned Osterling to expand the house again. He transformed the two-story Italianate house into a four-story French mansion, but the results inside and out were more baronial than happy. Recent additions are the limestone Renaissance Revival Frick Art Museum (1969–1970, Thomas C. Pratt for Pratt, Shaeffer and Slowik) and a garage for Frick's sumptuous cars.

More enchanting than the house are the grounds, with Frick's private greenhouse and the playhouse for his children. Immediately across Reynolds Street begin the several hundred forested acres of Frick's estate. In 1935, those acres became Frick Park, with John Russell Pope adding pavilions at the park

Frick Art & Historical Center ("Clayton" Henry Clay and Adelaide Childs Frick Estate)

entrances here and at the Forbes Avenue entrance. Currently a house museum, Clayton is one of the best of its type in the nation, less in artistic quality than in the obsessive retention of every article of clothing and its accompanying documentation.

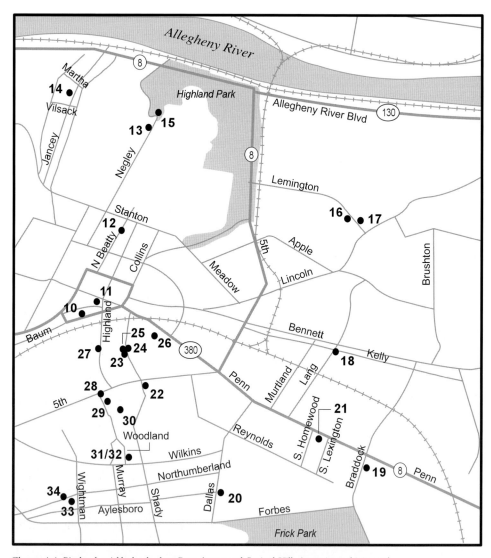

Characteristic Pittsburgh neighborhoods along Penn Avenue and Squirrel Hill. Approximate driving and walking time: at least than two hours.

From the 1850s, the Pennsylvania Railroad provided daily commuter trains from the congestion and pollution of downtown Pittsburgh to the emerging suburbs to the east. Shadyside emerged as a particularly distinguished suburb for an upper-middle class that now had the possibility of creating villas within easy reach of the city. Succeeding waves of development (based on the car and bus, since Shadyside station closed around 1950) kept to the same standard.

Squirrel Hill is Shadyside's uphill neighbor, at least in its wealthy half. (Realtors call this district "north of Forbes," to distinguish it from the densely packed streets south of Forbes Avenue.) The affluent north half contains striking houses by such modernist architects as Walter Gropius, Richard Meier, and local modernists, as well as many survivors in the various academic revivals from the 1890s to the 1920s. The names of many of the clients for these homes, such as Mellon, Thaw, Mesta, and Kaufmann, are renowned.

6.22 PITTSBURGH CENTER FOR THE ARTS.
(L. DILWORTH/ALAN AND SARAH SCAIFE AND CHARLES D. MARSHALL HOUSES)
1904; 1911–1912, Charles Barton Keen.
6300 Fifth Ave.

Pittsburgh Center for the Arts (Charles D. Marshall house)

The Pittsburgh Center for the Arts (PCA) uses two mansions and two outbuildings (a carriage house and a garage converted into kilns) on this prominent site. The Tudor Revival Scaife house of 1904 was given as a wedding present to Sarah Scaife in 1927 by her father, Richard B. Mellon, who lived in the 65-room mansion (designed by Alden & Harlow) next door. The Scaife house and the adjoining Georgian style Marshall house (designed by Philadelphia architect Keen) were, after 1945, put to use for Pennsylvania's largest community arts organization.

6.23 SELLERS-CARNAHAN HOUSE
(CALVARY EPISCOPAL CHURCH RECTORY)
1858. 400 Shady Ave.

It was probably its closeness to the Shadyside train station on the brand new rail line linking Pittsburgh to its burgeoning suburbs that induced wholesale grocer and banker Francis Sellers to purchase his ten acres of land here. His sprawling, L-shaped, Italianate-Gothic Revival brick house likely had its origins in an architectural pattern book design. The cross-gable roof and attic dormers were adorned with bargeboards when built (they are less elaborately decorated now), the two wooden porches have intricate balustrades, and there is an ornate porte-cochere. The house's name comes from its first and third owners. It also served for decades as the rectory for Calvary Episcopal Church, but has returned to use as a private residence. Though the grounds have been whittled down to a half-acre, this is one of the few homes to retain the park-like airiness that made Shadyside Pittsburgh's favorite mid-nineteenth-century village.

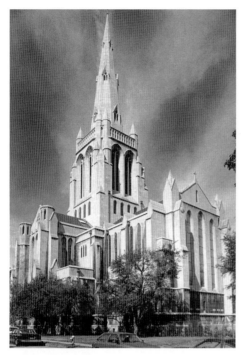

Calvary Episcopal Church

church design and building that ultimately fractured their partnership are readily evident.

6.25 SACRED HEART CHURCH
1924–1926, Carlton Strong; 1953, Kaiser, Neal, and Reid. 310 Shady Ave.

This is Strong's most prominent work in Pittsburgh, and, like the others, it is thoughtful and dramatic in concept and execution. Unlike Cram, whose Calvary Church (6.24) is externally austere but rich inside, Strong artfully captures the rich texturing of Gothic inside and out. The gable-topped facade, almost completely glazed, gives the church a sense of connection to the exterior that Cram's structure lacks. Strong traveled to Europe with the church's pastor to capture exactly the right note for this standard-bearer of Catholicism in a Protestant neighborhood. Particularly evocative is the forest-like wooden truss roof inside, its distinctive structure giving special meaning to the ship-like central volume of a church that we call a "nave."

6.24 CALVARY EPISCOPAL CHURCH
1906–1907, Ralph Adams Cram, for Cram, Goodhue, and Ferguson. 315 Shady Ave.

Almost a dozen churches and a synagogue met the needs of Shadyside's newly rich and pious residents in the two decades around 1900. All survive today, with Calvary Episcopal Church and Episcopal Church of the Ascension (6.42) standing like sentinels at Shadyside's east and west borders, and they are the two designs that are the most academically correct. With Henry Clay Frick among his patrons for Calvary Episcopal, Cram need not have worried about the budget. The church begins cool and almost brutal, then its limestone walls, emphasized by narrow vertical windows and prominent buttresses, culminate in a square tower and a skyward striving spire, one of Cram's best. The church turns rich and warm inside, with its wood trim and stained glass. Compared with his erstwhile partner Goodhue's First Baptist Church (2.4), the personality differences and approaches to

6.26 VILLAGE OF SHADYSIDE
1982–1987, UDA Architects.
100 Denniston St.

This was the first mark of the New Urbanism in western Pennsylvania: sixty-nine townhouses and seven condominiums (for a total of 215 residential units) on nine acres on the border between Shadyside and East Liberty. Making use of New Urbanism design concepts, this development repeated the key historical architectural design elements of the adjacent streets, in this case the dormers, bay windows, gables, front steps and decorative brick accents. This is most apparent in the first townhouses, standing immediately opposite a row of nineteenth-century homes. Their liveliness comes from their alternating tones of brick and their variations in setbacks, dormers, and entrance types, all the while respecting the streetline. The street units and the

Village of Shadyside

other townhouses grouped around internal promenades have first floor rear patios and second floor rear porches that overlook common yards between the buildings. The effect is of an old-style neighborhood. Only the guardhouse, the high walls, and the Penn Avenue gate locked against intruders suggest a harsher and more mundane reality.

6.27 HIGHLAND TOWERS
1913, Frederick G. Scheibler, Jr.
340–342 S. Highland Ave.

Of Scheibler's approximately eighty buildings in Pittsburgh, this four-story apartment block, designed for wealthy, progressive families, is the most confidently resolved. The usual influences Scheibler gleaned from architectural magazines and from the exhibitions of contemporary architecture held at the Carnegie Museum are evident in this stunning example of early Modernism. Its two entrances on either side of the recessed central facade of this U-shaped building are elevated from the street level, pushing the apartments away from the noisy street. Scheibler composed the exterior in yellow tapestry brick, dark blue tile, glass, and stucco. Each of the recessed apartments has a solarium that opens into a balcony; the central apartments look over a garden terrace.

The interior is rich, beginning with the deep blue art tiles at the entrances from Henry Mercer's Moravian Pottery and Tile works in Doylestown, Pennsylvania. Originally the floors were divided into four apartments, each with three bedrooms, two bathrooms, and servant's quarters. The apartments were equipped with the latest devices and had a safe, built-in oak and mahogany cabinets and bookcases. The building had vacuum cleaning outlets, a prototype air conditioning system, and a Modulated Vapor System for heating. An earlier Scheibler-designed apartment block, which incorporated commercial space and is more overtly Art Nouveau, is the Minnetonka Building of 1908 at 5421–5431 Walnut Street.

Highland Towers

Chatham College and Academic Revival houses

6.28 CHATHAM COLLEGE AND ACADEMIC REVIVAL HOUSES
1869–1920s. Bounded by Fifth, Wilkins, Shady, and Murray Hill aves.

Founded as the Pennsylvania Female College in 1869, Chatham College today encompasses a score of significant old houses along with newer custom-built buildings on its hillside campus. The earliest house, the Howe-Childs Gatehouse, dates from circa 1867, and the most prominent of the old mansions is steel magnate George Laughlin's vast Tudor Revival house designed by MacClure and Spahr. It was purchased by Andrew Mellon in 1917 and given to Chatham in 1940 by his son, Paul Mellon. The thirty-two-acre campus includes landscape elements designed for the Mellon estate by the Olmsted Brothers. Additional handsome mansions built by Pittsburgh's industrial elite after the Civil War still stand along Woodland Road and Beechwood Boulevard. Ranging in style from Tudor and Gothic Revival to Colonial Revival and Shingle style, they are a testimony to the sumptuousness of the era.

6.29 JEROME & JOAN APT HOUSE
1951–1953, A. James Speyer. 40 Woodland Rd.

Among the older houses of the Squirrel Hill neighborhood are some of the most distinguished modern designs in the city. James Speyer was born in one of the old mansions in the Woodland Road district, but, after studying under Mies van der Rohe, he became a committed modernist. Speyer joined Mies for graduate studies in 1938, just weeks after Mies became dean at the Armour Institute of Technology in Chicago, now the Illinois Institute of Technology (IIT). Speyer's achievements were fourfold: as teacher of architecture at IIT; as architect of some exquisitely detailed houses; as curator at the Art Institute of Chicago; and as famed exhibit designer there.

The background for the design of the Apt house was unusual. Joan Frank Apt had grown up across the road in a house designed by Walter Gropius and Marcel Breuer (6.30), and she knew Speyer. The site is steeply sloped, and a granite stairway descends the hillside to reach the house. The house's low rectangular base is Miesian, as are the great expanses of plate glass; the heavily wooded site also affords privacy. Other design decisions seem to have been client-driven, such as the two internal circulation systems, one for family members and one for servants. The architect's family summered next to the Kaufmanns at Fallingwater, and Frank Lloyd Wright's influence is apparent in the house's low ceilings and integration of the furnishings. The fireplace's dramatic arch in the living room is an H. H. Richardson influence.

6.30 CECELIA & ROBERT FRANK HOUSE
1939–1940, Walter Gropius and Marcel Breuer. 96 East Woodland Rd.

Renowned modernist Walter Gropius, founding director of Germany's Bauhaus, emigrated to the United States and to Harvard in 1937; a year later, he invited his former student, Marcel Breuer, to follow. The commission to design a house for the Frank family was the largest and most comprehensive commission of Gropius and Breuer's early American careers. It gave them an unprecedented occasion to expand their idea of a modernist house as a total work of art, replete with an extensive program of specially conceived furniture, which allowed Breuer to continue—

for the first, and virtually the only, time in America—experiments in laminated plywood begun in the mid-1930s in England.

Robert J. Frank. a Pittsburgh industrialist, heard Gropius lecture in 1938, and he visited Gropius's own house in Lincoln, Massachusetts, the following summer. By early 1939, he and the two Bauhaus masters had conceived a house as modern in its systems and attention to family comfort and ease of entertaining and recreation as in its materials and appearance. With its cladding in pinkish-colored Kasota stone over a welded steel frame, combined with huge areas of glazing in plate glass and glass brick, the house appears at once grand and stylish as well as functional and open—particularly in the large-scale strip windows, the huge sliding glass doors of the indoor swimming pool, and in the great open terrace that stretches through the block of the house above the pool. Gropius wrote his clients that the house would be "very noble" in appearance. The drama of the sweeping glass-curved stair window, linking the three principal floors, announces the flowing circulation within

that would greet guests once they alighted under the cantilevered porte-cochere. A games room and the pool occupy the ground floor, while a stair sweeps guests up to a reception area from which the second-floor dining and living rooms, cloak room and bar, and study with conservatory could all be reached at a step. A wishbone-shaped, travertine-clad fireplace core replaces conventional walls. The house is brilliantly integrated with its hillside site, so that the second floor is at grade with the rear garden, with its organically shaped lily pond and stepped retaining walls echoing the house's rustic stone base. The upper floor was given over to bedrooms, each with its own bath and dressing room, all accessed from the living area at the center of the plan with its monumental granite fireplace.

Because of the family's interest in discretion and privacy, the Frank house, four-car garage, and grounds constitute one of the unsung masterpieces of American house design. They have been preserved intact by Alan I. W. Frank, the youngest of the Frank's three children.

Cecelia and Robert Frank House

Frank A. Giovannitti House

6.31 FRANK A. GIOVANNITTI HOUSE
1979–1983, Richard Meier.
118 Woodland Rd.

The variety of architectural experiences a pedestrian might get from an inspection of Woodland Road is nowhere more pronounced than in the two postmodern residences standing at numbers 118 and 118-A. Meier's Giovannitti House stands directly next to the roadway, with Venturi's Abrams House behind. Meier's much-acclaimed design is at first glance a barely concealed reshuffling of his Smith House at Darien, Connecticut, of a dozen years before. Though keeping the same language of intersecting planes, solids, and voids, this three-story neo-Corbusian white cube takes on extraordinary vividness as it tucks itself into the hillside.

This affords privacy and a garden setting to the residents within the house and a reconsideration of one's relationship to nature to the streetside viewer.

6.32 BETTY & IRVING ABRAMS HOUSE
1979–1982, Venturi, Rauch, & Scott Brown.
118A Woodland Rd.

The clients had previously lived a few blocks away in a ranch house next to the stringently modernist Speyer House (6.33), which may have spurred them to Postmodernism here. Though they first considered the postmodernist architects Charles Moore and Michael Graves for the commission, they chose the firm of Venturi, Rauch, and Scott-Brown. The Philadelphia architects took as their point of departure the difficult setting of the proposed building site, slightly downgrade from Woodland Road, in a shallow valley split by a creek. The lot, one of five carved from the old Tudor Revival estate next door, contained an ornamental stone bridge from the 1920s that spanned the creek. The architects used the bridge as the main landscape feature that can be viewed from the oversized windows in the living room, and the creek's water fills ornamental pools at the front and rear of the residence.

Betty and Irving Abrams House

The dynamic, curvilinear form of the Abrams House emerges from the green and white wooden clapboards and the colored enamel panels that form strident, ray-like decorative motifs from the center of the facade over a gray background. The left half of the facade is dominated by an oversized, fan-shaped window that hints at a mill wheel—perhaps an allusion to the creek over which the structure is built.

The interior plan of the house is simple, allowing the architects to syncopate the large rectangles for the more important areas of the home, with smaller squares for secondary bedrooms and storage and utility rooms. Striking aspects of this interior are the changes in scale and the interplay of open and closed spaces. These effects are most notable in the living room where a balcony extends the full width of the house to create a snug sense of enclosure for a narrow bar on the floor below it. This enclosure acts as a foil for the adjacent living room, underscoring the unexpected 24-foot height of its gracefully curved ceiling.

The Abrams House represents the dynamic forms and dramatic juxtapositions for which the firm was acclaimed. By any measure, this quirky house on an inconvenient and water-logged site is an exceptional addition to the architectural pedigree of Woodland Road.

6.33 TILLIE S. SPEYER HOUSE
1963, A. James Speyer. Wightman and Northumberland sts.

Chicago-based architect Speyer returned to his hometown to create this house for his widowed mother, a sculptor of biomorphic abstracts. The severe temple-like block turns its back on the adjoining intersection of busy streets. The entire property is ringed by a high brick wall, with the bricks stacked rather than bonded to indicate their non-bearing role. Privacy also comes from the few windows, though the windows that face private spaces are large in size. The internal layout has a bank of side rooms

north and south off a two-story atrium. The rich woods set in the steel grid make the structure unexpectedly serene. This theme of serenity and contemplation extends to the sunken garden and adjoining channeled rivulet of water, which gave the sculptor the sense of a Japanese garden in the middle of Pittsburgh.

6.34 PFEIFFER HOUSE
1982, Arthur Lubetz Associates.
5553 Northumberland St.

This provocative three-story residence of dark brick, stone, aluminum siding, and metallic elements continues to surprise passers-by on a street of traditional-style homes. It has some modern neighbors, however: the Tillie Speyer house (6.33) is diagonally opposite, and Dahlen Ritchey's Tisherman House of 1948 (5627 Northumberland St.) is a tiny International Style house commissioned by Edgar Kaufmann, Sr. Lubetz designed this house for a newly arrived ALCOA executive and his wife. The executive wanted a new house, while his wife sought an urban townhouse she could modify. The Pfeiffer's House does both. The left half, tall and narrow like a townhouse (exclusive of a later garage and family room), is set frontally to the street, while the right half stands at right angles to it. This effectively renders the same building in two simultaneous views from front and side, with a bridge-like penthouse corridor connecting the two. Lubetz called the scheme

Pfeiffer House

"the juxtaposition of an urban townhouse and a suburban split-level . . . [an] investigation of architectural—and familial—dialectics."

6.35 ABRAAM STEINBERG HOUSE
1951–1952, Peter Berndtson and Cornelia Brierly Berndtson. 5139 Penton Rd.

This house for physician Steinberg is one of several Pittsburgh homes designed between 1947 and 1957 by two architects who met and trained at Frank Lloyd Wright's Taliesin in Spring Green, Wisconsin. Peter Berndtson designed most of them, and his wife and partner, Cornelia, collaborated on several and designed others on her own. Certainly the close fit of a house and its surroundings is a textbook definition of organic architecture. The brick, redwood, glass, and concrete house stands on the edge of a long, narrow, and steeply sloped lot. Two exterior walls of the house form a right angle to conform to the street grid, and the rounded rear wall echoes an inner circular garden that is open to the sky. This garden, visible from all of the major rooms, provides the true facade for the house. Interior spaces flow visually from one to the next, analogous to the ramps that physically unite its three levels. The organic theme is carried through in the house furnishings, built-in where possible, and in the same redwood that provides structure for the house. Invariably but unfairly compared to their teacher Wright, the Berndtsons were an important force in the adoption of modern architecture in post–World War II Pittsburgh.

6.36 SUNNYLEDGE HOTEL (SUNNYLEDGE, THE JAMES MCCLELLAND HOUSE)
1886–1888, Alexander W. Longfellow, for Longfellow, Alden, & Harlow; 1996–1997 conversion, Raymond Schinhofen. 5124 Fifth Ave.

James McClelland was a homeopathic doctor for Andrew Carnegie and the Frick, Mellon, and Scaife families. After rejecting a Queen Anne design for his house by a local architect, McClelland hired Longfellow, Alden, & Harlow of Boston. The house sits easily on a narrow bench of land against a small hillside, which softens the bulky massing and austerity of the unadorned brick walls. The front elevation has a deeply inset arched door, irregularly spaced windows, and textured brickwork. Massive square chimneys with decorative brickwork and corbelling rise from the hipped roof. McClelland's medical office curves out at the northeast corner to form an oversized tower with conical roof. His patients entered through a separate porch with exposed rafters. Inside, the entrance hall is paneled in wood, and a forest of thin wooden spindles form screens and the staircase banister.

The McClellands' younger daughter lived in Sunnyledge for ninety-four years, changing nothing. She endowed it as a private house museum, which would have had few equals for

Sunnyledge Hotel (Sunnyledge, the James McClelland House)

Gwinner-Harter House (William B. Negley House)

period authenticity, but her youthful curator survived her by very few years and the furnishings were auctioned. The family papers went to the Historical Society of Western Pennsylvania. Fortunately, when the home became a small hotel, the public rooms were kept intact, including samples of McClelland's old medicine bottles from a century ago.

6.37 GWINNER-HARTER HOUSE
(WILLIAM B. NEGLEY HOUSE)
1871–1872; 1912–1923 additions, Frederick J. Osterling; 1996 restoration, Edge Architects. 5061 Fifth Ave.

This is the second-oldest home of what remains from the days when Pittsburgh's Fifth Avenue rivaled Fifth Avenue in New York City. After World War I, many of the mansions in the Oakland section of Fifth Avenue in Oakland were demolished or turned into apartments, and this occurred here in the Shadyside neighborhood

after World War II. This three-story Second Empire style house built for attorney and banker William Negley is one of the few survivors. Edward Gwinner, a stone contractor, purchased the house in 1911 and commissioned Osterling to design a three-story addition to the west side of the house and a single-story, classically inspired porch in order to update the by then old-fashioned house. Gwinner expanded the small central entrance hall into a lavish marble room, with an extravagant staircase reminiscent of mansions in Newport, Rhode Island. In 1923, Osterling returned to design the interiors of three reception rooms; each is paneled in English oak and walnut, and two have carved limestone fireplace surrounds that reach the ceiling.

Dr. Leo Harter acquired the house in 1963 and began a decades-long restoration. In 1987 a fire on the third floor caused extensive damage to the house. Then, in 1995, Joedda Sampson, a major force in the renewal of Pittsburgh's historic properties, bought and

Shadyside Presbyterian

restored the house and hired Edge Architects for a contemporary redesign of the third floor's burned-out interior. The reborn house is the third in a row of superb Fifth Avenue mansions, after the coolly classical Hillman House (1924, E. P. Mellon) at number 5045 and the Rococo-style Moreland-Hoffstot House (1914, Paul Irwin) at number 5057. Older is the Gothic Revival Willow Cottage (Howe-Childs House), dating to around 1867, seven blocks away at 5918 Fifth Avenue, which has been handsomely restored and is part of Chatham College (6.28).

6.38 SHADYSIDE PRESBYTERIAN
1889–1892, Shepley, Rutan, and Coolidge; 1937–1938 interior renovation, Eyre and McIlvaine. 807 Amberson Ave.

Long one of Pittsburgh's wealthiest congregations, Shadyside Presbyterian was founded in 1867 by the prominent landowners Thomas Aiken and William Negley. After constructing two unsatisfactory churches on the same site, the congregation turned to the Boston-based successor firm to H. H. Richardson, whose style then dominated Pittsburgh. The predictable outcome was a restatement of Richardson's Trinity Church in Boston. Here the muscular central block and pyramidal cap clearly recall Trinity, but Shadyside Presbyterian is broader and has a lower profile. In more densely packed city streets, the church's understated grandeur would be lost, but, in this verdant setting amid nineteenth-century homes, the scaled-down facade, external narthex, and transept ends produce an unusually powerful neighborhood church. Another contextual touch is the inclusion of many windows, far more numerous here than in the Boston prototype, perhaps in response to Pittsburgh's dark and smoky skies.

6.39 RODEF SHALOM TEMPLE
1906–1907, Henry Hornbostel for Palmer and Hornbostel; 1989 renovation, The Ehrenkrantz Group and Eckstut. 4905 Fifth Ave.

This synagogue is the best of Hornbostel's three religious structures in Pittsburgh—the other two are Smithfield United Church (1925–1926; 620 Smithfield St.) and the former B'Nai Israel Synagogue of 1923–1924 at 327 North Negley Avenue. The congregation, which dates from 1856, used a synagogue in downtown Pittsburgh until it was attracted by the amenities of Oakland, coincidentally the same year that the neighboring St. Paul Cathedral relocated. The cream-colored brick structure has a square plan but culminates in a large squared dome of green tiles and glazed terra cotta ornament. The synagogue's compact massing and bright coloring are reminiscent of Byzantine structures, which were popular precedents at the time for synagogues.

The interior, as expected from the exterior massing, is a huge undivided volume underneath the Guastavino-tiled dome of light-colored herringbone tiles, which has an octagonal skylight. Stenciled color, gilded wood chandeliers, and oak paneling highlighted in gold leaf enrich the interior. A restoration in 1989 reversed water damage and improved the poor acoustics that had become an accepted but unloved attribute of the building.

6.40 MUDGE GRADUATE HOUSE, CARNEGIE MELLON UNIVERSITY (EDMUND AND PAULINE MUDGE HOUSE)
1922, Henry Gilchrist. 1000 Morewood Ave.

This smooth limestone mansion was the last of its generation to be built on Fifth Avenue. The house has a symmetrical facade, with large curved bays that extend three floors in height on each side of the one-story, semi-circular portico.

Rodef Shalom Temple

WQED Studios

A possible design source was the Shoenberger House that, in the 1920s, was still standing on Penn Avenue, downtown, as the Pittsburgh Club. Sympathetically extended with echoing wings when it became a college dormitory in the 1960s, Mudge House remains one of Shadyside's essential visual anchors.

6.41 WQED STUDIOS
1969, Paul Schweikher. 4802 Fifth Ave.

Created in 1952, WQED was the first publicly owned educational television station in the United States. As part of the cultural program of the Pittsburgh Renaissance, it gained fame as home to Mr. Rogers, the much-loved children's television personality. The combined state-of-the-art studios and administrative facilities encompass 66,000 square feet. The hallmarks of New Brutalism are visible throughout the building, from the raw poured concrete exterior to the unrestricted play of space inside. The plan of the complex is bilateral, with studios and conference rooms on the left side and offices housed in four blocks on the right. The subdued interior decor emphasizes texture over ornament, with rough concrete juxtaposed against polished oak and glass block partitions.

6.42 EPISCOPAL CHURCH OF THE ASCENSION
1896–1897, William Halsey Wood;
1897–1898, Alden & Harlow
4729 Ellsworth Ave.

This finely textured stone church is a beacon and a portal to the western border of Shadyside. Its massive square tower gave scale to the late nineteenth-century houses clustered around it, but now its neighbors are mainly apartment blocks. The building's style is Tudor Revival, with coursed sandstone outside and a dramatic timberwork roof inside. British church architecture was frequently used as inspiration for Episcopalian churches in the United States, and the New Jersey-based Wood did much to popularize it. Alden & Harlow completed the church after Wood died in 1897. The adjacent parish house (1909–1910) was designed by Janssen and Abbott.

T he Hill and the Bluff offer another example of two Pittsburgh neighborhoods
tightly linked. The first is oriented toward the Allegheny River and the second to
the Monongahela, with Fifth and Forbes avenues forming a corridor between them.
Both neighborhoods are a world away from downtown Pittsburgh in topography, social
function, scale, and architectural character, but anything that happens downtown for
good or ill impacts these two communities that stand immediately uphill.

The Hill had farmhouses on it around 1800; then, from the 1820s to the 1860s,
immigrants from Ireland and Germany settled here, followed by eastern Europeans,
notably Jews, and, from the 1880s to the 1920s, African-Americans from the South. The
Bluff was laid out on paper in the mid-nineteenth century. The rows of brick townhouses that survive in both areas date mainly from the 1860s to 1900.

6.43 OAK HILL (TERRACE VILLAGE)

*(Terrace Village) 1940, Marlier, Boyd,
Lee, and Pratt; 1996 renovations, Perfido
Weiskopf Architects; 1998, reconstruction as
Oak Hill, Goody Clancy; Perfido Weiskopf
Architects, and Graves Architects. Bounded
by Burrows and Reed sts., Bentley Dr., and
Herron Ave.*

Terrace Village was considered of sufficient importance that President Franklin Roosevelt
attended the ribbon cutting on October 11, 1940.
The chairman of the Federal Housing Authority
called it "one of the most dramatic housing sites
in the country," while Pittsburgh's mayor pre-
dicted that citizens would be "perfectly astounded
at the beauty of the place." The site was indeed
dramatic, encompassing the former Goat's and
Gazzam hills in a thickly wooded plot of several
hundred acres towering above the old neighborhood of Soho. Nonetheless, the location was
invisible to and inaccessible from the rest of Pittsburgh, a sure formula for decay. Eighty-three
identical three-story brick blocks housed a total
of 1,851 housing units on winding roads adjoining the University of Pittsburgh campus. The
blocks were flat-roofed and devoid of decoration,
fitting the objectives of Terrace Village to provide
basic, serviceable, and short-term housing.

By the 1990s, the units were perceived as
inadequate and dangerous. Six blocks were
demolished before the U.S. Department of
Housing and Urban Development (HUD)
inaugurated a Major Reconstruction of Public Housing (MROP) program in 1996. Eight
of the original blocks were transformed
through the elimination of common stairwells
and harsh spotlights, the creation of entrances
on both sides of the blocks, and the provision
of private entrances and yards. Carving the old
blocks into two-story duplex units on the
upper floors reduced building density and
eliminated perilous corridors. Hipped roofs
with gables further personalized the shapeless
old blocks, new brick outbuildings replaced
the dumpsters previously marring the street,
and decorative iron fencing and new trees and
shrubbery completed the dramatic transformation of these buildings from barracks into liv-
able apartments.

In 1998, 664 residential units in wood-
sheathed townhouses and brick-clad apartment buildings were built on the part of the
old Terrace Village adjacent to the University
of Pittsburgh campus. The results are impressive, but the process litigious. As of early 2007,
urban planners and the courts were still decid-
ing what will occupy the remaining vacant

portions of the Hill: student dormitories or dwellings for local residents.

6.44 NEW GRANADA THEATER (PYTHIAN TEMPLE)
1927, Louis A. S. Bellinger; 1937, Alfred M. Marks. 2007–2013 Centre Ave.

In the 1920s, African-Americans formed several chapters of the Knights of Pythias in Pittsburgh. A group of construction workers belonging to Union Local 111 commissioned Bellinger, Pittsburgh's first African-American architect of prominence, to design its lodge house. Born in South Carolina in 1891, Bellinger graduated from Howard University in 1914.

At first the building flourished, with a dining hall on the first floor, an auditorium on the second, and meeting rooms and offices on the third, but a downturn in economic conditions forced the sale of the temple in the 1930s to the Pittsburgh theater impresario Harry Hendel. Hendel, who had owned and lost an earlier Granada Theater, transferred its name to this building. The temple's dining hall became a theater, usually showing Yiddish movies, while the second floor housed the Savoy Ballroom, named for still another of Hendel's earlier businesses.

Bellinger's original design set three stories of windows in yellow brick below a cornice consisting of squared notches over a frieze of oval terra cotta tiles. In 1937, architect Marks added

New Granada Theater (Pythian Temple)

shimmering red, blue, and yellow glazed enamel panels to the ground floor. The marquee combines designs in blue, yellow, green, and red. The refurbished New Granada Theater remained the glory of the Hill for another three decades, hosting all the giants of the Jazz era: Count Basie, Cab Calloway, Ella Fitzgerald, Lionel Hampton, and Lena Horne. The New Granada closed after riots ripped through the Hill in the late 1960s. The Hill Community Development Corporation plans to rehabilitate it as part of Granada Square, a hub of educational, social, and artistic activities for the revived Hill of the future.

6.45 CRAWFORD SQUARE
1991–present, Urban Design Associates and Tai+Lee. Bounded by Crawford and Roberts sts. and Centre and Webster aves.

These attached townhouses of tan brick and wood are set in short blocks, with widened streets in the manner of the courts or private streets of nineteenth-century St. Louis or Boston. Lively in detail and staggered in response to the sloped grade, these hundreds of units would be a standout in any neighborhood, and they certainly are here between the desolation of the Lower Hill, with its acres of parking lots around the Mellon Arena (6.46), and the unattended old buildings of the Middle Hill.

Probably the most successful of any public project in post-Renaissance Pittsburgh, Crawford Square goes a long way toward healing the grievous urban wound inflicted by the Renaissance of the 1950s: the destruction of the Lower Hill and the severing of its remnant from the Golden Triangle. The twenty-three-acre site holds 350 rental units and 140 houses of mixed-income housing.

Three key groups were involved: Pittsburgh's Urban Redevelopment Authority (URA), a joint city-county agency; the developers McCormack Baron Associates of St. Louis; and Pittsburgh-based Urban Design Associates

Crawford Square

(UDA). The URA initiated the project in 1988 and hired McCormack Baron, based on the firm's successful results in Cincinnati and St. Louis. URA and the municipal agency enlisted UDA as designers, based on their success in getting community involvement in turning around weakened neighborhoods. UDA provided site planning and design for the first 203 rental units, while the first forty houses were designed by Tai + Lee.

Since Mellon Arena (6.46) and Crosstown Expressway (I-579) block the site to the west, UDA designed a plan with a strong north-south axis, using the existing street grid as a guide to reinforce a traditional urban fabric and to reintroduce connections to downtown. All buildings are two or three stories, each with front and rear yards. A pattern book codifies materials, colors, and facade elements, insuring that subsequent developers maintain a uniform look and feel in future expansions of the neighborhood.

Financing for this $55 million development came from the URA, the City of Pittsburgh, private lenders, and the philanthropic community. The reduced-rent units are provided by McCormack Baron, which gains tax benefits. Already in its short life, Crawford Square has

begun to revitalize the Hill. Even more important, it has provided a model for similar projects that are luring suburbanites back to the city, such as Washington's Landing, Lincoln at the North Shore, and Summerset at Frick Park.

6.46 MELLON ARENA (CIVIC ARENA)
1954–1961, Mitchell and Ritchey, architects; Ammann and Whitney, structural engineers; H. Rey Helvenston, superintending engineer. 66 Mario Lemieux Pl. (formerly 300 Auditorium Pl.).

The Civic Arena was, and still is, the subject of engineering admiration and urban regret. The project began when city councilman Abe Wolk proposed an open-air tent to house summer performances of the Civic Light Opera. Edgar Kaufmann, Sr., turned the concept into a glistening, retractable stainless steel dome. When its site was changed from Highland and then Schenley Park to the dense African-American neighborhood of the Lower Hill, the result was controversy: engineering marvel or racial harmony. The marvel won out, and 1,600 African-American families were dispersed through Pittsburgh's East

End. The ninety-five-acre redevelopment of the Lower Hill constituted Pittsburgh's largest, costliest, and most fractious urban renewal project, with far more headache and far less to show for it than Gateway Center (1.2). After the leveling of nearly 1,000 parcels of property, only Epiphany Catholic Church (1903, Edward Stotz) at 1018 Centre Avenue and the rebuilt Beth Hamedrash Hagodol Synagogue (1964, Liff/Justh) at 1230 Colwell Street remain as witnesses to the old neighborhood.

The Civic Arena was one of just three building complexes to emerge from the devastation: the other two were I. M. Pei's Washington Plaza Apartments (1964) and Edward Durrell Stone's Chatham Center of 1966. Only a few seasons were required to show the arena's impracticality for opera, though it remains a good venue for popular music and sports. Old as it now is, the arena has few betters in terms of clear-span roofs and retractable domes. The dome, approximately 417 feet in diameter and 109 feet high, is nearly circular in plan. The retractable shell is composed of six 220-ton steel leaves and two fixed leaves made of 7,800 stainless steel pieces, covering in all 170,000 square feet. The leaves roll back on carriage wheels that ride on 3,000 feet of steel rails, coming to rest under the two stationary leaves that are supported by a 260-foot cantilevered space frame. Nonetheless, the dome has not been opened in years.

Civic Arena

6.47 LOWER FIFTH AVENUE STOREFRONTS
c. 1900–1920. 800–1200 blocks Fifth Ave.

These five blocks of lower Fifth Avenue, a trough between the Hill and the Bluff, were one of the busiest wholesale marketplaces between New York City and Chicago, serving the proprietors of the small dry goods stores in the satellite steel towns surrounding Pittsburgh. Malls and factory outlets drove out the wholesale stores, but the original storefronts survive in almost unbroken rows. In the 1980s, many became law offices (they lie in the shadow of the Courthouse tower), providing luxurious accommodations at a fraction of Grant Street's rates. Other commercial enterprises followed. The result is a marketplace of a style and tone that no urban planner could possibly have foreseen when this district was marked for destruction.

6.48 DUQUESNE UNIVERSITY STUDENT UNION
1967, Paul Schweikher. Duquesne University Campus, Vickroy St.

Duquesne University opened in 1878 as the Pittsburgh Catholic College of the Holy Ghost, occupying this site on the Bluff overlooking the Monongahela River. In the 1960s, Duquesne erected two notable buildings of complementary but different appearance on opposite sides of Vickroy Street: the Student Union and Richard King Mellon Hall of Science (6.49). The Student Union was the first of several public buildings by Schweikher, who came to Pittsburgh in 1956 to head the architecture school at Carnegie Mellon University.

The Union is a massive, six-story poured-concrete building in which structure and materials function as both design and ornament. The building's best external features were the concrete scissor ramps at both ends of the rectangular building, but its severe aesthetics were compromised when the entrance ramp was replaced by double steps and the ground-floor interior resurfaced in brick in an attempt to

Richard King Mellon Hall of Science

make it warmer in tone. Schweikher's structuring of the Union has held up well in its programming, which houses spaces for recreation, dining, and activities for students and faculty. The two-story ballroom, illuminated by concealed clerestories, is a particularly grand space.

6.49 RICHARD KING MELLON HALL OF SCIENCE
1968, Ludwig Mies van der Rohe. Duquesne University Campus, Vickroy St.

Architect Paul Schweikher secured the Mellon Hall of Science commission for Mies. The building stands opposite the Union, close to the bluff of the Monongahela River. The rectangular four-story structure gives the impression of a horizontally oriented version of Mies's much admired Seagram Building in New York City. It is based on a 28-foot module of bronzed, heat-absorbing glass that, on the upper three floors, is subdivided by thin steel mullions and black, graphite-painted steel panels. The buff brick and glass first floor is recessed under the upper stories. Mellon Hall is visually adequate on the Bluff, but its power is best revealed when it is viewed from across the river on the slopes of South Side—another manifestation of Pittsburgh's abiding Acropolis complex.

CHAPTER 7:
ON THE PARKWAY EAST

The boroughs of Wilkinsburg, Churchill, and Monroeville line up in a row extending east of Pittsburgh, but they have little in common beyond a shared growth pattern as piketowns. A settlement at what is now Wilkinsburg existed even before the American Revolution. It was nicknamed Jewstown for its owner, Levy Andrew Levy of Philadelphia, but the town grew only after the turnpike to Philadelphia was cut through on the line of current Penn Avenue, early in the nineteenth century. A second boost in population and wealth came in 1852, when the Pennsylvania Railroad's tracks reached Wilkinsburg and initiated a century of commuter service to and from downtown. A third transportation artery brought Wilkinsburg to its peak importance early in the twentieth century, when the Lincoln Highway (US 30) incorporated Penn Avenue as part of its cross-country route to downtown and points west. Wilkinsburg was so pleased with this extra attention and the revenue it brought in that, in 1916, it erected a lifesize copper statue to Abraham Lincoln alongside the eponymous roadway. It still stands at the intersection of Penn Avenue and Ardmore Boulevard.

But highways give and highways take away: in 1939, New York City's Robert Moses designed an expressway linking downtown Pittsburgh to the western extension of the Pennsylvania Turnpike. Locally called Penn-Lincoln Parkway or Parkway East (officially it is I-376), the post-World War II road bypassed Wilkinsburg, with severe economic consequences from which the borough has not recovered. In 2003, the Martin Luther King, Jr., Busway, which runs busses alongside the Pennsylvania Railroad tracks, was extended to Wilkinsburg, but the impact of this link to downtown remains equivocal.

The original Pennsylvania Turnpike from Pittsburgh to Philadelphia was itself a direct successor to a Native American trail widened in 1758 by General Forbes in his victorious march to dislodge the French from the Forks of the Ohio. The military trail gave birth to Churchill, a borough that profited in the post–World War II era from its positioning along I-376. Even rosier, at least superficially, was the postwar fate of Monroeville, which burgeoned in population and size as Pittsburgh's main interchange on the modern turnpike. But growth came too fast: farmland, once plowed by early settlers such as the Mellons, gave way to malls that are indistinguishable from those found anywhere in the nation.

7.1 C.C. MELLOR LIBRARY AND EDGEWOOD CLUB
1916–1918, Edward B. Lee. 1 Pennwood Ave.

This private swim and tennis club includes spaces for meetings and a library. Incorporated in 1904, the club purchased this site from the Charles Mellor family. While seemingly Spanish-influenced in its stucco and elaborate tile roof, Arts-and-Crafts influences are much stronger as seen in its cottage-like outline, steeply pitched roof, dormer windows, garden-like atmosphere, and pergola. The Mellor complex occupies a corner site, the better to exploit the picturesque qualities of an exquisitely designed structure.

7.2 EDGEWOOD RAILROAD STATION
1902–1903, attributed to Frank Furness.
101 East Swissvale Ave.

This tiny station, with its passenger platform and adjoining baggage house, is all that remains of the Furness legacy in Pittsburgh. Time has eliminated his bank on Fourth Avenue, the elaborate B & O Terminal near the Smithfield Street Bridge, and two suburban railroad stations. The Edgewood station is a prosaic work, small-scaled and utilitarian, with a hipped roof, but nonetheless showing an aging Furness still capable of wringing expression from brick and shingle.

C. C. Mellor Library and Edgewood Club

Edgewood Railroad Station

7.3 THREE RIVERS CENTER FOR INDEPENDENT LIVING AND JANE HOLMES RESIDENCE AND GARDENS (HOME FOR AGED PROTESTANT WOMEN AND SHELTERING ARMS HOME FOR AGED PROTESTANTS)

1871, Barr and Moser. 900 Rebecca Ave.; 1881, Barr and Moser. 441 Swissvale Ave.

These two residences are important survivals of the decade following the Civil War. John U. Barr and Henry Moser constituted one of Pittsburgh's leading design firms for schools and civic buildings in the 1870s and 1880s. The former Home for Aged Protestant Women is characteristic of their work: brick, three stories high and nine bays long, with Italianate details. The Sheltering Arms Home (for both women and men) opened in 1881 as an enlargement of the Sheltering Arms Home for Wayward Girls of 1869. This new structure was architecturally more severe than the first, despite its first-floor verandah.

The patrons of these homes were two wealthy cousins who were both named Jane Holmes and were important charitable donors in Pittsburgh, decades before Andrew Carnegie changed the scale of giving. The two Holmes were energized by relief work during the Civil War, then continued their charitable endeavors in a postwar orphan asylum, schools for the deaf and blind, havens for the poor, and a home for incurables. Here the cousins were aided by a site donated by James Kelly, the developer of much of the land that became Brushton, Homewood, and Wilkinsburg. The Home for Aged Protestant Women was later renamed Rebecca Residence and the Sheltering Arms renamed the Jane Holmes Residence.

7.4 JOHN SINGER HOUSE
1863–1869. 1318 Singer Pl.

John F. Singer made his fortune supplying iron and steel to the Union army during the Civil War. Looking for a summer estate, Singer purchased thirty-five acres in what was then the rural village of Wilkinsburg. Singer began the house in 1863 and continued construction throughout the war. The architect could have been Joseph W. Kerr, Pittsburgh's dominant Gothic Revival designer in the 1850s and 1860s, but the house is too grand and too lavishly decorated to have come entirely from a pattern book, which was Kerr's usual mode of design.

With its finely cut stone construction and

thirty-five rooms, the Singer house achieved a degree of ostentation greater than any in Pittsburgh in that era. Austrian plasterers, English wood-carvers (some having just finished work on the Houses of Parliament), and German stone masons were imported for the construction. Singer spared no expense to acquire hand-carved work, as in the hardwood vergeboards and the delicate natural motifs in low relief under each bay window. Two somber mahogany porches were painted with crushed sandstone and gesso to emulate the stone walls of the house.

The house is cruciform in plan—typical of country houses at the time—with four steep gables and numerous dormers, each sumptuously decorated. The front steps, of Mexican slate, lead to an Italianate tiled foyer. The first floor's eighteen rooms feature elaborately carved mahogany window frames and doors, and every room has a mantel of a different imported marble.

The estate included an artificial lake, gatehouse where a Russian farm laborer lived, carriage house for Singer's "fine horse flesh," and private chapel where Singer led Episcopalian services. Singer's partner, Alexander Nimick, purchased adjoining property with the intent to build, but he never did, and, instead, Nimick Place turned into speculative tract housing.

After Singer's death in 1872, his wife and family left the estate. Westinghouse then used it as a boarding house for young executives, and, after that, it was broken up into apartments. The current owner is returning the mansion to a single-family dwelling.

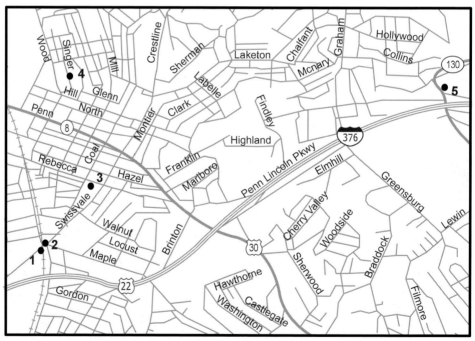

Wilkinsburg and the Parkway East. Approximate driving time: less than two hours.

John Singer House

7.5 BEULAH CHAPEL
(BEULAH PRESBYTERIAN CHURCH)
1837. 2500 McCrady Rd.

This finely proportioned small church in the community of Churchill is among the most evocative of the early buildings of the county, conveying in brick two centuries of change in social and physical context. It lies atop a ridge that slopes precipitously north to the Allegheny River and south to Turtle Creek.

Presbyterianism was the central faith of western Pennsylvania, arriving here early in the eighteenth century with the Ulster Scots driven from Northern Ireland by the first of the potato famines. Already in 1732, the Presbytery of Donegal was formed to maintain contact with the tiny congregations of farmers and traders west of the Susquehanna River. The British victory at Fort Duquesne in 1758 augmented the number of settlers, and itinerant preachers regularly visited the area. In 1809, the McRea family donated land for a church.

Beulah Chapel (Beulah Presbyterian Church)

The chapel (so named because a bigger church designed by Hoffman and Crumpton was built next door in 1956–1957) has the twinned doors characteristic of many early Southern churches. The bricks (Flemish bond on the facade, common bond elsewhere) were made on-site, the roof trusses are mortised and pegged, the floor beams are oak, and the delicate exterior moldings suggest a design holdover from the Federal era. The chapel is now raised on a modern basement. The Beulah chapel has an air of antiquity entirely appropriate as the mother church of the core denomination that settled western Pennsylvania.

7.6 SRI VENKATESWARA TEMPLE
1976, Sashi Patel. 1230 S. McCully Dr.

For those who enter Pittsburgh on the Parkway West (I-376), the temple is glimpsed from the highway on its wooded hillside. It was the first Hindu temple in the United States built by workmen from India, and it is modeled after the seventh-century Sri Venkateswara Temple in South India. Constructed of white stuccoed-brick, the large rectangular edifice has a facade dominated by a central stepped tower with massive teak doors at the base. Inside, the skylit colonnaded hall is supported on pillars carved with intricate foliate designs and accommodates several shrines with images of various deities. In the center of the hall is the altar to Lord Venkateswara, to whom the temple is dedicated.

7.7 HINDU JAIN TEMPLE
1981–1990, Sashi Patel. 615 Illini Dr.

Pittsburgh's second Hindu temple incorporates seven different deities within one structure. The clay-colored brick building follows the Nagradi architectural style of north-central India, with three gracious central towers

Sri Venkateswara Temple

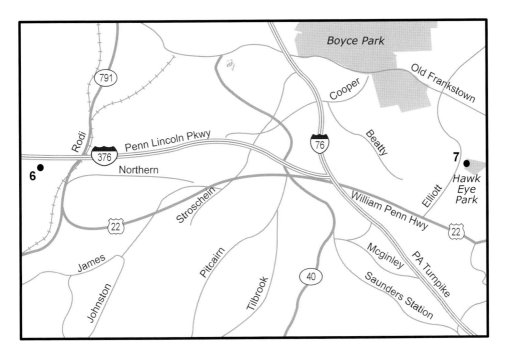

The Parkway East toward Monroeville. Approximatge driving time: one hour.

ringed with smaller versions. The exterior walls are articulated with horizontal brick bands, and the windows have elaborately carved surrounds. The hall-like interior is illuminated by skylights and features five free-standing altars honoring seven deities. Eleven master masons came from India to work on the project, using neither models nor scale drawings but instead proportioning all details of their carvings by religious formulas they had memorized. This was the first unified Hindu-Jain temple in the United States.

CHAPTER 8:
EARLY SETTLERS AND
TROLLEY SUBURBS

Were one to draw a crescent of about forty miles in circumference—from the Allegheny County Municipal Airport (3.19), near the Monongahela Valley, west to the Pittsburgh International Airport (5.8), not far from the Ohio Valley—the crescent would encompass a number of important settlement points for eighteenth-century Pittsburgh, together with a set of suburbs that were born early in the twentieth century. The south half of the crescent is, today, thick with the bedroom suburbs collectively called the South Hills, while its southwestern component remains so spottily settled that it lacks any name at all (theoretically it would be the West Hills).

In terms of development, this crescent marks the sleepiest part of the Pittsburgh orbit. Numerous farmhouses and selected isolated mansions survive from the early nineteenth century, but just a few of these nuclei transformed themselves into urban entities, compared to the dozens of parallel settlements east and north of Pittsburgh that did. The probable reason is the lack of access to major roads or rivers in this crescent. The South Hills had the Washington Pike to link it southward with the National Road (US 40), but real growth came only with the cutting of the trolley tunnel through Mt. Washington, in 1904. An even greater growth spurt came when the Liberty Tunnels, as a second cut through Mt. Washington, gave motorists similar access to the South Hills, in 1924. The theoretical West Hills remained cut off from Pittsburgh a good deal longer. It was served by just a few trolley lines, and it had no significant roadway until a parkway to the new airport opened in 1952.

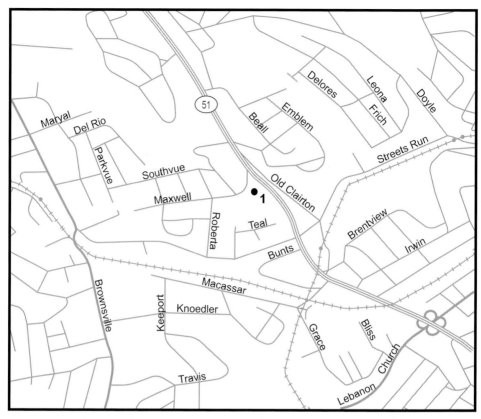

Early Settlers and Trolley Suburbs. Approximate time: one hour.

8.1 HOLY TRINITY SERBIAN ORTHODOX CHURCH
1967–1971, John Tomich. 4920 Old Clairton Rd.

Churches once comprised the building type that best expressed ethnic identity in Pittsburgh, as they did everywhere else in America, but they have played a minor a role in local architecture since World War II. This is one of the few postwar religious sites in Allegheny County that demands a visit, having liberated itself from denominational stereotypes while still deriving strength from architectural history. Holy Trinity uses uncompromising poured-concrete walls inside and out to evoke the ancient triconch plan of Byzantine architecture. What saves the church from being a mere pastiche of historic precedents and architectural clichés is what saved Richardson from falling into the same trap at his Courthouse and Jail (1.15): a highly personalized vision coupled with the artistic authority to carry it out.

8.2 SOUTH PARK AND OLIVER MILLER HOMESTEAD
(Park) 1927, with additions. (Homestead) Before 1808; c. 1830 addition.
PA 88 at Corrigan Dr.

The Oliver Miller Homestead on Stone Manse Drive in South Park is one of a trio of early and impressive stone houses still standing around

Holy Trinity Serbian Orthodox Church

Pittsburgh, joining the Woods House (3.8) and the Frew House (8.9). It is the best preserved of the three and the only one open to the public. Five generations of the family lived here from the eighteenth century through the 1920s, although the dates and ownership of the house are a matter of some conjecture. Oliver Miller had a log house here from c. 1780s, but it is uncertain whether he or his son, James, replaced that house with this stone construction. James did add the larger portion (c. 1830). Both sections are constructed of random rubble and are two stories in height.

The 2,000-acre park was established in 1927. About one-third of it is wooded, and the rest is greenspace and recreational areas. An 18-hole golf course is served by a clubhouse designed by Henry Hornbostel in 1938, when he was director of Allegheny County Parks from 1935 to 1939. The long rectangular structure's red brick walls are laid to create images of trees and golfers in relief designs. A stunning, concave corbeled arch that opens at the center of the building allows views across the landscape.

South Park and Oliver Miller Homestead

8.3 PETER BOYER HOUSE

c. 1840. 5679 Library Rd. (PA 88).

This unexpected survivor of the many Greek Revival mansions that once existed in and around Pittsburgh must always have been one of the more significant in architectural quality. The two-and-one-half-story frame house, with three tall dormer windows, has a two-story porch with piers at the ground level supporting Ionic columns on the second. It reminds us of a style that had enormous popularity in the region.

8.4 MISSION HILLS

1921–c. 1935. Bounded by Washington Rd. and Jefferson and Orchard drs.

Mission Hills is the most notable of the many tract developments of the interwar years. It is located in Mt. Lebanon, one of the chain of towns that forms the South Hills. Mission Hills was promoted by local realtor Lawrence Stevenson in 1921 on the model of its namesake, Jesse Clyde (also known as J. C.) Nichols's renowned subdivision in Kansas City. Stevenson put up 300 homes on three-acre lots in the variety of styles preferred at that time. The street plan did not replicate the regularity of Pittsburgh's street grid, and thus it avoided a flaw in many other South Hills developments. Medieval Revival styles predominate, but one can find anything from Louisiana plantations to California bungalows. Visual continuity is maintained by the gently curving streets, common setback frontage, common sourcing of building materials, and design linkages through the employment of a limited number of architects. The landscaping is particularly noteworthy, with houses sited on the hillside slopes. Marked by pillars and small parkways, the entrances from Washington Road give coherence and legibility to the street layout. The development is strictly a form of bedroom suburbia, but the tight town center of Mt.

Mission Hills

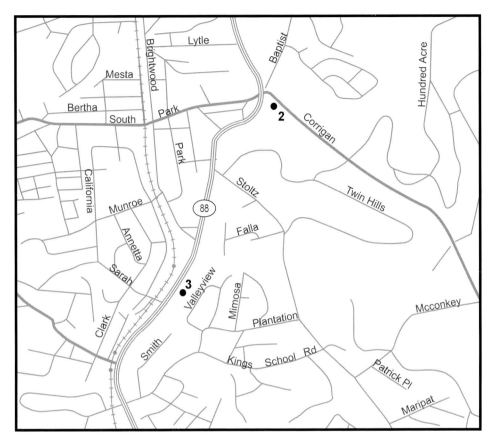

Early Settlers around South Park. Approximate driving time: one hour

Lebanon is only a few minutes away on foot. The trolley to Pittsburgh—renamed the "T"—functions better than ever.

8.5 ST. BERNARD'S CHURCH

1933–1947, William R. Perry for Comes, Perry and McMullen. 311 Washington Rd.

This Gothic Revival Catholic church is highly visible thanks to its bulk, the vigorous coloring of its materials, and its location on the high spine of the old Washington Pike. It is the latest, and best, of a trio of churches built along the former pike during the interwar years. The others are the rock-faced Gothic Revival Mt.

Lebanon United Methodist Church of 1923 by Charles Bier (at 3319 West Liberty Ave.) and the twin-towered Gothic Revival Mt. Lebanon United Presbyterian Church (255 Washington Ave.) designed by J. Lewis Beatty in 1929. Perry designed numerous churches and schools in western Pennsylvania and the Midwest. The most visible of Perry's local works today are this church and the former St. Philomena Church and School (now the Community Day School) of 1922 at 6424 Forward Avenue in Squirrel Hill.

St. Bernard's is constructed of coursed but rough-faced stones that range in color from gray to brown and red. Its interior is magnifi-

St. Bernard's Church

cent, thanks to Perry's first-hand knowledge of medieval architecture in southern France and Catalonia in northeastern Spain. Diaphragm arches in stone set up a rhythm along the wooden roof, and a ribbed dome covers the sanctuary. Especially impressive are the murals by Jan Henryk de Rosen that adorn the church and that include scenes from the New Testament and the life of St. Bernard. The church's capitals are by Frank Aretz, and the stained glass is by Alfred Fisher in the main church and by A. Leo Pitassi in the lower church.

8.6 WOODVILLE PLANTATION (JOHN AND PRESLEY NEVILLE HOUSE)
c. 1780; c. 1785. 1375 Washington Pike (PA 50 East) at Thomas Run Rd.

This National Historic Landmark at the edge of Chartiers Creek is a mecca for student field-trips, because it illustrates well the radically different way the region might have turned out had it not industrialized so soon after this house was built. When General John Neville built his log house (now the kitchen) on his 7,000-acre land grant, he registered the plantation as part of Virginia, since he refused to recognize Pennsylvania's claim to the region.

This plantation aspired to be Mount Vernon, especially as its living room, entrance hall, parlors, and bedrooms were added to the kitchen nucleus. This was to be expected, perhaps, for John Neville was a blood relative of Martha Washington and an intimate of her husband, George Washington. Many Virginians visited Woodville, and, in 1825, it was honored by a visit from the Marquis de LaFayette, a friend of John Neville's heir, Presley. Neville was one of the largest slave-holders in the area, but no slave structures survive. The house remained in the ownership of Neville's descendants until 1973, at which point the parlor wallpaper was sixteen layers deep.

8.7 ST. LUKE'S PROTESTANT EPISCOPAL CHURCH (OLD ST. LUKE'S)
1851–1852, attributed to John Notman.
330 Old Washington Pike at Church St.

This may be the earliest Episcopal church site west of the Allegheny Mountains, beginning with services in a log garrison in 1765. A wood-frame church was constructed in 1790 under the patronage of General John Neville and Major William Lea. This small, Gothic Revival stone structure is the second on the site. The church was attributed to Philadelphia's Notman by James Van Trump because of the church's archaicizing appearance and Notman's work on the Episcopal church of St. Peter (demolished) in Pittsburgh in 1852. Although the small wooden vestibule is a modern reconstruction, the church and the pioneer burial ground, with graves dating from the early 1800s, make an excellent reminder of Pittsburgh's pre-industrial era.

8.8 THORNBURG
1900–1909, Samuel Thornburg McClarren and others. Bounded by Baldwin Ave. and Hamilton Rd.

Frank Thornburg and his cousin, David, established this trolley suburb on some 200 acres of their ancestor's 400-acre estate. The houses range in style from Queen Anne to Colonial Revival, Shingle, Spanish Mission, and Arts and Crafts.

Woodville Plantation (John and Presley Neville House)

Thornburg

The latter two styles were introduced after Thornburg's visit to California in 1905. Another cousin, architect Samuel McClarren, designed most of the suburb's houses, including Frank Thornburg's Shingle style house at 1132 Lehigh Road in 1907. Other highlights are the Cobblestone House in Shingle style, with cobblestone garnish (c. 1905), at 1137 Cornell Avenue, and a Colonial Revival mansion, with a two-story Ionic portico (c. 1906, C. E. Willoughby), at 1080 Stanford Road.

8.9 JOHN FREW HOUSE
c. 1790; c. 1840. 105 Sterrett St.

John Frew's one-room deep, three-story stone farmhouse stands just within the northernmost border of Pittsburgh, contiguous with the trolley suburb of Crafton. The walls are set in random rubble, probably made from fieldstones that the Frews removed from their farmland. The rubble walls have large cut quoins at the corners. When a one-and-one-half story brick

extension was added later, the two structures were incorporated under a single roof.

The Frew House, the contemporary Woods house in Hazelwood (3.8), and the Miller homestead in South Park (8.2) are important reminders that Pittsburgh's basic urban function, after its earliest years as a military outpost, was to gather and sell the foodstuffs that poured in from thousands of pioneer farms such as this one.

John Frew House

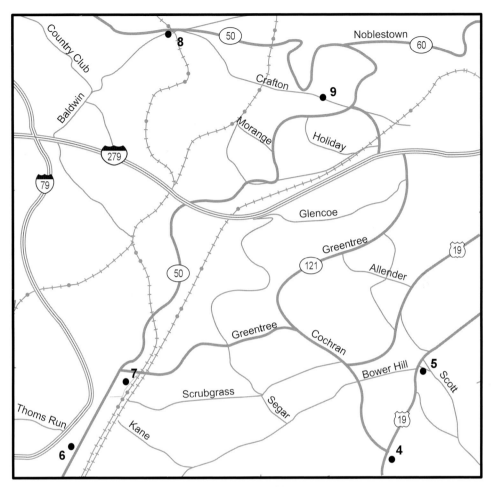

Mt. Lebanon and the Washington Pike. Approximate driving time: a half-day.

CHAPTER 9:
DAY TRIPS FROM PITTSBURGH

by Lu Donnelly

There are numerous day and weekend trips using Pittsburgh as the base. History is closer to the surface the farther one ventures from the city and nowhere more so than in the buildings in small towns and rural areas. Many of these will be part of the BUS series volume, *Buildings of Pennsylvania: Pittsburgh and Western Pennsylvania* (2009). Two highlights are presented here: an easy day trip to the north, to the Utopian settlements at Harmony and Economy, and a long day (or easy weekend) trip to the south, to Frank Lloyd Wright's masterful Fallingwater and Kentuck Knob, to historic Fort Necessity, where George Washington fought the French in 1754, and to other historic properties along and near the National Road (US 40).

TO THE NORTH: UTOPIAN SETTLEMENTS AT
HARMONY AND OLD ECONOMY (9.1)

This day trip via I-79 in Butler and Beaver counties, less than an hour from downtown Pittsburgh, reveals two sites that were built by the Harmonists, the millennial group that architectural historian Talbot Hamlin called "this successful if erratic celibate cult." The dozens of red-brick homes and institutional buildings are an extraordinarily rich combination of Germanic building techniques, the fashionable styles that the Harmonists absorbed upon landing in the United States in the earliest years of the nineteenth century, and influences from other communal societies such as the Shakers and Moravians.

The Harmonists followed George Rapp (1757–1847), a religious reformer and philosopher who preached that the church should be free from the state and adhere to the words of the *Holy Bible*. He believed the world would soon end, and only those who lived in accordance with God's word would attain salvation. But Rapp also believed that success in business and an appreciation for technological advances were pleasing to God. Thus, while the group lived separately from American society, speak-

Frederick Rapp House, 523 Main Street, Harmony

ing a German dialect and living chastely, they sought to be economically self-sufficient by building towns and industries that later had a nationwide impact. They excelled in textile manufacturing and adopted many new technologies in their efficient mills; later, they invested in oil and railroads.

The Harmonists first settled in southwestern Butler County in 1805 on 5,000 acres purchased the year before from another German émigré. Within five years, 2,000 acres of their village (named "Harmonie") were under cultivation, with 130 houses and outbuildings in place. Despite the Harmonists' industriousness, they could not overcome two obstacles: their lands were too small and too far from the Ohio River, and the soils were not amenable to the growing of grapes, a necessary component of their profitable wine-making.

Architectural highlights in Harmony include approximately twenty extant buildings with Harmonist origins. Frederick Reichert Rapp, who was the adopted stonemason son of George Rapp and the society's business manager, designed a number of buildings in Harmony and in the Harmonists' later towns in New Harmony, Indiana, and in Economy, Pennsylvania. The brick house Frederick Rapp designed for himself in 1811 at 523 Main Street is the most elaborate Harmonist house in town, with a fanlight over the entry and Flemish bond brickwork. The Harmony Museum at 218 Mercer Street, built in 1809 as a warehouse and granary, with a vaulted wine cellar, displays Harmonist history. Only one of the many barns built by the Harmonists in their three villages remains, at 303 Mercer Road. The Harmonist cemetery at 831 Edmond Street is perched on a rise at the southeast edge of town. Its unmarked graves reflect the Harmonist belief that all are equal in death. (For directions to, and information on, Harmony, call 888.821.4822 or go online at www.harmonymuseum.org.)

The Harmonists left Harmony and moved to western Indiana in 1815, staying until 1825. They returned to western Pennsylvania, creating a settlement they called Economy, this time on the banks of the Ohio River at what today is the town of Ambridge. To drive from Harmony to Ambridge, take PA 68 West through the town of Zelienople. This joins PA 989 South (Glen Eden Rd.) and PA 65 south, along the Ohio River. Going south, turn right at 14th Street, right onto Merchant Street, and left to the Old Economy Village Visitors Center on 16th Street. (The telephone number is 724.266.4500; the Website is www.oldeconomyvillage.org.)

Both of the Harmonist towns in Pennsylvania were laid out in grids, with houses fronting directly on the streets. The log houses (and, later, the brick homes) had side entrances from their gardens and were generally two stories, with two rooms and a hall per floor. Celibate men and women were assigned to quasi-family units while they lived in the small houses.

The most informative building in Economy is the Feast Hall of 1826, a large red brick gambrel-roofed building with a clipped gable end, which contains a large spiritual meeting place above and a museum below. St. John's Lutheran Church (1828–1831) has a square brick bell tower with an octagonal cupola containing a one-handed clock that chimes at fifteen-minute intervals, marking the schedule for the Harmonists as they worked throughout the village. The homes of George and Frederick Rapp were built across the street and act as a parlor for all of Economy. The houses mix elements of Colonial (portico) and Federal forms (fanlight) with a German-vernacular jerkin head roofline to impress and remind visitors of the group's German roots.

The Granary (1824) is a simple, gable-roofed frame barn with half-timbering and ventilation for the storage of a year's worth of grain. The Garden (1824) contains a pavilion and a rustic hut, with a

Doorway to Feast Hall in Old Economy

Greek Revival interior dedicated to the memories of George and Frederick Rapp. The Harmony Society grew rich (at one point, it was the largest shareholder of the New York Central Railroad) but declined in numbers after the 1820s. It was disbanded in 1910, and its assets were taken over by the Commonwealth of Pennsylvania.

From Ambridge it is an easy and dramatic drive of about forty-five minutes back to Pittsburgh on PA 65 South, following the Ohio River.

A day trip to Frank Lloyd Wright's Fallingwater and Kentuck Knob should always begin with reservations (724.329.8501 or www.paconserve.org for the former; 724.329.1901 or www.kentuckknob.com for the latter). Both are located about seventy miles southeast of downtown Pittsburgh, with a driving time of at least an hour and a half.

Fallingwater is considered the most important American house since Thomas Jefferson's Monticello (near Charlottesville, Virginia) and one of the most important buildings of the twentieth century. It represents the dramatic synthesis of a remote natural site, an innovative design, and the dynamic relationship between Edgar J. Kaufmann, Sr., and Frank Lloyd Wright. Built between 1936 and 1939 as a weekend retreat for the department store owner, his wife, Liliane, and their son, Edgar, Jr., the house reflects the family's sophisticated taste and sensibility. Frank Lloyd Wright cantilevered it over Bear Run's waterfall on a tract of wooded mountain land formerly used as the Kaufmann Department Store's employee summer camp. He mimicked the local layered rock strata by using quarried sandstone defined by smooth concrete cantilevers, with openings of plate glass and steel. A boulder near the waterfall was incorporated into the basement walls of the house, creating a rugged hearth for the living room fireplace.

The house and surrounding land were donated to the Western Pennsylvania Conservancy by Edgar Kaufmann, Jr., in 1963, and the Conservancy commissioned industrial designer Paul Mayen (working with architects Curry, Martin and Highberger) to design a visitor's center of concrete, cedar, and glass that relates to the house but does not conflict with it. The visitor center's trio of ecologically mindful pavilions houses a restaurant, museum shop, and permanent exhibition space.

Fallingwater

Near the entrance to Fallingwater, on the east side of PA 381 are two older barns that the Western Pennsylvania Conservancy commissioned Bohlin Cywinski Jackson to adapt as offices and a community center. The re-use was given a Green Design Citation and awarded the American Institute of Architects (AIA) of Pittsburgh's 2005 Silver Medal as an extraordinary work of architecture.

After visiting Fallingwater, follow PA 381 South to Kentuck Road, turn right, and watch for Kentuck Knob on the left. The former I. N. Hagan house, called Kentuck Knob for the geological site on which it sits, is one of a handful of customized houses that Frank Lloyd Wright designed in the 1950s that were variants on his modular Usonian prototypes from the 1930s. Here, between 1953 and 1956, Wright, by then eighty-seven years old, used his familiar design based on an equilateral triangle. The chevron-shaped house curls around a west-facing courtyard, blending comfortably into the contours of the land. The anchor of the design is a hexagonal core of native stone that rises from the long, low profile of the copper roof at the intersection of the living room and bedroom wings. The cantilevered cypress eaves have hexagonal openings that allow the low rays of the winter sun to penetrate the interior, while blocking the higher angle of the summer sun. Wright crafted the interior finishes and built-in furniture with red cypress from Virginia's Tidewater region. Bring a picnic lunch and eat it on the grounds among over three

Kentuck Knob

dozen modern sculptures collected by the present owners Lord Peter and Lady Palumbo. They purchased the house and 79 forested acres from the Hagans in 1985 and opened it to the public in 1996.

If you have time after your visit to Kentuck Knob, return to PA 381 and turn right (south) to the intersection with US 40, which is the old National Road. The National Road is the nation's first federally funded and planned roadway that began, in 1806, in Cumberland, Maryland, before reaching Wheeling, West Virginia, and the Ohio River by 1821. From Wheeling, the National Road was extended west, helping to open up settlement and commerce in Ohio, Indiana, and Illinois. The road reached the Mississippi River in 1851 at two locations in Illinois: Alton and East St. Louis. Today, the road is part of a major restoration effort of both the highway and its associated buildings and towns.

When taken west from its intersection with PA 381, the National Road (US 40) will lead you to several other tour opportunities that can extend your visit overnight. Fort Necessity, the first public site you encounter, is a reconstruction of the wooden palisade that sheltered George Washington before his defeat in July 1754 by the French. The Fort Necessity site is operated by the National Park Service and includes a visitor's center. Adjacent to the fort is the Mount Washington Tavern of 1827–1828. While built well after Washington's time here, the handsome brick tavern and inn is emblematic of much of the architecture seen along the road throughout the early nineteenth century. This inn was managed by a woman in the 1840s, when operating an inn was one of the few respectable and profitable occupations afforded women at the time. General Braddock's grave is nearby and is clearly marked. (For more information on the National Road, go to http://www.nps.gov/fone/natlroad.htm; on Fort Necessity and the Mount Washington Tavern, go to http://www.nps.gov/archive/fone/mwt.htm.)

If time allows, take US 40 Business (not the bypass US 40) and drive through the small village of Hopwood, where you will pass six two-story sandstone inns/residences dating from 1816 to 1839. As late as 1882, Hopwood had seven inns, and three remain on the south side of US 40 Business: the former Morris Tavern (1818), now the volunteer fire station (National Pike at Paul Street); the former Monroe Tavern (c. 1825, 1208 National Pike); and the former Moses Hopwood Tavern (c. 1816, 1182 National Pike), now Chez Gerard Restaurant. The Benjamin Hayden House (c. 1820, 1225 National Pike), on the north side of the road, is now Dean's Barber Shop, and two other 1823 stone houses in the same block (at 1223 and 1213 National Pike) complete the ensemble. Nowhere else along the National Road in Pennsylvania is there such an authentic collection of stone inns that graphically illustrate what a piketown looked like in the early nineteenth century.

Reconstruction of Fort Necessity

Entering Uniontown, you will pass the Fayette County Courthouse (1890–1892), at 61 East Main St., looking like Pittsburgh's Allegheny County Courthouse and Jail (1.15) by H. H. Richardson, but designed three years later by William Kauffman (no relation to the department store magnate) and his business partner, Edward Butz. At 27 East Main Street (US 40) Thomas Lamb designed a vaudeville theater for Uniontown in 1922, now called the State Theatre Center for the Arts. It has been rehabilitated and is a live performance site for the town. At 50 West Main Street Daniel Burnham designed a twelve-story limestone bank building in 1901–1902 for J. V. Thompson, the colorful king of the coal land barons, who overextended himself and lost his fortune. Thompson built two banks at the corner of East Main and Morgantown streets, on the left the gold-domed bank of 1900 called the Thompson-Ruby building accommodated the firm's offices until the larger Burnham-designed building was complete. Turn left onto

Morgantown Street and at 79 West Fayette Street Trinity United Presbyterian Church (1894–1895, William Kauffman) echoes Richardson's Romanesque Trinity Church in Boston. It has a group of Tiffany Studio windows lighting the auditorium style sanctuary. Follow Morgantown Street to Judith Street and turn left.

At the northeast corner of Judith and Union streets stands a tiny modern house designed by

Mount Washington Tavern, c. 1920, on the old National Road

Richard Neutra in 1959 for a pharmaceutical wholesaler and his wife. It is privately owned and not open to the public. This is the only Neutra house in western Pennsylvania. Using walls of different heights and textures, the house is arranged as two rectangles adjacent, but not plumb. A reddish-brown-stained board-and-batten wall with a short curve at its end extends slightly beyond the garage and gently propels the visitor to the entry, where another solid plane, rendered in golden sandstone, separates public welcome from private entrance by shielding the long bedroom wing.

For more information about Uniontown, go to http://www.uniontownonline.com and http://www.nationalroadpa.org. The return to downtown Pittsburgh is best accomplished by following Morgantown Street (PA 51) north out of Uniontown. Follow it all the way to the Liberty Tunnel, heading into downtown.

Academic Revival An ambiguous term referring to various historicist styles taught at and promoted by architecture schools and flourishing in the United States from the late nineteenth through the early twentieth centuries. These include classical and medieval revivals, as well as English and Spanish Colonial revivals.

American Renaissance The period in art and architecture from the U.S. centennial in 1876 to World War I that was marked by national self-confidence and international power. In a more social general sense this period is often referred to as the Gilded Age and can be understood as a cultural manifestation of the Progressive movement. Large-scale building projects featuring architecture, painting, and sculpture as an integrated whole are characteristic of the American Renaissance, which is also related to Beaux-Arts Classicism in the United States.

Art Deco A style inspired by the 1925 Exposition Internationale des Arts Décoratifs et Industriels Moderne, held in Paris. It is characterized by faceted forms and patterns and flattened decorative fields, rich materials (including polished metal and exotic wood), and an overall sleekness of design. It was used frequently in commercial and residential architecture during the late 1920s and early 1930s.

Art Nouveau A style that originated in Belgium and France in the 1890s and flourished briefly across Europe and the United States. It is characterized by undulating and whiplash lines and sensuous curvilinear forms inspired by the natural world and some non-Western sources.

Arts and Crafts A late-nineteenth-and early-twentieth-century movement that emerged in England and spread to the United States. Inspired by William Morris and initially a reaction to industrialization, it emphasized the importance of hand crafting and beauty in everyday objects and environments. Its works are characterized by simplified forms and construction and the straightforward use of materials.

Baroque A style of art and architecture that flourished in Europe and its colonies during the seventeenth and eighteenth centuries. Based on the classically derived architecture of the Renaissance, but more dynamic and dramatic, Baroque architecture favored ovals and trapezoids, curved and undulating walls, and complex, interlocking forms. It was a monumental and richly ornamental style.

Bauhaus (1) Work in any of the visual arts by the faculty and students of the Bauhaus, the innovative design school founded by Walter Gropius (1883–1969) and an active force in German Modernism from 1919 until 1933. (2) Work in any of the visual arts by the former faculty and students of the Bauhaus or by individuals influenced by them. In architecture, the term International Style is more generally used.

Beaux-Arts A historicist design on a monumental scale that was taught at the Ecole des Beaux-Arts in Paris and disseminated internationally throughout the nineteenth century and early twentieth century. The term is generally applied to an eclectic classicism of the 1850s through the 1920s. Beaux-Arts does not connote a single style, but rather an architecture derived from a variety of historical sources, especially Roman, Renaissance, and Baroque. It also connotes the disciplined development of a parti into a fully visualized design.

Brutalism (see **New Brutalism**)

Byzantine A term applied to the art and architecture of the Eastern Roman Empire centered on Byzantium (later Constantinople and then Istanbul) from the sixth to the fifteenth centuries. It is characterized by domes, round arches, and richly carved capitals and mosaics.

Chicago School A diverse group of architects associated with the development of the tall (i.e., six- to twenty-story) commercial building in Chicago during the 1880s and 1890s. The work of this group is characterized by its use of new engineering methods (metal frame construction and floating foundations) and robust architectural forms. William Le Baron Jenney and the firms of Burnham and Root and Adler and Sullivan are identified with this group.

City Beautiful A movement in architecture, landscape architecture, and planning in the United States from the 1890s through the 1920s, advocating the beautification of cities, emulating the world's fairs, and employing a monumental Beaux-Arts classical style. City Beautiful schemes emphasized civic centers, boulevards, and waterfront improvements, and sometimes they included comprehensive metropolitan plans for parks, infrastructure, and transportation.

Colonial Revival Generally understood to mean the revival of forms from British colonial design, the Colonial Revival began in New England in the 1860s, flourished after the U.S. Centennial in 1876, and continues nationwide into the present, especially in residential design. Typical elements include classically derived pediments, cornices, and dormers.

Federal A version of neoclassical architecture in the United States that was popular from New England to Virginia and in other regions influenced by the Northeast. The name refers to the establishment of the federal government in 1789. It flourished from the 1790s through the 1820s. It is sometimes called the American Adam style.

Gothic An architectural style prevalent in Europe during the Middle Ages (from the twelfth century into the fifteenth in Italy and into the sixteenth century in the rest of Europe) and best embodied by cathedrals. It is characterized by pointed arches and ribbed vaults and by the dominance of openings over masonry mass in the wall. Gothic was preceded by the Romanesque and followed by the Renaissance.

Gothic Revival A movement in Europe and North America devoted to reviving the forms and the spirit of Gothic architecture and the allied arts. It originated in the mid-eighteenth century and flourished during the nineteenth century. For some building types, notably churches, it was used frequently into the twentieth century.

Greek Revival A movement in Europe and North America devoted to reviving the forms and spirit of classical Greek architecture, sculpture, and decorative arts. It originated in the mid-eighteenth century, culminated in the 1830s, and continued into the 1850s. Its most recognizable architectural feature is the pedimented temple front. It is sometimes viewed as the first popular style in the United States, where it was used frequently for public buildings and private residences.

Green Architecture, Green Building A term originating in the late twentieth century that designates ecologically conscious architectural design. Green buildings are characterized by their energy efficiency, use of sustainable materials, and minimal environmental impact. The term generally refers to building technologies and mechanical systems rather than a form or style.

Guastavino vaults A system of tile construction developed by Spanish engineer Rafael Guastavino and used extensively in the United States in the late nineteenth and early twentieth centuries. Based on traditional Catalan techniques, these vaults use standardized tiles and Portland cement laid in a herringbone pattern in three to four staggered layers. They are extremely strong, lightweight and can be built without scaffolding.

International Style A style that originated in Europe in the 1920s and flourished across the globe into the 1970s, it is characterized by the expression of volume and surface, the suppression of historicist ornament, and the avoidance of axial symmetry and features the prominent use of such twentieth-century building materials as steel, reinforced concrete, and plate glass. Le Corbusier was a pioneer of the style, but the term was originally applied by Henry-Russell Hitchcock and Philip Johnson to the new, non-traditional, mostly European, architecture of the 1920s in their 1932 exhibition at the Museum of Modern Art in New York City and in their accompanying book, The International Style. (See, also, Bauhaus.)

Italian Renaissance The period in Western civilization identified with a rediscovery or rebirth (*rinascimento*) of classical Roman learning, art, and architecture. Renaissance architecture began in Italy in the mid-1400s (Early Renaissance) and reached a peak in the early to mid-1500s (High Renaissance). The Renaissance in art and architecture was preceded by the Gothic and followed by the Baroque.

Italianate An eclectic revival style derived from Italian Romanesque and Renaissance architecture, originating in England and Germany in the early nineteenth century and prevalent in the United States between the 1840s and 1880s not only in houses, but also in Main Street commercial buildings. It is characterized by prominent window heads (inverted u-shaped or pedimented), overhanging eaves, and bracketed cornices.

milltown An incorporated community, generally larger than a village, in which the focus of economic and social life is a "mill," generally a textile factory but often a steel plant in western Pennsylvania.

Modernism, modernist A movement in the visual arts, culture, and world history generally that dominated much of the twentieth century in Europe and North America. With roots in the Enlightenment and Industrial Revolution and linked with the forces of social modernity, Modernism deliberately broke from the traditional and emphasized innovation and progress. In the visual arts, this meant rejecting classicism and historicism and seeking inspiration in the forms and ideas of the present. While diverse styles were associated with Modernism in architecture from the late nineteenth century onward, the International Style was dominant after the 1920s.

Neoclassicism, neoclassical A broad movement in the visual arts that drew its inspiration from ancient Greece and Rome. It began in the mid-eighteenth century, with the advent of archaeology, and extended into the mid-nineteenth century. In architecture, it encompasses both a strict revivalism that copied classical models and motifs as well as more inventive interpretations.

New Brutalism, Brutalism An architectural style of the 1950s through 1970s, characterized by complex massing and a frank expression of structural members, building systems, and, especially, building materials. Shutter-marked concrete is the dominant material of New Brutalism, which is an extension of Modernism. As a term, it is sometimes applied to the work of Louis Kahn, Paul Rudolph, and the later work of Le Corbusier.

parti A basic solution or elemental concept for the arrangement of spaces or forms prior to the development and elaboration of a design.

piketown An incorporated community, generally larger than a village, whose distinguishing feature is its location on a "pike" or major roadway.

Postmodernism, postmodern, postmodernist A term applied to architecture that involves a reaction against the ideas and works of various twentieth-century modern movements, particularly the Bauhaus and International Style. Beginning in the 1960s and flourishing in the 1980s, postmodern architecture uses historicist and populist elements, but these are often merely applied to buildings that, in every other respect, are products of Modernism.

Queen Anne This term generally refers to an eclectic architectural style of the 1860s through 1910s in England and the United States that revived forms of postmedieval vernacular architecture and the architecture of the Georgian period (1714–1830), including those popular during the reign of Queen Anne (1702–1714). It is characterized by asymmetry in plan, complex roof forms, projecting bays and oriels, the use of red brick, and classical motifs such as broken pediments and pilasters.

Renaissance Revival A term that refers either to Italianate architecture of the 1840s through 1880s or to Beaux-Arts architecture of the 1880s through 1920s. In the decorative arts, it refers to an eclectic furniture style incorporating Renaissance, Baroque, and Néo-Grec architectural motifs and utilizing wood marquetry, incised lines (often gilded), and ormolu and porcelain ornaments.

Richardsonian Romanesque A style of architecture of the late nineteenth century that shows the influence of Henry Hobson Richardson (1838–1886). It is characterized by the eclectic use of round arches, rustication, and Romanesque details, and frequently it features prominent masonry and asymmetrical compositions. The style was especially popular for public buildings such as courthouses and libraries.

Rococo A decorative style associated primarily with interiors that emerged in France in the early eighteenth century as a reaction to the Baroque. It is marked by elegant, curvilinear ornament, a light scale, and delicate colors; its use of classical forms is relatively diffuse.

Romanesque Revival A term that refers either to the architecture that appeared in the United States as early as the 1840s that revived the forms of Romanesque architecture of the eleventh and twelfth centuries in Europe or to the forms of Richardsonian architecture that appeared after the 1870s. In either case, it is characterized by massive masonry and repeated arches whose undersides are a full semi-circle.

Second Empire Not strictly a style but a term for a period in French history that coincides with the rule of Napoleon III (1852–1870). Derived from Visconti and Lefuel's New Louvre in Paris, the Second Empire Style is characterized by mansard roofs, pedimented dormers, classical columns, and French Renaissance decorative motifs. In the United States, it was used frequently from the 1850s through the 1880s for a variety of building types and especially in governmental and institutional architecture.

Shingle Style A term applied to American domestic architecture of the 1870s through the 1890s, in which wood shingles dominate the roof and exterior wall planes. Rooms open widely into one another and to the outdoors, and the ample living hall or stair hall is often the dominant feature of the interior. The term was coined in the 1940s by architectural historian Vincent Scully for a series of seaside and suburban houses of the northeastern United States. The Shingle Style is a version of the Queen Anne Style and was used in the early work of Henry Hobson Richardson and the firm McKim, Mead and White.

Spanish Colonial Revival The revival of forms from Spanish colonial and provincial Mexican design; more specifically, to the architecture of Mexico as derived from the Spanish Baroque of the seventeenth and eighteenth centuries. It began in Florida and California in the 1880s and continues nationwide into the present. Spanish Colonial is characterized by stucco on brick walls, low roof lines covered with reddish tile, and often ornate, low-relief carvings on doors and windows in a style popularized by the Churriguera family of architects in Spain c. 1700.

Spanish Mission Revival A specific form of the Spanish Colonial Revival, this style originated in the 1890s and was popular in residential and institutional buildings. It makes use of forms and materials derived from Spanish mission architecture of the eighteenth and early nineteenth centuries in the southwestern United States and Mexico. The Spanish Mission Revival features unadorned, plaster-covered walls, clay roof tiles, and covered arcades.

Tudor Revival This term is applied to eclectic works or elements of those works that emu-late forms in the visual arts of the Tudor period (1485–1603) in English history. It was especially popular in houses and is characterized by steeply pitched gabled roofs, decorative half-timbering, and tall, narrow windows. It is sometimes called the Elizabethan Manor Style and Neo-Tudor Style.

Urban renewal This term refers to the efforts in the 1950s and 1960s to combat the decline of American cities caused by suburban expansion after World War II. Underwritten by the federal government and sponsored by local municipalities, these efforts physically transformed urban centers through the destruction of dense, older commercial and residential districts. Typical urban renewal projects included the construction of new highways, public housing, downtown parking lots, and cultural or government centers. Based loosely on modernist planning ideas, these projects were usually separated from the existing urban fabric and included widely spaced buildings and open plazas. By the 1970s, urban renewal was widely considered a failure.

Usonian A term originated by Frank Lloyd Wright to refer to the modest and relatively affordable houses he designed for middle-class clients beginning in the 1930s. Smaller than his prairie houses, the Usonians were generally single story, built slab-on-grade, with brick piers and natural wood siding. They featured car ports, cantilevered overhangs, clerestory windows, and an extensive use of built-ins.

Venetian Renaissance The period in the history of Venice when the rediscovery of classical Roman learning, art, and architecture that had earlier swept through the rest of the Italian peninsula finally reached the city state on the Adriatic Sea. This period reached its artistic peak in the middle of the sixteenth century as exemplified in the work of architects Andrea Palladio and Jacobo Sansovino and the painters Titian and Veronese.

Victorian A term for a period in British,

British colonial, and Anglo-American history, from the coronation of Queen Victoria in 1837 to her death in 1901. Though not a specific style, Victorian connotes the various forms of eclecticism that were predominant in architecture in the mid- to late-nineteenth century. These include Greek Revival, Gothic Revival, High Victorian Gothic, Queen Anne, and others.

voussoir A wedge-shaped masonry unit used in the construction of an arch. Its tapered sides coincide with the radii of the arch.

SUGGESTED FILMS AND READINGS

FILMS

As of June 2007, at least sixty movies have been filmed in Pittsburgh. The following are among the more noteworthy and entertaining:

Perils of Pauline (1914)
Angels in the Outfield (1951)
Night of the Living Dead (1968)
The Deer Hunter (1978)
Flashdance (1982)
Mrs. Soffel (1984)
Dominick and Eugene (1988)
The Silence of the Lambs (1990)
Hoffa (1992)
Desperate Measures (1996)
Inspector Gadget (1998)
Wonder Boys (1999)
The War That Made America (2004)
The Mysteries of Pittsburgh (2006)

For a more extensive list, see:
www.pghfilm.org

READINGS

The books and articles listed below are key readings to understanding Pittsburgh's history, geography, and architecture. Among other important but unpublished sources are the Allegheny County Survey at the Pittsburgh History and Landmarks Foundation and the ephemera (clippings, atlases, and photographs) at Carnegie Library and the Senator John Heinz Pittsburgh Regional History Center.

Alberts, Robert C. *The Shaping of the Point: Pittsburgh's Renaissance Park*. Pittsburgh: University of Pittsburgh Press, 1981.

Aurand, Martin. *The Progressive Architecture of Frederick G. Scheibler, Jr.* Pittsburgh: University of Pittsburgh Press, 1994.

―――. *The Spectator and the Topographical City*. Pittsburgh: University of Pittsburgh Press, 2006.

Baldwin, Leland. *Pittsburgh: The Story of a City*. Pittsburgh: University of Pittsburgh Press, 1970.

Barnett, Jonathan. "Designing Downtown Pittsburgh." *Architectural Record* 170:1 (January 1982): 90–107.

Bauman, John F. and Edward K. Muller. *Before Renaissance: Planning in Pittsburgh, 1889–1943*. Pittsburgh: University of Pittsburgh Press, in association with the Center for American Places, 2006.

Bolden, Frank E., Larry Glasco, and Eliza Smith, eds. *A Legacy in Bricks and Mortar: African American Landmarks in Allegheny County*. Pittsburgh: Pittsburgh History and Landmarks Foundation, 1995.

Borowiec, Andrew. *Along the Ohio*. Baltimore: The Johns Hopkins University Press, in association with the Center for American Places, 2000.

Brignano, Mary. *The Power of Pittsburgh*. Pittsburgh: Duquesne Light Company, 1996.

Brown, Mark M., Lu Donnelly, and David G. Wilkins. *The History of the Duquesne Club*. Pittsburgh: Duquesne Club, 1989.

Carnegie, Andrew. *The Autobiography of Andrew Carnegie*. New York: Houghton Mifflin, 1920.

Couvares, Francis G. *The Remaking of Pittsburgh: Class and Culture in an Industrializing City, 1877-1919*. Albany: State University of New York Press, 1984.

Davenport, Marcia. *The Valley of Decision*. New York: C. Scribner, 1942.

Demarest, David and Eugene Levy. "A Relict Industrial Landscape: Pittsburgh's Coke Region." *Landscape* 29:2 (1986): 29-36.

———. "Remnants of an Industrial Landscape." *Pittsburgh History* 72 (1989): 128-39.

———. "Touring the Coke Region." *Pittsburgh History* 74 (1991): 100-13.

Dennis, Neal. *Historic Houses of the Sewickley Valley*. Sewickley, PA: White Oak Publishing, 1996.

Fifield, Barringer. *Seeing Pittsburgh*. Pittsburgh: University of Pittsburgh Press, 1996.

Floyd, Margaret Henderson. *Architecture after Richardson: Regionalism before Modernism—Longfellow, Alden, and Harlow in Boston and Pittsburgh*. Chicago: University of Chicago Press, in association with the Pittsburgh History and Landmarks Foundation, 1994.

Gay, Vernon and Marilyn Evert. *Discovering Pittsburgh's Sculpture*. Pittsburgh: University of Pittsburgh Press, 1983.

Greenwald, Maurine W. and Margo Anderson, eds. *Pittsburgh Surveyed: Social Science and Social Reform in the Early Twentieth Century*. Pittsburgh: University of Pittsburgh Press, 1996.

Hays, Samuel P., ed. *City at the Point: Essays on the Social History of Pittsburgh*. Pittsburgh: University of Pittsburgh Press, 1989.

Jacques, Charles J., Jr. *Kennywood: Roller Coaster Capital of the World*. Natrona Heights, PA: Amusement Park Journal, 1982.

Jucha, Robert. "The Anatomy of a Streetcar Suburb: A Development History of Shadyside." *Western Pennsylvania Historical Magazine* 62 (1979): 301-19.

Kidney, Walter C. *Allegheny Cemetery: A Romantic Landscape in Pittsburgh*. Pittsburgh: Pittsburgh History and Landmarks Foundation, 1990.

———. *Henry Hornbostel: An Architect's Master Touch*. Pittsburgh: Pittsburgh History and Landmarks Foundation, in association with Robert Rinehart Publishers, 2002.

———. *Oakland*. Charleston, S.C.: Arcadia, in association with Pittsburgh History and Landmarks Foundation and the Carnegie Library of Pittsburgh, 2005.

———. *Pittsburgh's Landmark Architecture: The Historic Buildings of Pittsburgh and Allegheny County*. 2nd. edition. Pittsburgh: Pittsburgh History and Landmarks Foundation, 2001.

Lubove, Roy. *Twentieth-Century Pittsburgh*. 2 vols. Pittsburgh: University of Pittsburgh Press, 1996.

Miller, Donald. *The Architecture of Benno Janssen.* Pittsburgh: Carnegie Mellon University, 1997.

———— and Aaron Sheon. *Organic Vision: The Architecture of Peter Berndtson.* Pittsburgh: Hexagon Press, 1980.

Oberlin, Loriann H., Evan M. Pattak, and Jenn Phillips. *Insider's Guide to Pittsburgh.* Guilford, CT: The Globe Pequot Press, 2005.

Raitz, Karl, ed. *A Guide to the National Road.* Baltimore: The Johns Hopkins University Press, in association with the Center for American Places, 1996.

————. *The National Road.* Baltimore: The Johns Hopkins University Press, in association with the Center for American Places, 1996.

Regan, Bob and Tim Fabian. *The Bridges of Pittsburgh.* Pittsburgh: Local History Company, 2006.

Rinehart, Mary Roberts. *Best Mysteries of Mary Roberts Rinehart: Four Complete Novels by America's First Lady of Mystery.* Pleasantville NY: Reader's Digest, 2002.

Rivers of Steel National Heritage Area. Routes to Roots: A Driving Guide. Pittsburgh: Steel Industry Heritage Corporation, 2004.

Schuyler, Montgomery. "The Building of Pittsburgh." *Architectural Record* 30 (August 1911): 205-14.

Stotz, Charles M. *The Architectural Heritage of Early Western Pennsylvania.* Pittsburgh: University of Pittsburgh Press, 1936. Rev. ed. with new introduction, 1995.

————. *Outposts of the War for Empire: The French and English in Western Pennsylvania: Their Armies, Their Forts, Their People: 1749-1764.* Pittsburgh: University of Pittsburgh Press, 2005.

Swauger, James L. "Archaeological Salvage at the Site of Forts Pitt and Duquesne, Pittsburgh, Pennsylvania: 1940 through 1965." In *The Scope of Historical Archaeology: Essays in Honor of John L. Cotter,* edited by David G. Orr and Daniel G. Crozier. Philadelphia: Laboratory of Anthropology, Temple University, 1984.

Tannler, Albert M. "Architecture with a Dash of Paprika: Titus de Bobula in Pittsburgh," *Pittsburgh Tribune-Review, Focus* 28:11 (January 19, 2003), 8-11.

————. "The Joseph Urban Room." *Pittsburgh History and Landmarks Foundation News* 146 (June 1997): 8-9.

————. *A List of Pittsburgh and Allegheny County Buildings and Architects: 1950-2005.* Pittsburgh: Pittsburgh History and Landmarks Foundation, 2005.

————. "Louis Arnett Stuart Bellinger (1891-1946)." In *African American Architects: A Biographical Dictionary 1865-1945,* edited by Dreck S. Wilson. New York: Routledge, 2004.

————. "Quentin S. Beck: A Man Ahead of His Time," *Pittsburgh Tribune-Review, Focus* 21:48 (October 5, 1997): 6-7.

————. "Renaissance Man: Grosvenor Atterbury." *Pittsburgh Tribune-Review, Focus* 29:23 (April 11, 2004): 8-11.

————. "Richard Kiehnel: Architect of International Modernism and Tropical Splendor." *Pittsburgh Tribune-Review Focus* 21:30 (June 9, 1996): 6-7.

————. "Samuel Thornburg McClarren: A Player of Architectural Themes and Variations," *Pittsburgh Tribune-Review, Focus* 22:12 (January 25, 1998): 8-9.

————. "Swan Acres: First Modern Subdivision," *Pittsburgh Tribune-Review, Focus* 21:30 (June 1, 1997): 8-9.

————. "Temple of the Skies: Observatory Hill Renaissance of Art and Science," *Pittsburgh Tribune-Review, Focus* 30:15 (February 13, 2005): 8-10.

Tarr, Joel, ed. *Devastation and Renewal: An Environmental History of Pittsburgh and its Region.* Pittsburgh: University of Pittsburgh Press, 2005.

Teaford, Jon C. *The Rough Road to Renaissance: Urban Revitalization in America, 1940–1985.* Baltimore: The Johns Hopkins University Press, in association with the Center for American Places, 1990.

Toker, Franklin. *Fallingwater Rising: Frank Lloyd Wright, E. J. Kaufmann and America's Most Extraordinary House.* New York: Knopf, 2003.

————. "In the Grand Manner: The P&LE Station in Pittsburgh." *Carnegie Magazine* 53:3 (March 1979): 4–21.

————. *Pittsburgh: An Urban Portrait.* University Park, PA: Pennsylvania State University Press, 1986.

————. "Reversing an Urban Image: New Architecture in Pittsburgh, 1890–1980." In *Pittsburgh-Sheffield Sister Cities: Proceedings of the Pittsburgh-Sheffield Symposium on Industrial Cities,* 1981, edited by Joel A. Tarr. Pittsburgh: Carnegie Mellon University, 1986.

————. "Richardson *en concours*: the Pittsburgh Courthouse." *Carnegie Magazine* 51:9 (November 1977): 13–29.

Van Slyck, Abigail A. *Free to All: Carnegie Libraries & American Culture: 1890–1920.* Chicago: University of Chicago Press, 1995.

Van Trump, James D. *An American Palace of Culture: The Carnegie Institute and Carnegie Library of Pittsburgh.* Pittsburgh: Carnegie Institute, 1970.

————. *Life and Architecture in Pittsburgh.* Pittsburgh: Pittsburgh History and Landmarks Foundation, 1983.

————. *Majesty of the Law: The Courthouses of Allegheny County.* Pittsburgh: Pittsburgh History and Landmarks Foundation, 1988.

———— and Arthur P. Ziegler, Jr. *Landmark Architecture of Allegheny County Pennsylvania,* 1967.

ILLUSTRATION CREDITS

All photographs are by the author, except as noted below, and all contemporary maps were prepared by Ken Steif and Mark Mattson for the Society of Architectural Historians. No illustration may be reproduced without permission.

ii Jim Judkis

xii Jim Judkis

2 Historic Urban Plans

6 Historic Urban Plans

8 University of Pittsburgh Archives

9 University of Pittsburgh Archives (Norman Schumm, photographer)

14 Maurice Tierney

15 Left: Fifth Avenue Place
Right: Tulane University, Curtis & Davis Papers

16 PPG Place

17 Right: Dollar Savings Bank

19 PHLF (Pittsburgh History and Landmarks Foundation)

21 Left: Astorino (Ed Massery, photographer)
Right: Oxford Centre

22 City of Pittsburgh
(Mike Rizzo, photographer)

23 Allegheny County Department of Public Works

26 Mellon Financial Services
(Jeff Comella, photographer)

27 Left: Mellon Financial Services (Jeff Comella, photographer)
Right: Macy's Department Store

28 HABS/HAER (Historic American Buildings Survey/Historic American Engineering Survey), Library of Congress
(Nicholas Traub, photographer)

31 Left: PNC Financial Services Group
Right: Dominion Gas
(Clyde Hare, photographer)

34 Left: Dominion Gas
(Clyde Hare, photographer)
Right: HABS/HAER, Library of Congress
(Nicholas Traub, photographer)

35 HABS/HAER, Library of Congress
(Nicholas Traub, photographer)

36 Pennsylvania Apartments

37 USX Corporation

38 HABS/HAER, Library of Congress
(Nicholas Traub, photographer)

40 Carnegie Mellon University

53 Carnegie Museums of Pittsburgh

55 Carnegie Mellon University

59 Maurice Tierney

61 Union Switch & Signal Systems and The Design Alliance (Ed Massery, photographer)

62 PHLF

66 PHLF

67 PHLF

69 University of Pittsburgh, Department of the History of Art and Architecture

70 Angel's Arms Condominiums (Gregory Shearer, photographer)

71 HABS/HAER, Library of Congress (Nicholas Traub, photographer)

77 Carnegie Library of Braddock

78 HABS/HAER, Library of Congress (Joseph Elliott, photographer)

86 Carnegie Museums of Pittsburgh

87 Carnegie Museums of Pittsburgh

91 Community College of Allegheny County

97 The Mattress Factory

98 Jim Judkis

101 University of Pittsburgh Archives (Ray Cristina, photographer)

102 HABS/HAER, Library of Congress (Nicholas Traub, photographer)

103 Lu Donnelly

106 Carnegie Library of Pittsburgh

107 PHLF

114 Maurice Tierney

117 Top: Maurice Tierney
Bottom: HABS/HAER, Library of Congress (Nicholas Traub, photographer)

118 HABS/HAER, Library of Congress (Nicholas Traub, photographer)

119 Top: HABS/HAER, Library of Congress (Nicholas Traub, photographer)

122 Maurice Tierney

125 Astorino (Ed Massery, photographer)

128 Chatham University

130 HABS/HAER, Library of Congress (Nicholas Traub, photographer)

131 Maurice Tierney

133 HABS/HAER, Library of Congress (Nicholas Traub, photographer)

134 Bottom: PHLF

135 PHLF

136 Left: Maurice Tierney

137 Bottom: VisitPittsburgh

139 PHLF

140 Maurice Tierney

141 Top: UDA Architects

142 PHLF

146 Maurice Tierney

148 Timothy Engleman

150 WQED Multimedia

152 HABS/HAER, Library of Congress (Nicholas Traub, photographer)

154 Public Auditorium Authority of Pittsburgh & Allegheny County (Ken Balzer, photographer)

155 Duquesne University (Hedrick-Blessing, photographer)

156 Maurice Tierney

161 Top: Maurice Tierney

162 *Pittsburgh Post-Gazette* (V. Campbell, Jr., photographer)

164 PHLF

168 PHLF

170 PHLF

171 PHLF

172 Top: PHLF
Bottom: Charles M. Stotz, *The Early Architecture of Western Pennsylvania*

174 Western Pennsylvania Conservancy (Harold Corsini, photographer)

178 Western Pennsylvania Conservancy (Harold Corsini, photographer)

179 HABS/HAER, Library of Congress

181 HABS/HAER, Library of Congress

INDEX

SIDEBARS

1.1 Bridges in Pittsburgh, 20
1.2 The War of the Three Henrys, 25
2.1 Schenley Park, 56–57
3.1 Inclines in Pittsburgh, 67
3.2 Rising by the Rivers, 72–73
4.1 Riverview Park and Allegheny Observatory, 101–02
4.2 Pittsburgh's Suburbs, 107

ENTRIES

Abrams (Betty and Irving) House (6.32), 144
ALCOA Building (see Regional Enterprise Tower) (1.22)
ALCOA Corporate Center (4.1), 84
Allegheny Arsenal (6.5), 128
Allegheny Cemetery (6.7), 130
Allegheny Commons East (4.14), 92
Allegheny County Airport (Allegheny County Municipal Airport) (3.19), 81
Allegheny County Courthouse and Jail (1.15), 22–24
Allegheny County Soldiers' and Sailors' Memorial (see Soldiers' and Sailors' National Military Museum and Memorial Hall) (2.1)
Allegheny General Hospital (4.22), 98
Alpha Terrace (6.12), 133
Anderson Manor (James Anderson House) (4.5), 87
Andy Warhol Museum (Frick and Lindsay) (4.3), 85
Angel's Arms Condominiums (St. Michael's Parish Complex) (3.7), 70
Apt (Jerome and Joan) House (6.29), 142
Arthur Lubetz Architectural Office (2.6), 46

Bank Center (see Point Park University Center) (1.7)

Baum Boulevard Dodge (Chrysler Sales and Service Building) (6.9), 132
Baywood (Alexander and Cordelia King House) (6.13), 133
Bedford School Apartments (Bedford School) (3.4), 68
Bedford Square (3.5), 68
Bell Telephone of Pennsylvania Building (see Verizon Building) (1.38)
Benedum Center for the Performing Arts (Stanley Theater) (1.27), 32
Benjamin Jones House (see Jones Hall, Community College of Allegheny County) 4.13), 92
Bessemer and Lake Erie Bridge (4.34), 111
Beulah Chapel (Beulah Presbyterian Church) (7.5), 161
Bloomfield Commercial Buildings (6.8), 131
Boyer (Peter) House (8.3), 168
Buhl Planetarium and Institute of Popular Science and Old Post Office Museum (see Children's Museum of Pittsburgh) (4.16)
Burke Building (1.6), 16–17

Calliope House (William and Mary Lea Frazier House) (4.7), 89
Calvary Episcopal Church (6.24), 140
Calvary Methodist Episcopal Church (4.9), 90
CAPA (see Pittsburgh High School for the Performing Arts) (1.32)
Carnegie Institute and Carnegie Library (2.14), 52
Carnegie Institute of Technology (see Carnegie Mellon University) (2.16)
Carnegie Library of Braddock (3.15), 76
Carnegie Library of Pittsburgh, Allegheny Branch (4.17), 95
Carnegie Mellon Research Institute (Mellon Institute for Industrial Research) (2.9), 47

Carnegie Mellon University (Carnegie Institute of Technology) (2.16 to 2.19), 54
Carnegie Science Center (4.4), 86
Carson (Rachel) House (4.35), 111
Cathedral of Learning (2.10), 48
C.C. Mellor Library and Edgewood Club (7.1), 158
Chatham College and Academic Revival Houses (6.28), 142
Chatham Village (3.1), 66
Chautauqua Lake Ice Company (see Senator John Heinz Pittsburgh Regional History Center) (6.1)
Chesterfield Road, Robinson and Dunsmith Streets (2.22), 60
Chrysler Sales and Service Building (see Baum Boulevard Dodge) (6.9)
Children's Museum of Pittsburgh (Buhl Planetarium and Institute of Popular Science and Old Post Office Museum) (4.16), 94
City-County Building (1.14), 22
Civic Arena (see Mellon Arena) (6.46)
"Clayton" Henry Clay and Adelaide Childs Frick Estate (see Frick Art & Historical Center) (6.21)
College of Fine Arts (2.18), 58
Colonel James Andrews House (see Heathside Cottage) (4.21)
Commercial Buildings in Bloomfield (6.8), 131
Community College of Allegheny County (4.12), 91
Consolidated Natural Gas Tower (see Dominion Tower) (1.26)
Crawford Square (6.45), 152

David L. Lawrence Convention Center (1.33), 35
Dollar Savings Bank (1.8), 17–18
Dominion Tower (Consolidated Natural Gas Tower) (1.26), 31
Dravo Building (see One Mellon Bank Center) (1.19)
Duquesne Club (1.24), 30
Duquesne University Student Union (6.48), 154

East Carson Street Storefronts (3.6), 69
East Liberty Presbyterian Church (6.11), 132
Eberhardt & Ober Brewery Company (see Penn Brewery) (4.26)
Edgewood Railroad Station (7.2), 158
Emmanuel Episcopal Church (4.8), 89
Episcopal Church of the Ascension (6.42), 150
Episcopal Church of the Good Shepherd (3.9), 71
Epping-Carpenter Company (see National Robotics Engineering Consortium) (6.6)
Equibank (see Two PNC Center) (1.25)
Evergreen Hamlet (4.30), 106

Fallingwater and Kentuck Knob (9.2), 179
The Federated Building (Liberty Center) (1.34), 35
Fifth Avenue Place (1.3), 15
First Baptist Church (2.4), 45
First Presbyterian Church and Trinity Cathedral (1.23), 30

Fort Pitt and the Blockhouse (1.1), 13–14
Fulton Building (see Renaissance Pittsburgh Hotel) (1.30)
Frank (Cecilia and Robert) House (6.30), 142
Frank Lloyd Wright, George Washington, and the National Road (9.2), 178
Frazier (William and Mary Lea) House (see Calliope House) (4.7)
Frew (John) House (8.9), 172
Frick Art & Historical Center (Clayton) (6.21), 137
Frick Building (1.16), 24

Gateway Center (1.2), 14–15

Giovannitti (Frank A.) House (6.31), 144
Gwinner-Harter House (William B. Negley House) (6.37), 147

Hamerschlag Hall (Machinery Hall) (2.19), 58
Harmony and Old Economy (9.1), 175
Heathside Cottage (Colonel James Andrews House) (4.21), 98
Heinz Chapel (2.11), 50
Heinz Hall (Penn Theater) (1.29), 33
Heinz Lofts (H. J. Heinz Company Factories) (4.25), 99
Henry Clay Frick Fine Arts Building (2.13), 51
Herr's Island (see Washington's Landing) (4.28)
Highland Park and the Zoo (6.15), 134
Highland Towers (6.27), 141
Hindu Jain Temple (7.7), 162
H. J. Heinz Company Factories (see Heinz Lofts) (4.25)
Holy Rosary Church (6.18), 136
Holy Trinity Serbian Orthodox Church (8.1), 166
Home for Aged Protestant Women and Sheltering Arms Home for the Aged Protestants (see Three Rivers Center for Independent Living and Jane Holmes Residence and Gardens) (7.3)
Homewood Cemetery (6.20), 136
Houses on Beech Avenue (4.11), 90
Houses on Liverpool Street (originally Locust Street) (4.6), 87

IBM Building (see United Steelworkers Building) (1.4)
Industrial Bank (1.9), 18
Immaculate Heart of Mary Roman Catholic Church (6.4), 127
Isaly's Dairy (see UPMC Magee Women's Hospital Administrative Offices) (2.21)

Jones Hall, Community College of Allegheny County (Benjamin Jones House) (4.13), 92

Kaufmann (Edgar and Liliane) House (see La Tourelle) (4.33)
Kaufmann's Department Store (see Macy's Department Store) (1.20)

Kennywood Park (3.13), 75

Kentuck Knob and Fallingwater (9.2), 178–79

King (Alexander and Cordelia) House (see Baywood) (6.13)

Koppers Building (1.37), 37

La Tourelle (Edgar and Liliane Kaufmann House) (4.33), 109

L. Dilworth/Alan and Sarah Scaife and Charles D. Marshall Houses (see Pittsburgh Center for the Arts) (6.22)

Lemington Elementary School (6.17), 135

Lemington Engine House No. 38 (see Lincoln-Larimer Fire Station) (6.16)

Liberty Center (see the Federated Building) (1.34)

Liberty Market (see Motor Square Garden/AAA East Central) (6.10)

Lincoln–Larimer Fire Station (Lemington Engine House No. 38) (6.16), 135

Locust Street (see Houses on Liverpool Street) (4.6)

Loft Buildings (1.39), 48

Longue Vue Club (4.37), 113

Lower Fifth Avenue Storefronts (6.47), 154

Lubetz (Arthur) Architectural Office (2.6), 46

Macy's Department Store (Kaufmann's Department Store) (1.20), 27

Margaret Morrison Carnegie Hall (Margaret Morrison Carnegie School for Women) (2.17), 55

The Mattress Factory (4.20), 97

McClelland (James) House (see Sunnyledge Hotel) (6.76)

McKees Rocks Bridge (5.4), 119

Mellon Arena (Civic Arena) (6.46), 153

Mellon Institute for Industrial Research (see Carnegie Mellon Research Institute) (2.9)

Mesta (George and Perle) House (3.10), 71

Mexican War Streets (4.18), 96

Midfield Terminal Complex, Pittsburgh International Airport (5.8), 121

Mission Hills (8.4), 168

Motor Square Garden/AAA East Central (Liberty Market) (6.10), 132

Mudge Graduate House, Carnegie Mellon (Edmund and Pauline Mudge House) (6.40), 149

The National Aviary in Pittsburgh (4.15), 94

National Carpatho-Rusyn Center (St. John the Baptist Greek Catholic Cathedral) (3.12), 75

National Robotics Engineering Consortium (Epping-Carpenter Company) (6.6), 129

Negley (William B.) House (see Gwinner-Harter House) (6.37)

Neville (John and Presley) House (see Woodville Plantation) (8.6)

New Granada Theater (Pythian Temple) (6.44), 152

Newington (Shields-Brooks House) (5.7), 120

North Shore Center and Allegheny Landing Park (4.2), 85

Oak Hill (Terrace Village) (6.43), 151

Oakland Square (2.20), 59

Old Heidelberg Apartments (6.19), 136

Old St. Luke's (see St. Luke's Protestant Episcopal Church) (8.7)

One Mellon Bank Center (Dravo Building) (1.19), 27

The Oratory (Ryan Catholic Newman Center) (2.5), 46

Orphan Asylum of Pittsburgh and Allegheny (see Renaissance Apartments) (4.19)

O'Reilly Theater (see Theater Square) (1.28)

Oxford Centre (1.13), 21–22

Park Brothers and Company, Ltd., Black Diamond Steel Works (see Ralph Meyer Company) (6.3)

Park Building (1.21), 28

Penn Brewery (Eberhardt and Ober Brewery Company) (4.26), 102

Penn Theatre (see Heinz Hall) (1.29)

Pennsylvania Drilling Company (Taylor–Wilson Manufacturing Company) (5.2), 116

Pennsylvania Salt Manufacturing Company Workers' Housing (4.36), 112

The Pennsylvanian Apartments (Pennsylvania Station, Union Station) (1.35), 36

Pennsylvania Station (see the Pennsylvania Apartments) (1.35)

Pfeiffer House (6.34), 145

Phipps Conservatory (2.15), 54

Pittsburgh & Lake Erie Railroad Steam Locomotive Repair Shop (5.3), 118

Pittsburgh & Lake Erie Railroad Terminal (see Station Square) (3.2)

Pittsburgh Athletic Association (2.2), 44

Pittsburgh Center for the Arts (L. Dilworth/Alan and Sarah Scaife and Charles D. Marshall houses) (6.22), 139

Pittsburgh High School for the Creative and Performing Arts (CAPA) (1.32), 34

Pittsburgh and Lake Erie Railroad Locomotive Repair Shop (5.3), 130

Pittsburgh Municipal Courts Facility (1.12), 21

Pittsburgh Technology Center (2.23), 61

Point Park University Center (1.7), 17

PPG Place (1.5), 16

The Priory and Grand Hall (St. Mary's Roman Catholic Church) (4.23), 99

Pythian Temple (see New Granada Theater) (6.44)

Ralph Meyer Company (Park Brothers and Company, Ltd., Black Diamond Steel Works) (6.3), 126

Regional Enterprise Tower (ALCOA Building) and Mellon Square (1.22), 28

Renaissance Apartments (Orphan Asylum of Pittsburgh and Allegheny) (4.19), 97

Renaissance Pittsburgh Hotel (Fulton Building) (1.30), 33

Rhodes (Joshua and Eliza) House (see Victoria House

Bed and Breakfast) (4.10)

Richard King Mellon Hall of Science, Duquesne University (6.49), 155

Roberto Clemente, Andy Warhol, and Rachel Carson Bridges (Sixth, Seventh, and Ninth Street bridges) (1.31), 33

Rodef Shalom Temple (6.39), 149

Ryan Catholic Newman Center (see the Oratory) (2.5)

Sacred Heart Church (6.25), 140

St. Anthony of Padua shrine (4.27), 103

St. Bernard's Church (8.5), 169

St. John the Baptist Greek Catholic Cathedral (see National Carpatho-Rusyn Center) (3.12)

St. John the Baptist Ukrainian Catholic Church (3.3), 68

St. Luke's Protestant Episcopal Church (Old St. Luke's) (8.7), 171

St. Mary's Roman Catholic Church (see The Priory and Grand Hall) (4.23)

St. Michael the Archangel Church (3.11), 71

St. Nicholas Church (4.29), 106

St. Michael's Parish Complex (see Angel's Arms Condominiums) (3.7)

St. Paul Cathedral (2.7), 47

Sauer (Frederick) Houses (4.31), 108

Schenley Farms (2.3), 45

Schenley Hotel (see William Pitt Student Union) (2.12)

Schwab (Charles) House (3.14), 76

Sellers-Carnahan House (6.23), 139

Senator John Heinz Pittsburgh Regional History Center (Chautauqua Lake Ice Company) (6.1), 125

Shady Side Academy (4.32), 108

Shadyside Presbyterian Church (6.38), 148

Shields-Brooks House (see Newington) (5.7)

Singer (John) House (7.4), 159

Sixth, Seventh, and Ninth Street Bridges (see Roberto Clemente, Andy Warhol, and Rachel Carson bridges) (1.31)

Sixteenth Street Bridge (4.24), 99

Smithfield Street Bridge (1.11), 19, 21

Software Engineering Institute (2.8), 47

Soldiers' and Sailors' National Military Museum and Memorial Hall (Allegheny County Soldiers' and Sailors' Memorial) (2.1), 43

South Park and Oliver Miller Homestead (8.2), 166

Speyer (Tillie S.) House (6.33), 145

Sri Venkateswara Temple (7.6), 162

Stanley Theater (see Benedum Center for the Performing Arts) (1.27)

Station Square (Pittsburgh & Lake Erie Railroad Terminal) (3.2), 66

Steinberg (Abraam) House (6.35), 146

Sunnyledge Hotel (Sunnyledge, the James McClelland House) (6.36), 146

Taylor-Wilson Manufacturing Company (see Pennsylvania Drilling Company) (5.2)

Terrace Village (see Oak Hill) (6.43)

Theater Square (Incorporating the O'Reilly Theater) (1.28), 32

Thornburg (8.8), 171

Three Rivers Center for Independent Living and Jane Holmes Residence and Gardens (Home for Aged Protestant Women and Sheltering Arms Home for Aged Protestants) (7.3), 151

Trinity Cathedral and Graveyard, and First Presbyterian Church (1.23), 30

Two Mellon Bank Center (Union Trust Building) (1.17), 26

Two PNC Center (Equibank) (1.25), 31

Union Station (see the Pennsylvania Apartments) (1.35)

Union Trust Building (see Two Mellon Bank Center) (1.17)

United Steelworkers Building (IBM Building) (1.4), 15–16

United States Steel Edgar Thomson Works (3.16), 77

UPMC Magee Women's Hospital Administrative Offices (Isaly's Dairy) (2.21), 60

USX Tower (United States Steel Building) (1.36), 37

Utopian Settlements at Harmony and Old Economy (9.1), 175

Verizon Building (1.38) (Bell Telephone of Pennsylvania Building), 38

Victoria House Bed-and-Breakfast (Joshua and Eliza Rhodes House) (4.10), 90

Village of Shadyside (6.26), 140

Vilsack Row (6.14), 133

Washington's Landing (Herr's Island) (4.28), 105

Watson-Standard Building and Cast-Iron Fronted Buildings (1.10), 18

Way Family Houses (5.6), 120

West End Bridge (5.1), 116

Westinghouse Air Brake Company (formerly 2425 Liberty Avenue) (6.2), 125

Westinghouse Air Brake Company complex and the Wilmerding plan (3.18), 78

Westinghouse Memorial Bridge (3.17), 78

William Penn Hotel (1.18), 26

William Pitt Student Union (Schenley Hotel) (2.12), 50

Wilpen Hall (William Penn Snyder House) (5.5), 119

Woods (John) House (3.8), 71

Woodville Plantation (John and Presley Neville House) (8.6), 170

WQED Studios (6.41), 150

ABOUT THE AUTHOR

Franklin Toker was born in Montréal in 1944 to a family that has lived in French Canada for seven generations. He obtained degrees from McGill University, Oberlin College, and Harvard University before joining the faculty of the University of Pittsburgh, where he is Professor of the History of Art and Architecture. Professor Toker is active in civic improvements relating to the architecture and urban history of Pittsburgh, and he has been a John Simon Guggenheim Memorial Foundation Fellow and a Senior Fellow of the National Endowment for the Humanities. His first book, *The Church of Notre-Dame in Montreal: An Architectural History* (McGill-Queen's University Press, 1970), was awarded the Hitchcock Book Award, granted annually by the Society of Architectural Historians for the best new book published in the previous two years by a North American author. His other books are *Pittsburgh: An Urban Portrait* (Pennsylvania State University Press, 1986) and *Fallingwater Rising: Frank Lloyd Wright, E. J. Kaufmann, and America's Most Extraordinary House* (Knopf, 2003). He is currently at work on a four-volume archaeological history of early medieval Florence and its cathedral.

The Center for American Places is a tax-exempt 501(c)(3) nonprofit organization, founded in 1990, whose educational mission is to enhance the public's understanding of, appreciation for, and affection for the places of America and the world—whether urban, suburban, rural, or wild. Underpinning this mission is the belief that books provide an indispensable foundation for comprehending and caring for the places where we live, work, and explore. Books live. Books endure. Books make a difference. Books are gifts to civilization.

With offices in Santa Fe, New Mexico, and Staunton, Virginia, Center editors have brought to publication more than 300 books under the Center's own imprint or in association with numerous publishing partners. Center books have won or shared more than 100 editorial awards and citations, including multiple best-book honors in more than thirty academic fields.

The Center is also engaged in other outreach programs that emphasize the interpretation of place through exhibitions, lectures, seminars, workshops, and field research. The Center's Cotton Mather Library in Arthur, Nebraska, its Martha A. Strawn Photographic Library in Davidson, North Carolina, and a ten-acre reserve along the Santa Fe River in Florida are available as retreats upon request.

The Center strives every day to make a difference through books, research, and education. For more information, please send inquiries to P.O. Box 23225, Santa Fe, NM 87502, U.S.A., or visit the Center's Website (www.americanplaces.org).

ABOUT THE BOOK:
Buildings of Pittsburgh was issued in an edition of 500 hardcover and 2,500 softcover copies. The text was set in Bembo with Futura display. The paper is Garda Silk, 80lb. weight. The book was printed and bound by Friesens in Canada.

FOR THE CENTER FOR AMERICAN PLACES:
GEORGE F. THOMPSON, *President and Publisher*
A. LENORE LAUTIGAR, *Publishing Liaison and Associate Editor*
CATHERINE R. BABBIE, *Editorial and Production Assistant*
PURNA MAKARAM, *Manuscript Editor*
ANGELA C. TAORMINA, *Compositor*
DAVID SKOLKIN, *Book Designer and Art Director*